A HISTORY OF BRITAIN VOLUME TWO
PART 2: THE BRITISH WARS

The British Wars is a compelling chronicle of the changes that transformed every strand and strata of British life, faith and thought from 1603 to 1776. Simon Schama explores the forces that tore Britain apart during two centuries of dynamic change—transforming outlooks, allegiances and boundaries.

The British wars began in 1637 with the Prayer Book riots. Over the next 200 years, other battles would rage on other battlegrounds. Most would be wars of faith—waged on wide-ranging grounds of political or religious conviction. The struggle to pull Britain together at first succeeded only in tearing our nations further apart. But as wars of religious passions gave way to campaigns for profit, the British people did come together in the imperial enterprise of 'Britannia Incorporated'.

The story of that great alteration—revolution and reaction, inspiration and disenchantment—is brought vividly, sometimes disturbingly, to life in Schama's rich and teeming tapestry of The British Wars

A HISTORY OF

BRITAIN

VOLUME 2 PART 2

THE BRITISH WARS
1603–1776

Simon Schama

BBC
LARGE
PRINT

First published 2000
by
BBC Worldwide Limited
This Large Print edition published 2004
by
BBC Audiobooks Ltd
a subsidiary of BBC Worldwide Limited

ISBN 0 7540 5670 8

British Library Cataloguing in Publication Data available

Printed and bound in Great Britain by
Antony Rowe Ltd., Chippenham, Wiltshire

CONTENTS

For Martin Davidson and Janice Hadlow—
history-makers.

Narrative is linear. Action is solid. Alas for our chains and chainlets of 'causes' and 'effects' which we so assiduously track through the countless handbreadths of years and square miles when the whole is a broad, deep immensity and each atom is 'chained' and complected with all . . .

THOMAS CARLYLE, 'History' from *Fraser's Magazine*

Vico's fantasia *is indispensable to his conception of historical knowledge; it is unlike the knowledge that Julius Caesar is dead or that Rome was not built in a day or that thirteen is a prime number, or that the week has seven days; nor yet is it like knowledge of how to ride a bicycle or engage in statistical research or win a battle. It is more like knowing what it is to be poor, to belong to a nation, to be a revolutionary, to fall in love, to be seized by nameless terror, to be delighted by a work of art . . .*

ISAIAH BERLIN, *Giambattista Vico and Cultural History*

Man is the only animal that laughs and weeps; for he is the only animal that is struck with the difference between what things are and what they ought to be.

WILLIAM HAZLITT, *Lectures on the English Comic Writers*

ACKNOWLEDGEMENTS

Epic' is a word that suffers from over-use these days, but the history of *A History of Britain* certainly has a long roll-call of heroes—other than its author—without whose unflagging labours neither television programmes nor book could possibly have got made.

At BBC Worldwide Sally Potter and my excellent editor Belinda Wilkinson have remained heroically undaunted by the prospect of what had been commissioned as one short book turning into three. In every important sense this work has been a collaboration between myself and an exceptionally gifted and devoted group of colleagues at BBC Television, in particular Ian Bremner, Martin Davidson, Liz Hartford and Mike Ibeji. Melisa Akdogan, Ben Ledden and Ashley Gethin were exceptionally resourceful both in the libraries and on location. Had I not had the tireless and invariably considerate help of Sara Fletcher, I would have come unglued in locations throughout the British Isles. Tanya Hethorn, Tim Sutton and Mark Walden-Mills have, in crucial ways, helped the presenter present. Susan Harvey in Factual Publicity has been the gentlest and friendliest of promoters. It's been a source of great happiness to work closely with John Harle on the music for the series. Laurence Rees, Glenwyn Benson and Janice Hadlow have all cast a benevolently critical eye on our work when it most mattered and have been our most generous supporters. Alan Yentob and Greg Dyke have both given us the sense of how much *A History of Britain* matters to the BBC.

I'm deeply grateful to a number of colleagues who were kind enough to read both scripts and chapters for errors, in particular John Brewer, Ann Hughes, Holger Hoock, Peter Marshall, Steven Pincus and David Haycock. Any that remain are, of course, my own responsibility.

In a much larger and deeper sense, though, I owe an enormous debt of gratitude to the wisdom and erudition of teachers (including schoolteachers), from whom I first learned the great contentions of British and colonial history in the seventeenth and eighteenth centuries, and of friends and colleagues, whose scholarship and critical analysis is still a source of exhilarating illumination. Though they may well take exception to some (or many) of the views expressed in this book, I hope that the overdue thanks offered, in particular to David Armitage, Roy Avery, Robert Baynes, Mark Kishlansky, Sir John Plumb, Roy Porter, Kevin Sharpe and Quentin Skinner, will not go amiss.

My agents at PFD—Michael Sissons and Rosemary Scoular—have been, as ever, towers of strength on whom I lean, and occasionally collapse. My thanks, too, to James Gill, Sophie Laurimore and Carol Macarthur. Provost Jonathan Cole at Columbia University has been exceptionally kind in allowing me the necessary leave to work on the series and I'm delighted to have played a part in pioneering the on-line seminar, produced jointly by BBC Education and Columbia in partnership with Fathom.Com, about the eighteenth-century British Empire. Jennifer Scott was an extraordinary colleague in the production of that innovative departure in popular historical education.

Shifting back and forth between book and

script-writing is likely to make the head spin, and certain to make the writer-presenter generally impossible to be around. So I'm, as always, more grateful than I can say to my friends for submitting to recitations from the Schama book of lamentations —thank you, again—Clare Beavan, Lily Brett, John Brewer, Tina Brown, Jan Dalley, Alison Dominitz, Harry Evans, Amanda Foreman, Eliot Friedman, Mindy Engel Friedman, Andrew Motion, David Rankin, David Remnick, Anthony Silverstone, Beverly Silverstone, Jill Slotover, Stella Tillyard, Bing Taylor and Leon Wieseltier. To my nearest and dearest—Ginny, Chloe and Gabe—I give my heartfelt thanks for riding the storms of their unreasonably cranky Dad and husband, and for the calm waters and always-open harbour of their love.

PREFACE

If it's a truism that being British has never been a matter of straightforward allegiance, never was this more glaringly obvious than during the two centuries narrated by this book. Was this country an archipelago or an empire, a republic or a monarchy? 'Great Britain' began as a grandiose fantasy in the head of James VI of Scotland and I of England, and ended as a startling imperial reality on the bloodied ramparts of Seringapatam. The confident chroniclers of the mind-boggling transformation, from sub-insular realms to global empire, liked to imagine that this history was somehow pre-ordained, unfolding naturally from the imperatives of geography and from a shared sense of the inevitability of a parliamentary monarchy. But never was a nation's destiny less predictable, or *less* determined by the markers of topography, which said nothing about whether its bounds should be on the Tweed or the coast of Sligo, the Appalachians or the Bay of Bengal, nor whether those who decided such things should be thought of as the servants of the Crown or the representatives of the people.

It was these battles for allegiance—the British Wars, between and within the nations of our archipelago, and then beyond in the wider world, between different and fiercely argued ideas about our historical and political inheritance—that made us what we became. The creation of our identity was a baptism of blood.

But the slaughters were not always mindless.

Crucially, for our future, they were often, even excessively, mindful. The Victorian historians, especially Macaulay, who believed the good fortune of British birth to be a reward won by the sacrifices of ancestors, are habitually berated in much modern scholarship for their detestably insular smugness, their fatuous error of reading history 'backwards' and their habit of projecting on periods—entirely innocent of parliamentary civics—their own nineteenth-century preoccupations. Read those books, it's said, and you are in a world drained of historical free will, of the uncertainty of outcomes, a past ordered to march in lock-step to the drumbeat of the Protestant, parliamentary future. But a dip, or better yet, a prolonged immersion in the great narratives of the last century—Gardiner, Carlyle, and, to be sure, Macaulay—suggest, to this lay reader anyway, anything *but* imprisonment in a universe of self-fulfilling prophecies. At their most powerful, those wonderfully *complicated* texts deliver the reader into a world shaking with terror, chaos and cruelty.

But it is true, certainly, that many of the grand narratives assumed that the long story they told was one of a battle of beliefs, rather than a mere imbroglio of interests, and that the eventual, admittedly partial, success of the party of liberty represented a genuine turning point in the political history of the world. If to tell the story again, and yet insist that that much is true, is to reveal oneself as that most hopeless anachronism, a born-again Whig, so be it.

New York, 2001

xiv

CHAPTER FOUR

UNFINISHED BUSINESS

Not long after Cromwell died, John Dryden wrote, with premature optimism, 'No Civill broyles have since his death arose / But Faction now by Habit does obey'. The question on everyone's mind—could the Protectorate survive the loss of Oliver—was about to be answered resoundingly in the negative. At first it seemed as though Oliver's named successor, his eldest surviving son, Richard, might make a go of it. Loyal addresses poured in, and the thirty-one-year-old was recognized as decent, honest, well meaning and quite without his father's alarming irascibility. His greatest asset was that no one could think of any reason to dislike him. But this was also a liability. Richard's conspicuous inability to command Oliver's selectively deployed menace made him politically defenceless as well as clueless. His father had known all along that Richard was too amiable for his calling, too softly seated upon the cushions of life's many pleasures. He made no one break out in a sweat, either of exertion or of fear. This became a problem when Richard, faced with the usual choice of depending on the army or the pragmatists, opted heavily for men like Ashley Cooper and Montagu. However conservative Oliver might have seemed, the generals, beginning with Fleetwood, felt that through the brotherhood of arms they could always recall him to the colours of the 'Good Old Cause'. Richard, on the other

1

hand, seemed more the plaything than the master of his civil servants. So out of a sense of self-preservation—for themselves and for the republic—the generals made common cause with the same Rump politicians they had ousted in 1653. It may be that by the spring of 1659 they felt they had no choice, for the generals were themselves being hard pressed by junior officers, angry about forty-month arrears of pay; about the political purges that had taken place in the last years of Oliver's Protectorate and about the systematic policy of replacing them with the old county militias under the control of the gentry.

In April that year, after a petition bearing 20,000 signatures calling for the return of the Rump Parliament was presented to the Protector, and after he had been given to understand that if he failed to heed it a military insurrection was in the offing, Richard abdicated. He was summarily ordered to depart from Whitehall with his family (including his younger brother Henry, who might have made a much more formidable successor). The Rump Parliament (all forty-two members of it who showed up) was recalled. The Protectorate, which hard-core republicans like Ludlow had never ceased to regard as a defiled thing, was abolished and the Commonwealth restored. But what was immediately restored with it, of course, was the ferocious mutual hostility of the republican politicians and zealot soldiers, which had caused its disappearance in the first place. Without Oliver Cromwell to hold the ring they proceeded to tear each other, and what remained of the kingless state, to pieces, spinning into an anarchy from which the only possible escape was the return of the monarch. The extraordinary irony about the restoration of Charles II is not that he became king because the country desperately needed a successor to Charles I. He became king because it desperately needed a successor to Oliver Cromwell.

As late as August 1659, when an attempted royalist rising led by Colonel George Booth was easily suppressed, it seemed that the odds against the imminent return of Charles II were still prohibitively steep. But the fratricidal self-destruction of all the alternative contenders for power—not just Rump against army, but even Rumper against Rumper (Vane and Haselrig were at each other's throats and Ludlow hated both of them)—precluded any kind of republican stability. Opposing factions argued furiously about whether there should be one house of parliament or two, whether an upper house should be elected or appointed, while the real house, the house of the republic, was burning down around them. Crazily short-sighted though it seems in retrospect (no crazier in truth than many other revolutionary situations), the parties concerned were much more interested in destroying their immediate enemies than in agreeing on a secure republican regime that might have locked out a monarchy for the foreseeable future. It was, indeed, the republicans who killed the republic.

Somehow, England in 1659 got sucked into a temporal worm-hole to emerge ten years earlier, in 1649, when everything—government, religion, social order—had been fluid, and no one quite knew how any of those matters might be resolved. Suddenly, in 1659, the pamphlet market was once

3

again flooded with experimental proposals, tracts and broadsides. The country was back in its Torricellian gap, the void-in-a-void. Leveller tracts reappeared and with them a surge of apprehension among the horsey classes that democracy was about to strike down the counties. Fifth Monarchists like Christopher Feake belatedly declared that the real kingdom of Christ had not after all been frustrated, only postponed by Cromwell, the Antichrist. George Fox, in one of his brief vacations from prison, published *Fifty-Nine Particulars* 'to bring the nation into a Garden, a free nation, a free people', to abolish the fee-gouging of lawyers, to take care of the blind and lame; to ban the carrying of swords, daggers and guns for all those who did not require them in their office; and, not least, a reform dear to his heart, to improve the conditions of gaols so that 'prisoners might not lie in their own dung and piss'.

The pragmatic survivors from the government of the Protectorate stood back from all this ferment in horrified disbelief. At the Rota Club in London, William Petty could sit down with James Harrington to discuss the latter's *Oceana*, in which, for the first time, the necessary connection between property and political power was exposed. But not for a minute could they countenance his 'agrarian law' limiting the size of landed estates. Experiments were not good for business, and they could see that the economy was suffering from the breakdown of orderly government. Shops were closed, trade stopped and tax strikes were threatened. Customs and excise dues went uncollected. Goldsmiths moved their stock out of London for safe-keeping. And it was more than ever obvious that a choice between inflexible republican zealots, who represented only themselves, and military dictatorship was no choice at all. They had built a formidable state—commercially dynamic, fearsome on the high seas, dependable in its revenues, scientific in its administration, a state built in partnership with, not against, the gentry of the counties. Before it was irreparably lost they needed to do their utmost to restore the stability enjoyed under the Protectorate. And since neither the republicans nor the generals would provide it, where else was there to go except to Charles Stuart? With any luck he would be the next Protector.

Like many sea-changes in British history, this was not a gradual but a sudden decision, made by men such as Montagu, Lord Broghill and William Petty, who all voted with their feet at some point between the summer of 1659 and the end of the year. When John Evelyn decided to publish his royalist *Apology* late that year he made much of the fact that he was committing a capital offence. But he went ahead all the same and was gratified, though not perhaps surprised, that it was 'universally taken up'. It was a sign of things to come that the man he approached to get a copy to Charles II was the Commonwealth's own Lieutenant of the Tower, Herbert Morley. Evelyn believed this man would not betray him, since they were old schoolfellows. But he would still never have dared entrust him with the mission had he not also believed the Lieutenant was acting from prescient self-interest. Countless others did the same. Thomas Hobbes's axiom that allegiance ended when the state's capacity to protect had

5

irreversibly broken down could never have seemed more glaringly self-evident.

The man who finally pushed Britain over the edge to Restoration, 'Black George' Monck, was Hobbes's kind of general, someone for whom the tactics of self-preservation had been learned the hard way. He had been born into an old gentry family in Devon, and his strongest links were to the Grenville family, who themselves produced royalist heroes and parliamentary turncoats during the civil war. Monck, who early on was a one-man weathervane, had his doubts about the prospects as well as the rightness of the royal cause but was personally converted by a meeting with Charles I. He should have stayed doubtful. Captured at the battle of Nantwich in 1644, he spent the next two years in the Tower, where at least he met the Presbyterian seamstress Anne who later became his wife. In 1646 Monck took the Covenant oath and went to Ireland as a colonel for parliament. He became close to Cromwell, whom he first met in August 1649 and evidently came to trust and revere. He fought alongside Cromwell at the battle of Dunbar in 1650 and, although without any naval experience, was made a commander of the fleet during the war with the Dutch, in which he proved himself indisputably clever, tough and brave.

While the republic was disintegrating in England during 1659 Monck was in secure command of the army of Scotland. Although his old royalist allegiance made him a natural target for those who wanted him to come out early for Charles, Monck stayed aloof, not at all sure, for once, which way the wind was blowing, nor what would be the right, as well as the smart, thing to do.

What *was* apparent to those who still hoped for a republican military regime—Lambert and Fleetwood—was that they could not expect any support from Monck, whose army was the most coherent and concentrated in Britain. And although he attempted to muster what forces he could, even Lambert knew that without Monck they were finished. At the point when he realized his game was up Fleetwood commented bitterly that 'the Lord had blasted their Counsels and spat in their faces'. When Monck began his self-authorized march south from Coldstream near Berwick on 2 January 1660, with 7000 troops, it was as a soldier against rule by soldiers. But if it was clear what he was against—army interference in parliament—it was much less clear what he was for. The rump of the Rump, which had been restored at the mere prospect of his coming to London, hoped and assumed he was marching to protect *them*. But Monck kept his cards close to his chest and his powder dry, and at some point en route he was obviously impressed by the wild enthusiasm, not for preserving the Rump but for getting rid of it. The cry, nearly universal, was for a 'free' parliament, which meant the return of all the members of the Long Parliament who had been shut out by Pride's Purge.

By the time Monck got to London at the beginning of February, the call for a 'free parliament' had developed from a campaign for constitutional amendment to something more like a desperate cry to get the country out of the chaotic hell that the Commonwealth had become. It was also, increasingly, the royalism that dared not (yet) quite speak its name. If appeals for liberty had once meant the end of kingship, now they very definitely meant its reinstatement. Even blind John Milton, standing by in impotent dismay as the republic unravelled, conceded its unpopularity in his last published attempt to reverse the rush back to monarchy. In his *Readie and Easie Way to Establish a Free Commonwealth* he argued that a minority had the right to force the majority to accept freedom, while the majority could not coerce the minority into sharing their subjection as fellow-slaves. But the crowds of apprentices in London (as in Bristol and Exeter) who mounted demonstrations for the 'free parliament' that everyone knew would open the door for the king did not want to be forced to be free. They wanted to be subjects. Women offered their own verdict on the Rump by lifting their skirts, bending over and shouting: 'Kiss my parliament!'

On 11 February Samuel Pepys, who for five years had been a clerk in the Exchequer (the protégé of his powerful kinsman Edward Montagu), stood at the end of Strand Bridge and counted bonfires. There were thirty-one on the bridge alone. 'At one end of the street, you would think there was a whole lane of fire, and so hot that we were fain to keep still on the further side,' he wrote in his diary. The entire city seemed to have been turned into one great open-air spit, on which rumps—some fowl, some beef—were being roasted. The streets were greasy with celebration. It was not just meat that was being cooked, but the Commonwealth. Earlier that day it had been decided to readmit the members of parliament who had been shut out by Pride's Purge over eleven years before. Pending a new 'free' parliament,

Londoners were voting, as usual, with their bellies. There were carillons of carving knives on the city streets. 'The butchers at the Maypole in the Strand', wrote Pepys, 'rang a peal with their knifes when they were going to sacrifice their rump.'

History was now respooling fast. Men who had not shown themselves in politics for many years, like Sir Thomas Fairfax, reappeared along with their colleagues from the Long Parliament who had never forgotten the humiliation of their 'seclusion' in 1648. Two of the 'birds' of 1642, Denzil Holles and Arthur Haselrig, now faced each other, doubtless in mutual mortification—one of them about to be a republican on the run, the other headed for a Stuart peerage. But the pragmatists, not least Montagu, passed smoothly from one regime to the other. The parliament, which had first assembled twenty years before, now—heavily nudged by Monck's soldiers and an armed royalist militia—killed itself off, ordering its own dissolution and the 'free election' that all concerned knew would produce a parliament for Restoration.

Although, in a last gesture of piety towards the civil-war parliamentarians, royalists who had actually fought for Charles I were excluded, a hundred of them were none the less elected and duly took their seats in the 'Convention' Parliament of March 1660. Another fifty-eight members were unequivocal royalist supporters. Virtually the same number—close to 150—were parliamentarians, although that did not make them republicans. Most of them belonged to the gentry, who had all along wanted a reformed monarchy. And now, so they hoped, they would at last get one. The terms that they sent with Monck and their

9

commissioners to Charles II at Breda in the Netherlands were calculated to test his willingness for a reconciliation: an amnesty for those on the parliamentary side in the civil war (the regicide signers of Charles I's death warrant excepted), a degree of liberty for 'tender consciences' and guarantees against reversing the changes in property that had taken place during the interregnum. But the Convention Parliament did not insist, as a precondition, on the king committing himself to executing these policies. For his part, Charles's response from Breda on 4 April was shrewdly handled, offering a forty-day period of 'grace' for amnesties but leaving any exceptions to the discretion of later parliaments, the same going for matters of religion and property. To make parliament, rather than himself, the arbiter of these matters already seemed to advertise that the son would not go the way of the father.

On 23 May 1660, Samuel Pepys watched Charles, along with his younger brothers and his cousin the boy Prince of Orange (later to be King William III) come on board the flagship of the Commonwealth, the *Naseby,* at Scheveningen near The Hague. Pepys kissed their royal hands to the sound of 'infinite shooting of guns' and took dinner 'in a great deal of state'. After dinner the *Naseby*'s name was repainted as the *Royal Charles*. For Pepys and his patron Montagu, as well as for Monck and Thurloe—all Cromwellians—it was as painless as that. In the afternoon they set sail for England and the king

walking here and there, up and down (quite contrary to what I thought him to have been),

10

very active and stirring. Upon the Quarterdeck he fell in discourse of his escape from Worcester. Where it made me ready to weep to hear the stories that he told of his difficulties that he had passed through. As his travelling four days and three nights on foot, every step up to the knees in dirt, with nothing but a green coat and a pair of country breeches on and a pair of country shoes, that made him so sore all over his feet that he could scarce stir.

Pepys listened and listened, obviously agog. This was not what he had anticipated. The tall man with his mother's black curly hair, dark eyes and thick lips was a spell-binder—someone who could, when he chose, scatter magic. Literally days after disembarking, Charles had touched 600 sufferers from scrofula in one emphatic demonstration of the healing power of the king. Thirteen years before, parliament had appointed a commission to draft a declaration denouncing the practice of touching for the 'king's evil' as an absurd superstition. But here were the hordes of ordinary people, some with swollen or tumorous lymph glands, others with styes or mouth blisters, all convinced that royal magic had returned. In twenty years, 90,000 of the scrofulous would receive the royal touch and a gold chain to hang around their necks.

John Evelyn, who had endured the kingless decade with unrepentant royalism burning in his breast, could hardly credit what was happening: 'The greedinesse of all sorts, men, women & children, to see his Majesty & kisse his hands, in so much as he had scarce leasure to Eate for some

11

dayes.' Even as hard-bitten an old Presbyterian as Denzil Holles of Dorchester, who had fought Charles I at Edgehill, now addressed his son with slavish adulation as 'the light of their [the people's] eyes, the breath of their nostrils, their delight and all their hope'. On 29 May, Charles II's birthday, not far from where Pepys had counted bonfires, Evelyn watched the cavalcade of 20,000 horse and foot escorting the king through London,

> brandishing their swords and shouting with unexpressable joy; The wayes straw'd with flowers, the bells ringing . . . I stood in the strand, & beheld it, & blessed God. And all this without one drop of bloud, & by that very army, which rebell'd against him: but it was the Lord's doing . . . for such a Restauration was never seene in the mention of any history, antient or modern, since the returne of the [Jews from their] Babylonan Captivity, nor so joyfull a day, & so bright, ever seene in this nation: this hapning when to expect or effect it, was past all humane policy.

Not everyone was celebrating in the heady days of May 1660. Edmund Ludlow, fortieth on the list of fifty-nine signatories of the death warrant of the king, watched the same revels with mounting disgust and disbelief. Jerusalem had suddenly become Sodom. What could you expect? 'The Dissolution and Drunkenness of that Night,' he hurrumphed, 'was so great and scandalous, in a Nation which had not been acquainted with such Disorders for many Years past, that the King . . . caused a Proclamation to be publish'd, forbidding the drinking of Healths. But resolving, for his own part, to be oblig'd to no Rule of any Kind, he publickly violated his own Order in a few days, at a Debauch in the Mulberry Garden.' Above all, Ludlow was horrified to see 'the Horse that had formerly belonged to our army, now put upon an Employment so different from that which they had first undertaken; especially . . . that for the most part . . . they consisted of such as had engaged themselves from a Spirit of Liberty.'

On 30 January 1661—the anniversary of Charles I's execution—the remains of Oliver Cromwell, his son-in-law, Ireton, and John Bradshaw, who had presided over the court that had judged the king, were 'dragged', as Evelyn gleefully wrote, 'out of their superbe Tombs [in Westminster among the kings], to Tyburne, & hanged on the Gallows there from 9 in the morning 'til 6 at night, & then buried under that fatal & ignominious Monument, in a deepe pitt.' Evelyn thought back to the chaotic magnificence of Cromwell's funeral in 1658. It had been just two and a half years between embalming and dismemberment. 'Oh,' he exclaimed 'the stupendious, & inscrutable Judgements of God.'

As far as Ludlow was concerned, Cromwell got what he deserved. For it had been his betrayal of the nation's liberties and his greed for power that had killed the republic. But now the unswerving friends of liberty were paying the price. Dismay was followed by consternation and fear as army 'grandees' were abruptly turned into fugitives or supplicants desperately working the good offices of men who had been timely turncoats. The republicans looked on in horror as old friends and

13

comrades associated with the death of Charles were brought before punitive tribunals, swiftly condemned and subjected to hanging and live quartering. Two of the regicides were dragged on a sled to Tyburn while facing the decapitated head of a third, the Fifth Monarchist 'Saint' Major-General Thomas Harrison. Ludlow made contingency plans for a rapid escape. Milton, now quite blind, reflected on the iniquities that must have deserved this rod across their backs.

What of those who *had* jumped in time, who had been instrumental in bringing about the Restoration? Did these rituals of revenge make them just a little nervous? In May 1661 Samuel Pepys stood in the immense, glimmering cave of Westminster Abbey on the coronation day of Charles II and watched while fistfuls of silver and gold were flung high in the air, the coins and medals ringing as they hit the stone slabs. But the shower of treasure did not fall on his shoulders, positioned as he was at a properly respectful distance from the throne. The tailor's son may have come a long way from Fleet Street, but he was still just clerk to the Navy Board. So he was obliged to observe while his betters scrambled for the royal bounty, like so many bridesmaids scuffling for the nosegay. 'I could not come of any,' he complained ruefully to his diary.

What could he 'come of'? What could men like Pepys expect from the new reign? It was one thing to purr contentedly as he was massaged by the famous royal affability; another to be completely confident that men who had served what was now euphemistically referred to as 'The Old State' would find the same favour in the kingdom. The

14

presence, both political and physical, of the portly Lord Chancellor Clarendon—who had inflated alarmingly along with his new peerage—helped calm some of these anxieties. Clarendon was, without question, the ballast of the Restoration, the man who could bring a dose of political sobriety to the understandable inebriation of the vindicated Cavaliers. In the Long Parliament, as Edward Hyde, he had been a reformer. But so much had since happened to make those mild changes pale into insignificance that Clarendon's moderation could now pass as the staunchest royalist conservatism. Without surrendering the legitimate prerogative of the Crown, Clarendon was anxious to reanchor it in a stable constitution: parliament and king engaged in trusting, mutual dependence. While Pepys, along with many of the younger servants of the Restoration, was as apt as any courtier to snigger and cavil at Clarendon's weighty self-importance, he was actually very grateful for his settling authority. Clarendon, he knew, was unlikely to spurn the talents of ex-officers of the Protectorate—especially in so critical an area of expertise as the navy—merely to keep the kingdom pure. Purity did not seem to be much on Charles II's mind. So Pepys would have been gratified, but not perhaps surprised, to see his patron Edward Montagu promoted to the earldom of Sandwich. Pepys was also enough of a realist to appreciate that, if some carcasses had to be thrown to the baying hounds of the Cavaliers, he had better make sure his was not one of them. No one with so well-developed a sense of irony would have missed the fact that those who were now most incriminated by the posthumous notoriety of Cromwell were—like

15

Vane, Bradshaw, Ludlow and Harrison—precisely the republicans who had most hated him! So, with his wife Elizabeth, Pepys could move into his new lodgings at the Navy Board secure in the knowledge that this new state, like the old state, needed capable, industrious men like him; men who knew where to find things like guns, ships, men and money. Especially money.

All the same, though, he was bound to have felt just a little uncomfortable amid the obscure gorgeousness of the coronation. The serried ranks of bishops and barons were men who seemed to know by instinct, as well as by education, how to play their parts in this ponderously antique performance. What would Cromwell have made of the apparition of the 'King's Champion' riding, in full coat of mail, into Westminster Hall during the banquet and flinging down his gage to challenge anyone who might impugn his royal master?

Well, perhaps King Oliver might even have suffered this nonsense as a necessary mummery, a plaything for the landed and the hare-brained. But he would certainly not, like Charles, have rounded up the scrofulous to be touched 'for the king's evil'. Could the ironic, urbanely quizzical Charles really believe in all this foolishness? It was the same Charles, after all, who patronized the natural philosophers of Gresham College, and who endorsed a 'Royal Society' as a fellowship of the learned who might converse and even dispute without destructive acrimony. To some, in fact, the king himself seemed to be of this inquisitive mind, poring as he did over the latest time-pieces and telescopes, scrutinizing the universe as an ingeniously constructed apparatus put together by

16

the Celestial Mechanic.

So, when all was said and done, could Charles be expected to preside over a realm of even-tempered reason? The Declaration of Breda, issued in April 1660, had promised 'Liberty to tender Consciences' precisely as an antidote to 'the Passion and the uncharitablenesse of the times [which] have produced severall Opinions in Religion, by which men are engaged in parties and animosities against each other'. But what transpired in the first years of his reign hardly fulfilled the promised hopes of 'freedom of conversation'. Charles may have wished to be sweetly reasonable, but the 'Cavalier' Parliament, elected in March and April 1661—and not replaced until 1679—was much more interested in vindication than moderation. The old soldiers who had bled for the king (either in their persons or in their purses) doubtless felt the savage punishments meted out to the republicans were merited by the enormity of their crimes. But the real thirsters after satisfaction were the clergy, especially the bishops, who after the downfall of Laud had suffered humiliations inconceivable in the history of the English Church: the imprisonment and execution of the Archbishop, expulsion from the House of Lords and extirpation from their own dioceses, the very name and office of bishop made shameful. Now the mitres and monstrances were back, nowhere more triumphantly than at Ely, where Christopher Wren's formidable uncle Matthew was restored after years of unrepentant incarceration in the Tower of London where he had shared a cell with Laud. Matthew was Zadok glorified, Oded set up on high, and he let it be known in no uncertain terms that the pernicious

17

pack of 'fanatics and sectaries' who had desecrated the sanctity of the Church of England would never again be allowed to delude the credulous and make trouble in the house of the Lord.

A pathetic Fifth Monarchist riot in London in January 1661, which mobilized all of fifty supporters to its cause, gave the militant bishops and their allies in the subsequent Cavalier Parliament all the pretext they needed to reject the efforts of both Clarendon and the king to loosen the severity of the restored Church of England. For all the grandeur of his demeanour, Clarendon was a pragmatist and had no interest in provoking and perpetuating disaffection. Better the Puritans should scowl from within than from without the Church. So he had hoped that either the Church of England's dogma could be broadened enough to allow some of the Nonconformists to be reconciled, or else that the penalties for active conformity might be unenforced. The king wanted the same leniency for Catholics. But prelates like Wren and Gilbert Sheldon were having none of this. So notwithstanding the fact that it represented everything the Lord Chancellor opposed, parliament enacted a series of punitive acts known collectively as the 'Clarendon Code' and expressly designed to strangle the life out of non-Anglican Christian worship. Knowing that the sects had drawn their strength from urban artisans and merchants, dissenting ministers were banished to a distance at least 5 miles outside town limits. Strict examination of the orthodoxy of professing clergy was to be enforced, and those tainted with the least signs of Nonconformity weeded out. And of course it was not just the wilder fringe cults—the Muggletonians and the Seekers—that were the target of all this draconian scrutiny. The acts were intended to marginalize, and then uproot, the entirety of English Presbyterian Calvinism. Presbyterian opposition to the republic in the 1650s and support for the Restoration was as of no consequence now. The bishops were adamant in their belief (not unfounded) that Puritan heterodoxy had been the great engine of disaffection against Church and king. If those institutions were to be made secure against a repetition of rebellion, the opposite conclusion from Clarendon's middle way had to be embraced. English Calvinism needed to be wiped out.

So—astonishingly—a whole culture of teaching, preaching, praying and singing, a culture that had so deeply coloured faith and politics for at least two generations, was made to go away. If it survived at all it did so with permission, not as of right but furtively and apologetically. In 1662 on the anniversary of the St Bartholomew's Eve massacre, hundreds of Nonconformist (overwhelmingly Puritan-Presbyterian) ministers were evicted from their livings. In December of the same year the king issued a Declaration of Indulgence, expressing his intent to ask the Cavalier Parliament to grant him power to dispense with the Act of Uniformity, but he was defeated in March 1663 by his own, much more intransigent parliament! In November 1663, Pepys heard his clerk Will Hewer's 'Uncle Blackborne' speak with quiet but deep resentment of the 'many pious Ministers of God—some thousands of them [who] do now, beg their bread' and of 'how highly the present Clergy carry themselfs everywhere, so as that they are hated and

19

laughed at by everybody'.

This transformation of a highly visible and even more highly audible culture into a closeted, family Church was one of the great disappearing acts in English history. It was neither permanent nor universal. Dissenting Christianity would survive and revive (especially in the next century). And the enforced collapse of Calvinism encouraged recruits to Nonconforming Churches like the Quakers, which were free from political suspicion. But the future of British history was profoundly affected in ways as yet undiscernible to the confident bishops and the Cavaliers who made the Clarendon Code. What they did was not so much eliminate Puritanism as displace it, sending it into exile from where, in the future, it would cause at least as much trouble to the British monarchy as it had in the past: places like Belfast and Boston.

The shutting of mouths was completed by the closing of presses. The repeal of the act requiring triennial elections brutally pruned back the young growth of competitive politics. A licensing act now effectively gagged the free press of the Commonwealth by giving a publishing monopoly over works of history and politics to the orthodox university presses or the officially regulated Stationers Company. The unrepentant old Laudian journalist Roger l'Estrange was given effective censorship authority over London's master-printers, whose numbers, he proposed, should be cut from sixty to twenty. Bad things could happen to those who flouted that authority, however idiosyncratic their publications. John Heydon, for example, was thrown into prison merely for casting the king's horoscope—deemed a seditious act—

and publishers like Giles Calvert, who had specialized in treatises of political theory, ended up in Newgate. Clubs, such as the Rota, where competing arguments about the constitution and government had been freely debated in 1659, were shut down; coffee-houses, where the agitators had met, were patrolled and spied on.

For the prophets and preachers, the printers and journalists cast out into the wilderness, their dispersal handed the realm to Pharisees, harlots and parasitical courtiers. But it was not necessary to be a Puritan 'fanatic' to be scandalized by the profligacy and promiscuousness of Charles II's court. Even to staunch Anglican Royalists like John Evelyn, the addiction of the king and his brother to debauchery was an affront to the Almighty by whose benevolent grace the king had been restored to his throne. But the king, now in the narcissistic prime of his mid-thirties, was impervious to criticism. He lolled on downy pillows of flattery, assiduously fluffed up by a succession of fawning poets (many of whom, like John Dryden and Edmund Waller, had once fawned on Cromwell), and would dandle his bastards on the royal couch along with his glossy spaniels and mistresses. There was an instinctive graciousness about the king (unlike his cynosure Louis XIV), which made it physically painful, if not outright impossible, for him to refuse favours to those women who had so unhesitatingly received him into their bed. The brightest and most ambitious of them made the most of the moment. Barbara Palmer, Lady Castlemaine, for example, insisted on being treated as a true consort, accumulating not just wealth but power, and at times dictating who might and who

21

might not be received by the king. As a helpless bystander to Charles's captivity between the sheets, Clarendon was in a state of infuriated torment. Under Cromwell, the aggressive (if intermittent) pursuit of virtue had threatened to undo the stability of government. Now, the equally aggressive pursuit of vice promised to have the same effect. For if sophisticated Londoners were unshocked by the fashion parade of over-frizzed curls and over-exposed bosoms, the same, so Clarendon feared, was not true of opinion in the shires. When the secret marriage of his own (pregnant) daughter, Anne Hyde, to Charles's brother, James, Duke of York, was announced, Clarendon was so aghast that he recommended the king behead her for her temerity. His horror was occasioned not just by James's reputation for lechery, which surpassed even that of the king, but by the inevitable whispering campaign that he had contrived the marriage to create a royal dynasty of Stuart-Hydes (something that duly came to pass but not exactly in the way Clarendon imagined or feared).

He was not alone in these anxieties. When things went very badly wrong with the government of the realm a few years later, in 1667, Sir George Carteret, Pepys' colleague at the Navy Board, reminded him that the want of 'at least a show of religion in the government, and sobriety' had been the cause which

> did set up and keep Oliver, though he was the greatest rogue in the world. And that it [decency] is so fixed in the nature of the common Englishman, that it will not out of him

22

. . . while all should be labouring to settle the Kingdom, they are at Court all in factions . . . and the King adheres to no man, but this day delivers himself up to this and the next to that, to the ruin of himself and business. That he is at the command of any woman like a slave [and] . . . cannot command himself in the presence of a woman he likes.

That the affairs of the flesh and the affairs of state need not necessarily be mutually exclusive is documented—exhaustively—by the diaries of Samuel Pepys. His hands were seldom still, whether they were busily penning memoranda on the state of the timber supply, or travelling through the underthings of the latest woman to take his fancy. But for Pepys these dalliances were not distraction so much as invigoration: the grope that refreshes.

3 October 1664 Talk also of great haste in the getting out another fleet and building some ships. Thence, with our heads full of business, we broke up, and I to my barbers and there only saw Jane and stroked her under the chin; and away to the Exchange and there long about several businesses, hoping to get money by them. And thence home to dinner . . . But meeting Bagwell's wife at the office before I went home, I took her into the office and there kissed her only. She rebuked me for doing it; saying, that did I do so much to many bodies else, it would be a stain to me. But I do not see but she takes it well enough; though in the main, I believe she is very honest.

To say his days were full would be an understatement. Apart from his business at the offices of the Navy Board, Pepys managed to take in several plays a week, meetings of the Royal Society, bibulous assemblies in taverns and musical recitals. Hungry for news, gossip or flirtation, Pepys roamed the capital by boat, by carriage or on his own two feet, searching for whatever he needed that particular hour, that particular day: information from the arsenal at Woolwich, or the dockyard managers at Deptford; girls who made themselves available in the alleys off Fleet Street; a shipyard carpenter's wife; the latest telescope from Richard Reeve's shop; the sleekest black-silk camelot suit coat from his tailor.

Pepys was one of the great inspectors, whether of the inviting curve of a woman's breast or the supplies of cordage available to the fleet. He was compulsive about tallies, not least of his own assets as well as the kingdom's, and was distressed whenever he detected shortfall. When he thought his long-suffering wife Elizabeth was frittering the substance of their fortune on dress he subjected her to bullying accusations, and when she presumed to argue back slapped her about the face (as he often did) for her temerity. This ugly side of his character, however, was seldom on show to his large circle of friends and colleagues, who took him to be the most companionable and learned of men. And Pepys was easiest amid like-minded fellows who shared his view that the accumulation of knowledge was the pillar, not just of understanding but of power. So he could be counted on as a booster of experimental and scientific projects designed for the benefit of the kingdom, like John Evelyn's proposals, set out in his *Fumifugium,* to make the verminous, insanitary, smoke-choked city safer and healthier, or William Petty's invention of the double-keeled boat—even when the king politely ignored the one and saw the other founder in its first sailing trial, drowning those on board.

It became apparent, in fact, that for Charles science was an amusement, an indulgence of toys like time-pieces and eye-pieces rather than a meticulously sustained inquiry. The king (like the rest of polite society) was charmed by Robert Hooke's engravings of the magnified louse in the *Micrographia,* and he was content to have his patronage attached to the deliberations of the Royal Society. But he also made sure to broadcast his bewilderment at the goings-on at Gresham College whereby grave men busied themselves 'spending time in weighing of ayre'. But it never occurred to Charles to see the proceedings of the Royal Society as more than the eccentric diversions of a gentlemen's club, certainly not as a model of inquiry and debate settled by experimental observation, favoured by the likes of Petty and Boyle. When calamity struck the kingdom, as it did in a succession of stunning hammer-blows between 1665 and 1667, the instinctive response of the king, as well as of his subjects, was to invoke not the illuminations of science and the arguments of reason but divine intercession through penance, fasting and prayer.

So the appearance of a comet in the summer of 1664 struck observers, not with astronomical wonder (though those in possession of Richard Reeve's telescope could observe its blazing tail with unparalleled clarity), but with the same dismay that this phenomenon had always inspired as a presage of disaster. Those like Clarendon who had bitterly opposed the war against the Dutch, into which the king had entered with such bellicose optimism, felt even queasier when they saw the dusty pallor trembling in the night sky, notwithstanding an early naval victory at Lowestoft. By the following summer, when the Dutch showed no sign of surrender and plague carts were carrying thousands to the burial pits every week, the Jeremiahs seemed vindicated in their prophecies that God's hand would be laid across the back of the sin-steeped kingdom. And there was not much that science could do about it, other than count London's dead with modern devotion to the seriousness of statistics and the mapping of the epidemic (8252 deaths in the first week of September, 6978 from the plague).

Understanding of the generation and transmission of the sickness was scarcely any more advanced than when it had first struck in 1348. Because it was thought that cats and dogs spread the plague, the Lord Mayor of London ordered a general slaughter: 40,000 dogs and perhaps (by Pepys's reckoning) 200,000 cats were duly massacred. That they were so swiftly rounded up and dispatched testified to the fact that what *had* modernized since the medieval epidemics was the policing of mortality. Daniel Defoe's heart-rending account of the harvest of bodies in 1665, *A Journal of the Plague Year*, was written more than half a century after the event, but was based on reliable memories of contemporaries, including one of Samuel Pepys's amanuenses, Paul Lorrain. What

Defoe describes is a culture divided into the mad and the methodical. Unhinged prophets walked naked in the streets roaring for repentance before the race was consumed altogether, while platoons of watchmen patrolled the streets enforcing the requirement that households become hermetically sealed at the first sign of infection. While the court, the aristocracy and the professions (including, of course, physicians) fled London just as fast as they could, common citizens were locked up by the watch in their own houses, prisoners of the contagion, left to succumb, starve or survive. The regulations may have been designed to seal off the country from the plague, but inevitably the infection always outran the ability to contain it, and in the meantime they condemned Londoners to be deprived of any hope of work or sustenance except what came their way by charity. The desperate who attempted to escape the net risked arrest and prosecution. From Alderman Hooker, Pepys heard of a saddler 'who had buried all the rest of his children of the plague; and himself and wife now being shut up, and in despair of escaping, did desire only to save the life of this [their surviving] little child; and so prevailed to have it received stark-naked into the arms of a friend, who brought it (having put it into new fresh clothes) to Greenwich'. And for once Pepys and his colleagues were moved enough to allow the child to stay there in safety.

One-sixth of London's population died in the plague of 1665. The misery ebbed with the onset of cool weather, but the trepidation hung around. Pepys was inhibited from wearing his fine new periwig for fear that it was made of hair cut from

27

infected bodies. Following astrology, as the almanacs reminded their preternaturally anxious readers, was numerology; the tail of the comet heralded the sign of the Beast, his number being, as everyone knew: 666. Sure enough, in the first week of September 1666, up from the bituminous regions of hell came the diabolical fire. Prophets like Walter Gostelo and Daniel Baker had long been warning that the new Sodom, steeped in lechery and luxury, would be consumed by the fiery wrath of an indignant Jehovah. But the more sober John Evelyn, watching thousands upon thousands arrive each day from the country, blocking the alleys with their carts, cramming the stinking, congested, drought-stricken city, also believed that, should a dry wind catch a casually released flame, a general ignition would occur.

Still, the violence of the conflagration caught almost everyone else unawares. The warm southeasterly, which blew in with the last dog days of August and the first of September, was feared as the carrier of contagion, rather than as a fire-lighter. So when, in the early hours of Sunday morning, 2 September, Sir Thomas Bludworth, the Lord Mayor of London, was woken from his sleep and told that the fire that had begun in the bakery of Thomas Farinor in Pudding Lane had already consumed much of Fish Street Hill and was advancing towards Thames Street, his response was: 'Pish! A woman might piss it out', before going back to sleep, irritated by the disturbance. As he snored on, the flames found their way into the warehouses flanking the Thames between London Bridge and the Tower, brim full of tallow, pitch, tar and brandy wines. A rolling fireball came roaring

28

and sucking out of the narrow streets, feeding on the overhanging timbered bays and gables. In an hour or two another 300 houses had been swallowed up by the fire. Panic took hold. People came flying out of their homes, pushing carts full of their possessions, making for the river where they dumped their wooden boxes in the grimy water to float and bob along in the spark-flecked darkness. The lanes became choked with traffic; faces were choked with scorching smoke. The elderly were carried through the streets in their beds or in improvised wheelbarrows. Told how serious the situation had become, Pepys got up before dawn, walked to the Tower and climbed to one of the high storeys from where he saw the fire working its way along London Bridge, devouring the piled-up houses and shops as it ate its way hungrily across the span. Only the pigeons stayed put in their windows and eaves until their feathers caught fire, leaving them to flutter pathetically, their wings alight.

Pepys made his way up-river, his boat navigating between the crates of household possessions as he kept his face away from the 'showers of firedrops' that flew with the wind. At Whitehall he told the king that only the immediate demolition of houses in the path of the fire, depriving it of kindling and creating fire-breaks, could contain the conflagration. For once Charles was not about to make light of the situation and gave orders that this should be done right away. A system of couriers between the City and the palace was established to keep the king informed of the progress of the fire. When Pepys got to the Lord Mayor, very much awake now 'like a man spent, with a hankercher about his neck', he found that Bludworth had gone from complacency to distraction: 'Lord what can I do? People will not obey me.' The Lord Mayor protested that he was pulling down houses as fast as he could but—not surprisingly—he was encountering resistance from those whose property (but not their persons) happened to be in the demolition zone. The truth was that Bludworth himself was still deeply reluctant to take action, worrying about the cost to house- and store-owners.

By the end of Sunday the fire, stoked by the wind, had destroyed the most densely populated core of the old city between the Tower and the Bridge. The thick pall of smoke, still lit here and there by bursts of flame, hung over London so thickly that it turned the September sun blood-red. John Evelyn, for whom the city's health and welfare had become a personal passion, was distraught.

O the miserable & calamitous speectacle, such as happly the whole world had not seene the like since the foundation of it, nor to be out don, 'til the universal Conflagration of it, all the skie were of a fiery aspect, like the top of a burning Oven, & the light seene above 40 miles round about for many nights. God grant mine eyes may never behold the like, who now saw above ten thousand houses all in one flame, the noise & crackling & thunder of the impetuous flames, the shreeking of Women & children, the hurry of people, the fall of towers, houses & churches was like an hideous storme . . . Thus I left it this afternoone burning, a resemblance of

Sodome, or the last day . . . It call'd to mind that passage of 4 *Heb: non enim hic habemus stabilem Civitatem*: the ruines resembling the picture of *Troy. London* was, but is no more!

* * *

On Monday, 3 September, the fire travelled beyond the huddle of houses, shops, taverns and warehouses, jumping the narrow Fleet river that bisected the old city, to reach the Royal Exchange and Lombard Street. 'Rattle, rattle, rattle was the noise which the fire struck upon the ear as if there had been a thousand iron chariots beating down upon the stones,' wrote Thomas Vincent of the experience of being trapped in the burning near the Exchange, 'whole streets at once in flames that issued forth as if they had been so many great forges.' Pepys now began to fear for his own property and possessions. While there was still time he sent his valuables off to a friend at Bethnal Green and, together with Sir William Penn, buried their official papers in a pit dug in Tower Street by the Navy Office. Then the two men, their shirts filthy with soot and smoke stains, dug their own deep hole. Into it went precious things: bottles of wine and Pepys's Parmesan cheese. At the end of the day he wanted to let his father know the terrible news that St Paul's and all Cheapside were on fire, 'but the post-house being burned, the letter could not go'. The next day, Tuesday, 4 September, was even worse, with the gusty breeze blowing the flames still further, north and west. On that terrifying Tuesday, the fire showed itself no respecter of the great public institutions of the city.

31

Over forty of the livery company halls went up in flames, and the Guildhall itself burned for twenty-four hours. By some miracle the city archives, which had been hastily stored in the crypt, survived. Not so the enormous stock of books kept by the sellers in the churchyard precincts of St Paul's. Seeing the fire coming straight towards the cathedral, they had made a panicky rush to store them in the booksellers' favoured chapel of St Faith's in the great church. Some managed to get their barrow-loads there; others, caught in the mass of human traffic and desperate not to be trapped, ended up dumping the books in the open yard. When the fire caught up with them it ignited the paper and parchment in a huge bonfire, the blackened pages flaking and flapping around amid the roaring air. But the books in St Faith's ended up no better off. For at the critical moment of the blaze most of the superstructure of the choir crashed into the chapel below, completing the incineration of the books. Then the lead on the roof liquefied: 'The stones of Pauless, flew like granados,' wrote Evelyn, who had been on a tour of inspection of the cathedral just a week before on 27 August; 'the Lead mealting downe the streetes in a streame, & the very pavements glowing with fiery rednesse, so as nor horse nor man was able to tread on them.'

The immensity of the disaster seemed to mock the pretensions of king and government to be a protector to the people. But unlike during the plague epidemic, when they had got themselves out of the capital as quickly as possible, Charles and his brother were very much in the thick of the efforts to contain and fight the fire. James was put in

32

charge of containment and demolition. There was not much that could be done with water. The summer's drought had reduced the levels of the city cisterns, and in any case most of the wooden pipes carrying water to the pumps and squirts had themselves been destroyed by the heat. But it was possible to fight fire with fire, and once the opposition to the demolition programme was finally overruled, and whole streets of houses blown up using military mines and tunnels, it began to have some noticeable effect. On Wednesday, 5 September, the wind started to drop. The conflagration began, at last, to be held in check.

The king himself was seen in the streets attended by just a few guards, doing what he did best—giving away gold (for once, to the deserving). But even his genuinely kindly presence could do little to abate the trauma experienced by the multitudes—now at least 100,000—who had been made homeless by the fire and who wandered about the smouldering ruins of the city. Tents had been set up at St George's Fields and Moorfields where the refugees camped in a state of shock. Evelyn saw many 'without a rag, or any necessary utinsils, bed or board, who from delicatnesse, riches & easy accomodations . . . were now reduc'd to extreamest misery & poverty'. By the end of the week, the tent cities of the homeless stretched all the way north through Islington and Primrose Hill to Highgate. If many were disconsolate at the catastrophe, just as many were in the grip of anger, looking for someone to blame for their predicament. So Charles went to the camp at Moorfields to quell the ugly rumours that the fire had been set by either the Papists or the Dutch—

or, in some improbably unholy alliance, by both. James intervened to stop a Dutch baker being lynched, but the French were still conspicuous targets. A Westminster School boy, William Taswell, saw one of them floored by a blacksmith with an iron bar. It had not been foreigners who had caused the disaster, Charles told the destitute and the homeless; it was, rather, the hand of God. And for whose transgressions, exactly, they might have asked, looking the king in the eye, had London been turned into a second Sodom?

When the rain started on 9 September, a week after the outbreak of the fire, allowing some early stocktaking, the scale of the devastation appalled even the pessimists. London, blackened and shattered, looked as though it had been broken by a cruel siege. Some 13,200 houses had been destroyed in 400 streets and courts. Eighty-seven churches, six chapels, much of St Paul's Cathedral and forty-four halls of the livery companies, as well as the Guildhall, the Exchange, the Custom House, Bridewell Prison, the great law courts, four bridges and three city gates, were gone. The damage was estimated at almost £10 million.

Of course, when Evelyn lamented 'London is no more', he was technically rather than demographically accurate. Three-quarters of the old City of London, the most densely populated core of shops, warehouses and small dwellings, had indeed been burned, but the metropolis now consisted of two cities (London and the rapidly expanding Westminster), or perhaps even three, with Southwark, Rotherhithe and Lambeth making another conurbation on the south bank. The fire had been contained before it could get through to the newer sprawling areas to the west and north, which housed both the very rich and the very poor. But it was precisely because the palace at Whitehall and the fashionable new streets, like Piccadilly where Clarendon had had his outrageously palatial town house built by Sir Roger Pratt, had been unscathed by the destruction that it was especially incumbent on the rich and powerful to show themselves solicitous about rebuilding the dwellings and public meeting-places of the less well-to-do. 'Restoration' might finally mean something other than so much poetic rhetoric. Now there was something solid, something serious to restore.

On 11 September, just two days after the rain had started, dousing any more fears of minor reignitions, the Savilian Professor of Astronomy at Oxford asked for an urgent audience with the king. Christopher Wren was then in his early thirties, a little younger than Charles. He could expect a cordial reception because his father, also Christopher, had been Dean of Windsor and had put his own life on the line during the civil war to preserve some of the treasures of the chapel, not least the archives of the Order of the Garter that Charles I had so passionately and so hopelessly cherished. Dean Wren had died before the Restoration, but his more famous and much more intransigent brother Matthew, the Bishop of Ely, had emerged from captivity determined to perpetuate Laud's programme for authority and beauteous decorum in the Church. The erstwhile Bishop of London, Gilbert Sheldon, now Archbishop of Canterbury, was one of young Christopher's patrons and had commended him to the king not just as someone capable of abstruse

35

mathematical demonstrations, but as a prodigy who could turn his nimbly versatile intellect to practical and architectural matters. Although Wren chose not to go, he had been asked, as early as 1661, if he could advise the king on the fortifications of Tangier, which were about to be passed to the Crown as a result of Charles's marriage to the Portuguese princess, Catherine of Braganza.

The flames had barely died away when Wren drafted for the king's inspection a plan for the rebuilding of the City of London. He must have worked on the project at startling speed, day and night, since he managed to anticipate by some days the more considered plans of two of his close friends among the Royal Society circle of scientists, John Evelyn and Robert Hooke. Wren's determination to get his ideas before the king's eyes in advance of any rival plans stemmed not so much from egotistical ambition (though Wren was no shrinking violet) as from his certainty that the breathtaking radicalism of the plan would shock conventional expectations of how the destroyed city should be rebuilt. Most of those expectations—including the king's—assumed that the buildings and streets of London would be reconstructed as and where they had stood before the fire. The immensely important exceptions to this assumption, embodied in the Rebuilding Act of February 1667, were the requirement to build in brick and stone, the ban on overhanging storeys and the broadening of selected streets so that an accidental fire on one side would not automatically catch on the other. Noxious industries that used combustible materials, like dyeing, tanning and brewing, were also to be moved out from the centre of town, preferably across the river.

Most of these prophylactic measures had been proposed by Evelyn's *Fumifugium* five years before. But Wren had his eye on something far more daring than fire precautions. He wanted an utter transformation of the old city: nothing short of the creation of a new Rome on the banks of the Thames, with a great domed basilica replacing the burnt-out Gothic hulk of old St Paul's. The vision, laid out so audaciously before Charles, was something Wren believed most perfectly expressed the spirit of a new Londinium: a marriage of antiquity and modernity, the colossal and the commercial, the sacred and the entrepreneurial. At its heart was a great oval piazza, but it was to be dominated by a Pantheon of business—a new, colonnaded Royal Exchange. Radiating out from its hub would be broad streets, optically calculated to afford sweeping, geometrically satisfying vistas of the public edifices and monuments (not least one to the fire itself). Studded throughout the new metropolis would be fifty-odd rebuilt churches, situated without any regard to the old boundaries of parishes, which Wren believed had been made redundant by the fire. New parishes could surely be redesigned about these architectural imperatives, not the other way round. Surely, as a man of science and high taste, the king could see the logic of this argument? Did he not want a capital worthy of all those odes eulogizing him as the new Augustus?

Charles, who had spent years in Paris watching that city transformed by architects such as François Mansart, Le Mercier and Louis Le Vau, was flattered by Wren's disarming instinct for grandeur.

37

And his initial reaction was to congratulate and encourage the young man on his visionary optimism. But—advised by harder heads on the Privy Council—he also knew that he was no Pharaoh (or Bourbon) who could simply order it into existence. The merchants, brokers and tradesmen wanted the life of the city to resume just as quickly as possible, and just where it had been interrupted by the fire. The thousands whose bread depended on their work for those enterprises could not afford to wait around until some gleaming vision of the phoenix-metropolis had been realized. Even the very limited scale of alteration (the broader streets) required compensation to be paid to those displaced by the building, derived from a tax (on shipped 'sea coal') that needed authorizing by parliament. And parliament, even a Cavalier parliament, was not in the utopia business. Those country gentlemen may have had the great text-books of architectural and city design, antique and neo-classical—Vitruvius, Palladio and Serlio—in their libraries, but, with rare exceptions, the vellum gathered dust and the folios stayed uncut.

So Wren's marvellous vision was doomed to be unrealized. He would, though—over three decades —get to build a fair number of his churches, themselves wonders of the new architecture, which thoughtfully combined Protestant concern for the centrality of preaching (through his acoustically calibrated interiors) with steeples, tiered with tempietti and balustrades, pilasters and columns, translated from baroque Rome and Paris to London. And Wren would, of course, give the country the greatest of all its sacred buildings: not just a new cathedral, but a national basilica.

Even had he wanted to, Wren would never have escaped St Paul's, the rebuilding of which gave him such grief and such glory. His uncle Matthew's cellmate Laud, at the height of his power, had imposed a massive fund-raiser on the country for the renovation of the dangerously unsound ancient structure (whose spire had fallen from the tower in an earlier fire in 1561). And before his execution, Laud had set aside £800 in his will to further the work of renovation. For Matthew the task of bringing St Paul's back, not just from architectural peril but from desecration, was the true meaning of the Restoration: a cleansing of profanity. When the parliamentarian army had come to London in 1647 and 1648, cavalry troopers had stalled their horses there; and after the king's execution the statues of Charles and James that had surmounted Inigo Jones's west portico had been pulled down and smashed. The cathedral plate had been melted down for the army, the stained glass shattered, pews and choir stalls chopped up for firewood. The royalist antiquarian William Dugdale's instinct that a terrible iconoclasm was at hand had been proved only too accurate, but happily he had completed his detailed description of the fabric and interior of the cathedral before the worst could happen. So, armed with this inventory (beautifully illustrated by Wenceslaus Hollar), Bishop Wren, along with the then Bishop of London, Gilbert Sheldon, and the Dean, William Sancroft, appointed themselves the Nehemiahs of the purified temple.

Christopher's piety was of an altogether quieter kind than that of his uncle. But he was, in his way, a deeply pious Christian, and he was not going to shirk the challenge. Saturated in the literature of

Roman and Renaissance architectural theory, he had a lifelong ambition to transplant classical architecture into England in such a way as would be consistent with the Protestantism to which he was devoutly committed. Laud had offended, because his 'innovations' had come to be seen as somehow an alien, even sinister, presence. Christopher Wren wanted to make spiritually beautiful and architecturally grand building seem *at home* in England. The fact that we now think of Wren as a quintessentially English architect suggests how completely successful he was in achieving this ambition. But the truism blinds us to the immense and painfully protracted difficulty he had in squaring the circle of a classical, colossal style for a Protestant, parliamentary nation. Somehow Wren managed his life's work—although with innumerable compromises that embittered and saddened him—but the Stuart monarchy, which he believed would anchor itself through his public achievement, failed. His work at St Paul's began as the showpiece of the Restoration, but it would only be accomplished after a revolution. And these two events were, in fact, crucially and meaningfully connected. What tied them together was the old lethal dance between Romanophilia and Romanophobia.

Wren's connection with St Paul's began in 1663, when a Royal Commission was set up to examine the soundness or unsoundness of the structure after the ordeal of the Commonwealth. The Surveyor-General of the Royal Works was the poet Sir John Denham, and it was decided to take advice from architects who included the fashionable house-builder Roger Pratt and the unknown Oxford mathematician and astronomer Christopher Wren. Wren had had no formal architectural training and had been foisted on the commissioners by Sheldon, who had daringly commissioned him to build the ceremonial theatre in Oxford that bore his name. Wren had borrowed from the precedent of the ancient theatre of Marcellus in Rome to create an arena, and since, unlike its Italian counterpart, the building could not be open to the skies, he had enclosed it with a roof, supported by disguised buttresses and painted on the inside with a dazzling *trompe l'oeil* classical allegory. With this commission under way, Wren had no hesitation in disregarding the much more provisional recommendations of Pratt to repair and restore St Paul's, especially its great tower. Instead, he proposed the demolition of the tower altogether and the removal of its columns. Surmounting the crossing in its place would be a great ribbed dome, carried on a drum and supported from within by eight massive piers. More eccentrically, it was to be surmounted, not by a conventional lantern but by a pineapple spire—the fruit of choice for architectural ornament, it is true, and possibly a compliment to the king, whose garden at Kew had just presented him with the first home-grown specimen.

Roger Pratt was not amused. In fact he was incensed at the temerity of this unknown and inveighed to the bishop, his patron Clarendon and the king against the extravagance and impracticality of the scheme. But Charles, guided by Sheldon, was in fact enough taken with the suggestion to refrain from any sort of veto. And in the summer of 1665, while London was in the grip of the plague, Wren took a journey that, if anything, made him even more resolved to pursue his vision of a Romanized basilica. His sojourn was not in Rome but in Paris. But architecturally speaking, Rome was *in* Paris in the person of its great genius Gian Lorenzo Bernini, whom Wren duly visited at his house where he saw the drawings of his stupendously audacious (and unrealized) plans for the east front of the Louvre. The contrapuntal rhythms of Bernini's rendering of the façade, swelling and receding, convex and concave, obviously made an impact on the impressionable Wren, since he too aimed for that kind of music in stone in the most ambitious of his own plans for St Paul's. But the rebuilding of Louis XIV's Paris and the great classical houses of the Ile de France, like Vaux-le-Vicomte, while more formally austere than Bernini's building language, gave Wren an opportunity to see at first hand how domed churches and colleges could be successfully transplanted into settings very different from Rome. French architects had felt free to play with the possibilities offered by different kinds of cupola: Bramante's hemispherical plan for St Peter's or Michelangelo's loftier, more tapered version. And Wren must also have admired the energy and clarity with which the royal architects carved their way through the clutter of medieval streets parallel to the Seine to create great axial thoroughfares converging on spacious squares, the house façades harmonized by classical pilasters.

When Wren arrived back in London his head was buzzing with creative ingenuity, and he was impatient to press on with his ideas for the all-out, rather than makeshift, reconstruction of St Paul's.

On 27 August 1666, in the company of John Evelyn as well as the still intensely antagonistic Pratt, a tour of inspection of the cathedral was made. Plumb lines dropped from the top of the columns supporting the tower found that they leaned, in some cases as much as 6 inches or a foot away from true perpendicular—a variation that Pratt had a hard time accounting for as the prescient intention of the original Gothic architects, concerned to allow for settling. But it was, of course, the great fire, which broke out six days later, rather than any invincibility of Wren's arguments, which settled the matter. Even *after* the fire, though, it was by no means a foregone conclusion that Wren would be allowed to implement his Romanizing dream. For much as Charles might have *liked* to have been Louis XIV and to be able to order grandeur into existence with a wave of his cane, he was not and he could not. Parliament had to be consulted when money needed to be spent, and the Cathedral Chapter's concerns, which were often practical rather than aesthetic, had to be listened to.

Wren, however, was only intermittently paying attention. The summer of 1667 had added yet another body blow to the credibility of the restored monarchy to be the divinely appointed protector of the nation. Charles and his governments had been unable to protect the country from plague and fire. And now they had shown themselves incapable of fulfilling the elementary obligation of defending the country against foreign invasion. Astoundingly in June, a Dutch fleet commanded by the great admiral Michiel de Ruyter had sailed up the river Medway with impunity, landed soldiers at Sheerness, stormed the river forts at Upnor and

Chatham, broken the barrier chain and destroyed or captured the better part of the English fleet. The king's flagship, the *Royal Charles* (which as the *Naseby* had been the terror of the North Sea), was taken back to Amsterdam in triumph.

Panic was followed by a bitter sense of humiliation, which in turn was followed by fury. As an official of the Navy Board, Pepys was lucky to escape with his position more or less intact; his senior, Peter Pett, was hounded from his place and sent to the Tower. Predictably, the hue and cry turned on the most conspicuous scapegoat, Lord Chancellor Clarendon—even though he had been vocal in criticizing the decision to go to war as recklessly ill-advised. His grandiose house was attacked, and Clarendon became genuinely frightened that, with talk of impeachment in the air, he might suffer the same fate as Strafford. Before that could happen he took himself back into the exile from which the Restoration had rescued him. Always hag-ridden by the ghosts of history, he would now try to exorcise them by writing it. And the partisan masterpiece that is his *History of the Rebellion and Civil Wars in England* was the result.

The shock of 1667 only made the need for some sort of triumphalist statement, testifying to the undimmed grandeur of Crown, Church and country, more urgent. Perhaps the Almighty might smile a little more generously on his afflicted kingdom if a great Solomonic temple could be built to extol him. And Clarendon's fall had also removed as an obstruction his pet architect, Pratt, who prudently chose to occupy himself henceforth with gentlemen's estates, including his own. In due course Wren became the new Surveyor-General.

But the relatively modest scale of his first design for a new St Paul's suggested that he was still conscious that funds were tight. Following the practice of the great Italian masters he admired so much, Sebastiano Serlio and Andrea Palladio, in 1669 Wren had the carver Richard Clear and the master-joiner William Clear build a scale model, which was put on display at Whitehall for the king's delectation. From the surviving fragments and drawings, it is apparent that Wren had not yet taken the great leap of imagination that would produce a truly stunning design. The cupola from his 1663 plan remained, but it was oddly attached (over a square base) to a conventionally rectangular nave, made somewhat grander by the colonnade, which was to be built along its exterior length. Most controversially, the dome dominated the east end of the church—the end that had been most badly damaged by the fire. The immediate concern of the Chapter was to have a new choir built as quickly as possible so that some semblance of church worship could be restored, before the rest of the rebuilding was tackled. But since that choir was now housed within the domed structure, acceptance of the plan was to become committed to its most ambitious, time-consuming and expensive feature.

The king liked Wren's first plan enough to allow his new Surveyor-General (who at last felt secure enough to resign his chair of astronomy at Oxford) to go ahead with the enormous project of demolition that had to precede any construction. Since the ruined and burnt-out walls of old St Paul's had, paradoxically, been strengthened by all the molten lead that had poured down them from the roof, the demolition took on the aspect of a military siege. An army of labourers, miners and excavators was drafted to the site, with Wren himself and his assistants directing the campaign from their custom-built office opposite the north side of the churchyard. While the work was under way Wren and his friends from the Royal Society, Evelyn and Hooke, took advantage of the excavations, dug deep enough to assure the architect that he was not imposing his monumental structure on sand, to see what remains of previous antiquity might surface. From the account given by his son in his biographical *Parentalia*, the finds were more extraordinary than anything that could have been anticipated, and they made a profound, even emotional impression on the always historically minded Christopher. The story of a labourer bringing Wren a stone to mark some spot in the works, and discovering that it bore the prophetic lapidary inscription *Resurgam* ('I will arise') is well known. But this is the least of it. For as the excavators dug they travelled back down through London's history, through the medieval and Norman foundations, discovering an ancient burial site. Saxon pins and jewellery were uncovered and then, deeper down, the remains of a Roman mortuary: urns that had contained the ashes of the dead, fragments of vividly decorated pottery. Wren and his friends and colleagues busied themselves in their shirtsleeves in the trenches of the dig, sorting, dating, arranging and classifying. Even deeper still they found, to their amazement, seashells buried in the sandy rock, so that in his mind's eye the architect saw the archaic geology of the place, Ludgate Hill, no hill at all but a low strand washed by the ocean and the primitive Thames a 'sinus of the sea'.

With antiquity made immediate, and Roman London, especially, staring him in the face, Wren's architectural imagination suddenly took wing. His second design, again translated by the Clears into an exquisite model 18 feet long, spoke of a pure revelation, an act of inspired courage that produced from Wren the most beautiful building never to be built in Britain.

Wren's design of 1673–4 confronted the awkwardness of attaching a domed crossing and choir to a traditional nave (like setting a new head on an old body) by doing away with the nave altogether, in fact, by creating the kind of church that had never been seen in Britain before. Instead of a long corridor opening up at the crossing into a tall lantern (like his uncle's church at Ely), Wren envisioned a vast scooped-out central basilica, full of light and air and sound: a Greek cross, three of the arms being equilateral, the fourth slightly elongated to provide an entrance vestibule. The vestibule, fronted by a flight of noble steps, would itself be surmounted by a smaller rotunda, serving as a kind of architectural overture to the immense cupola that lay beyond. The exterior walls of the Greek cross would be convex, setting up an exhilarating counterpoint with the concave circularity of the drum on which the great dome rested.

Wren had evidently not forgotten Bernini. But to the stunned *cognoscenti* who examined the model in the Convocation House, this was evidently just the problem. They had asked for a new St Paul's. And what Wren had given them was a new St Peter's. Had he fronted it with a set of enfolding colonnaded *braccia,* as in Bernini's new piazza, he could not possibly have done anything more aggressively Roman. The immediate and overpowering sense that they had been given something disturbingly alien, something that, as was pointed out, looked nothing like any known English cathedral, was especially ironic since Wren prided himself on having created an expressly Protestant house of worship. By abolishing a conventional nave-and-choir design and the screen barriers that separated them, he thought to bring the congregation closer to the essential experience of Anglican-Protestant worship, which, after all, was the sermon. His, he was convinced, was a church built for the auditory reception of Christ's word, not for the glimpsed exposure of visual mystery down a darkened tunnel, as in Catholic sacred spectacle. He may even (with some justification) have felt that, just as the teachers of the Reformation justified their emphasis on word over image from what they took to be the aural evangelism of the early Christian fathers, so he was returning to those days of conversion when the great pagan temples had been made over into basilicas for the true faith.

At the outset it was not clear that the king was among those who were shocked into opposition. But the Chapter, in particular the vocal and formidable Dr Edward Stillingfleet, was appalled and confounded by the Great Model. However impeccably Protestant Wren might have thought it, they could not help but read it as a Catholic structure, something that belonged to the Rome of Pope Alexander VII rather than to the Anglican capital of King Charles II. The Chapter was anxious not to repeat the mistakes of the Laudian campaign for sacred beautification, which had been attacked as popery by the back door. They insisted on a design that reverted to the traditional Latin cross with its long nave and separated choir, not least because they knew that the whole cathedral was very seldom used, and that, other than on holy days, they needed only the smaller space of the choir for daily services. Before long these many arguments began to make a decisive impression on the king. Around 1672 his brother James had been received back into the Roman Church, and Charles himself, as Pepys later discovered, had been privately and secretly moving in that direction himself. That only increased the necessity of *not* building something that looked to most people like the temple of the Pope.

Crestfallen at the reception of the Great Model, Wren mounted a campaign to try to have the king overrule the objections of the Cathedral Chapter. But persuade, argue, even implore as Wren tried, Charles had made up his mind. While no objection was raised to some sort of domed crossing, Wren was ordered to meet the Chapter's complaints by reverting to a traditional Latin cross. Almost as if in a sulky demonstration of the impossibility of squaring (or rectangularizing) the circle, that first 'Warrant' design was the most absurdly incongruous of all Wren's plans, obediently attaching a long nave to a bizarre double-tiered dome consisting of a Bramante-like squat circular base with a peculiar Michelangelesque onion dome on top: an Anglican pagoda. After the inevitable failure of this monstrosity, it would take Wren years to come up with a more acceptable compromise, largely by surreptitiously ignoring some of the restraints and reverting to his original vision of 1663, in which there would be two grandiose statements on the cathedral—the mighty dome at the east end and a great portico at the west, the two connected by a spacious nave.

That is the cathedral as it stands today, more or less. But it's impossible to sit in the nave, with its echoes bouncing off the columns, and not dream of Wren's banished basilica, where perfect sound would have been bathed in limpid pools of light. Although he carried on with his work at St Paul's, Wren was devastated by the rejection. It was said that, as he heard the king's final decision, tears stood in his eyes. And although he was supposed to have been consoled by the grant of his knighthood, Wren's cup of sorrow overflowed during 1674. He was defeated in an attempt to win election to the House of Commons for Oxford and endured the death of first a child, and then of his wife, in 1675. His ambition to convert London into a new Rome had been a victim of terrible timing. For between the inception of the idea and Wren's attempt to persuade the earthly powers of its 'beauty and convenience', something ugly had happened to English politics. That something was the return of the prime patriotic neurosis: anti-Catholicism.

It had never really gone away, of course. Between the Gunpowder and the Popish plots the equation of Catholicism with 'enslavement' to the demonic power of tyrannical, Jesuitical Rome shrank to the margins of the great events of the mid-century wars and revolution. And understandably so, since by the Restoration probably not much more than 1 per cent of the population of England (probably rather more in Scotland) remained actively practising Catholics. But the power of anti-Catholicism as a polarizing force in politics, and the ease by which it could be exploited to unleash uncontainable forces of hysteria, fury and panic, were out of all proportion to the reality of the threat. In 1641 it had been the perception that Charles I was secretly behind the Irish insurrection and that he would use Catholic soldiers against both the Scots and English that had convinced men like Pym and Cromwell that the king could no longer be safely entrusted with control of the militia. In that sense at least, anti-Catholicism had been the proximate cause of the civil war. In 1649 Cromwell's conviction that a royalist army in Ireland might still be used to reverse the victory of parliament made him determined to annihilate resistance in that country and created in the wake of his conquests the first kingless Britain. Running through two centuries of British history like a scarlet thread—from Walsingham's security state in the 1570s to the Gordon Riots in the 1780s—was the adamant conviction that Rome's war on heresy had ruled out the possibility of being loyal to both Church and king (or Commonwealth). Even those, like Cromwell, who had passionately believed in religious liberty, axiomatically denied that liberty to Catholics. Milton, the great guardian of the free conscience, refused to allow that Catholics were, in fact, Christians at all. For at least a century—ever since the publication of Foxe's *Actes and Monuments* (the 'Book of Martyrs')—national identity had been hammered out against the anvil

51

of a perennially threatening, fiendishly devious, politically tyrannical and spiritually demonic Rome. The only question had been which power had been better able to protect the heart of the nation from the dagger of the Antichrist pointed at it—king or Commonwealth, parliament or Protector?

The credentials of the Protectorate as an Anglo-Protestant warrior-state, much vaunted by Cromwell in a rabidly anti-Spanish oration to parliament, had taken a fatal blow when the 'Western Enterprise' in the Caribbean came to ignominious grief on Hispaniola. And the religious and political anarchy of 1659 had provided a perfect opening for the Restoration monarchy to advertise itself as ensuring strength through a return to order and conformity. This is, indeed, what Clarendon and Archbishop Sheldon genuinely believed: that a return to the unquestioned authority of the Church of England, not some deluded and divisive liberty of conscience, was the best bulwark against the subversion of 'fanatics'—whether Calvinist, Quaker or Catholic. And through the honeymoon years of Charles II's reign, notwithstanding his attempt to pass a Declaration of Indulgence in 1662, the assumption among the vast majority of the county gentry was that this was the staunch opinion of the king as well. Whatever his shortcomings as a model of upstanding Christian propriety, Charles at least went through the motions of Anglican observance, and when taxed with the consequences of his relentless lechery responded disarmingly that he did not believe 'God would damn a man for a little irregular pleasure'.

But elegant flippancy only took you so far. In good times it advanced general merriment, a quality the Restoration consciously promoted against the public grimness of the Protectorate. In bad times, though, the banter could suddenly seem wan and facetious. (Evelyn, the devoted monarchist, quickly sickened of it as so much political confectionery.) The avalanche of misfortune that crashed down on England after 1665 raised questions among the more pious gentry in the shires, who were by no means all unreconstructed Presbyterians, about the seriousness with which Charles took his coronation vow to be the Defender of the Faith. The shamelessness of his debauchery, the squalid promiscuousness with which he took both mistresses and spaniels into his bed (sometimes, it was said not inaccurately, at the same time), undoubtedly had a cumulative effect on men who identified with the supposedly independent, old-fashioned virtues of 'country' as against the licentious sink and rapacious self-promotion of the 'court'. It was an article of country-Cavalier faith that their displeasure with court and courtiers would never affect their allegiance to the king himself. But over the long stretch of bad years, country suspicion and hostility towards those around the king deepened, and with it came anxiety that the king's proverbial laziness, self-indulgence and irresolution (so unlike his sainted father) might yet lead the country into crisis, even before Charles had deigned to notice it. John Evelyn, who always had his ear to the ground when it came to the prejudices of the gentry, echoed them by judging that Charles, who 'would doubtless

53

have been an excellent prince, had he been less addicted to women, who made him uneasy and always in want to supply their unmeasurable profusion', was sovereign of everything except himself.

Towards the end of the decade, these fears, for a while amorphous and unarticulated, began to take on much crisper definition. There was, to begin with, the disturbing fact of royal childlessness. The barrenness of the Portuguese Catholic queen, Catherine of Braganza—in unhappy contrast to the fecundity of Charles's many mistresses—was surely some sort of punishment laid on the kingdom. If you looked at the world through the correct— which was to say the most conspiratorially acute— lenses, you saw right away something so rotten that it could only have originated in the filthy stews of the Whore of Babylon (aka the Jesuit-ridden Papacy). Fatal sterility and spendthrift concupiscence were part of the same plan—to sap the vitals of sturdy Protestant England.

Fruitlessness led to fretfulness. Without a direct heir, the next in line to the throne was the king's brother, James, Duke of York, whose own confessional allegiances seemed much closer to those of the Queen Mother, Henrietta Maria, still very much alive and very much the unrepentant Catholic, utterly convinced that the downfall of her husband had been his wishful thinking that a strong monarchy could be created in an Anglican, parliamentary country. James, described as 'the most unguarded ogler in England', was every bit as much of an unappetizing lecher as his older brother, but, unlike Charles, managed to alternate hearty bouts of lust with equally fierce orgies of sanctimoniousness. James's first marriage, to Clarendon's daughter Anne Hyde, had shown that he could indeed produce children, at least daughters. Demoted by James's mistresses to an object of ridicule, Anne sought consolation in the Hyde family weakness, the table, and like her father expanded in girth as she declined in dignity. When she died in 1671, leaving the two girls, Mary and Anne, who would both become queen and who resisted their father's efforts to make them follow him back into the arms of the Roman Church, James lost no time in taking a second wife in 1673: the unquestionably Catholic (and strikingly beautiful) Mary of Modena.

With that marriage, and the prospect of a Catholic heir, the threshold of anti-Catholic hysteria dramatically lowered. A year or so earlier, James had gone public for the first time, declaring his return to the Roman Church by conspicuously failing to attend Anglican communion at Easter. This calculated advertisement of his confessional allegiance put the Anglican hierarchy and the gentry in the shires on notice that, unless something changed, they could expect a Papist king and perhaps a Papist dynasty to follow. Hackles rose in Hampshire. Paranoid though the reaction was, had the guardians of the Anglican settlement known the whole truth their suspicions would have turned to apoplexy. For on 25 January 1669 (significantly, the feast of the conversion of St Paul) Charles II had expressed his regrets to his brother that he was not able to profess openly the faith to which he too was genuinely drawn. No one (other than the Pope himself) could have been gladder to hear of this than Louis XIV, who had been targeting his own secret weapon—the glamorous Louise de Kéroualle—directly at the place he knew it was bound to score a direct hit: Charles II's bed. It certainly did no harm to the French king's strategy. For Louise cantered between the royal sheets, routing her rivals, as brilliantly as Louis triumphed on the battlefield, and Charles was helplessly seduced by both of them. Louise bore Charles a son in 1672 and in 1673 was made Duchess of Portsmouth. And in 1670, Charles was grateful enough to sign a clandestine treaty with Louis. Although he was encouraged in this direction by some of his inner circle of ministers—particularly Lord Ashley, Henry Bennet, Lord Arlington, and Thomas Clifford—the terms of the treaty were shocking enough to be kept from the majority of the Privy Council and especially the dourly suspicious Scot, John Maitland, Earl of Lauderdale. This was just as well, since any objective observer would have to conclude that what Charles had done, in his obtuse recklessness, was to mortgage his sovereignty to the king of France, or rather replace dependence on an English parliament by dependence on the bounty of the French purse. In return for a Versailles hand-out, handsome enough to free Charles from the inconvenience of having to go cap in hand every few years to parliament, the English king had committed himself to easing the conditions of English Catholics and perhaps, when a suitable occasion arose, even declaring his own true confessional allegiance. And there was more. Charles had committed himself to joining Louis's surprise attack on the Protestant Dutch Republic, a policy much easier to justify in England as payback for the humiliation of 1667.

To suggestions that some sort of deal had been made with France, Charles II simply lied, flatly denying there had been any under-the-table treaty. In fact, the provisions of the secret Treaty of Dover exceeded the most feverish nightmares of anti-Catholic conspiracy theorists. The birthright that Charles had casually bartered away was, after all, not his to give away but parliament's. And there was still worse. Had the king bothered to reflect in any detail on the issues that had caused so much grief for his father in 1641, he might have recalled that the suspicion that Charles I was about to call in a foreign, Catholic (Irish) army had been top of the list. That had been the red rag waved at the parliamentary bull, which more than anything else had provoked them to strip the king of his control of the militia. It had, in fact, triggered the civil war. So what did his son do in 1670 but agree to the importation of *French* troops in the event of facing his own domestic rebellion?

Some of Charles's ministers who led him into this suicidally reckless stratagem had their own reasons. Clifford, as it would be discovered before he committed suicide, was a secret Catholic. Lord Arlington probably was, too, although he justified the Declaration of Indulgence of March 1672 essentially as a measure designed to strengthen, not weaken, the security of the state, especially against Nonconformists notorious for their unreconciled republicanism. For while the Declaration meant that Catholics were now allowed to worship in *private* houses (a detail that did nothing to allay suspicions), Dissenters, ostensibly receiving even-handed treatment, were required to apply for the official licensing of their places of gathering and worship.

The dramatic, undeclared opening of Charles's second war against the Dutch in May 1672 and the success of both English warships and Louis XIV's armies, who occupied two-thirds of the country, reducing the most powerful state in the world to chaos, was such an unalloyed source of gloating to patriotic opinion, still smarting from the débâcle of 1667, that for a while it silenced questions about the king's motives for issuing the Declaration of Indulgence. But quite quickly the war deteriorated and with it any kind of consensus. The young Prince of Orange, William III, took over as the Captain and Admiral-General of the panic-stricken Dutch Republic, on the brink, so it seemed, of annihilation. The scapegoats of the nightmare, the brothers De Witt, who had led the Republic to the great victory of 1667 and then into this catastrophe, were physically torn to pieces on the streets of The Hague. William, who had been kept powerless by Jan De Witt, shed no tears. But nor did he capitulate to the aggression. Instead of coming to terms, as expected, with the kings of France and England (both of whom were his relatives), William became an overnight Protestant hero by rallying his Fatherland to all-out defiant resistance. Flattering comparisons were made with his great-grandfather, William the Silent. The dykes were once again cut, as they had been almost exactly a century before, and Louis XIV's army, like Philip II's, became literally bogged down. Instead of mopping up resistance, it sank into the peaty mire. Dutch fleets began to inflict brutal attacks on English and French ships, and very quickly the war consensus inside the English government unravelled as defeats presented irresistible opportunities for critics among the country party to present the botched war and the Declaration of Indulgence as a sell-out to the Gallo-Catholic menace.

The incoming administration, committed to making a separate peace with the Dutch and reversing the Declaration of Indulgence, was led by Thomas Osborne, shortly to be Lord Danby. Although every bit as ambitious and self-seeking as the men he replaced, Danby was the very first English politician to present himself to the nation, quite self-consciously, as the Voice of the Shires: the country gentleman's friend and mouthpiece, fiercely Anglican, staunchly conservative, unquestionably royalist, but in an English, not a Frenchified, way. His government set its seal on power by forcing (on pain of denying the king revenues) the rescinding of the Declaration of Indulgence. In its place was put an anti-Catholic Test Act, which required all holders of any public office—including magistrates, members of parliament and officers of state, or of the army and navy—to deny the Catholic doctrine of transubstantiation and to conform in every way with the Anglican settlement. Thus the two pillars of Charles's rapprochement with Louis—toleration for Catholics and the anti-Dutch war—were simultaneously shattered. Privately, Charles let his regrets be known but complained that his hands were tied by parliament. Privately, Louis thought any king who would permit such contemptible insolence was hardly worthy of the office. Most incomprehensible of all to him was Charles's willingness to see his own brother, the next in line to the throne, deprived of his high office as Lord High Admiral for refusing to take a 'Test' imposed on royal blood by a noisy rabble of presumptuous commoners.

After the upheaval of 1672–3, the five years of the Danby regime that followed are often presented as some sort of placid recuperation, in which the potentially explosive nature of anti-Catholicism had been neutralized by heavy doses of Anglican rectitude and all around happiness with the status quo. By this account the even more tumultuous, near-revolutionary crisis that followed the 'revelation' of the fake Popish Plot came out of a clear blue sky as well as out of the criminally paranoid brains of Titus Oates and Israel Tonge. But their bizarre allegations of Catholic plots to assassinate the king and replace him with the Duke of York could not possibly have sent the country into the most extreme political convulsion it had experienced since the civil war unless the ground had been very well prepared in the preceding years. For if Danby's original claim to power had rested on his promise to purge the body politic of anything resembling pro-French Catholicism, many of his critics came to the conclusion that the remedy seemed worse than the disease. Danby's management of members of parliament as something like a 'Crown' party; his manipulation of patronage conditional on political obedience; his attempt to make office-holders sign a formal renunciation of any resistance to the monarch on any grounds; and his willingness to perpetuate, indefinitely, the life of the already long-lived Cavalier Parliament of 1661, all seemed evidence that he was actually making English government over in the image of the absolutism he professed to abhor.

These critics were not altogether wrong. Before the 1670s, opposition to governments had been moved by, and expressed in, dislike of particular men (Strafford or Clarendon) and particular measures (ship money). Not since 1640–42 had politics been articulated in such sharply ideological terms. And it was the adversaries of the power of the Crown, so apparently entrenched by Danby, who made the going. Lord Shaftesbury, who as Anthony Ashley Cooper had been successively a Barebone's MP, a Cromwellian Councillor of State and a Restoration Chancellor of the Exchequer, has been seen as the epitome of the scoundrelly opportunist, reaching for whatever politics was most likely to propel him into power and keep him there. And Shaftesbury was certainly not free of opportunism. He had, after all, been evicted from office by Danby and was impatient for revenge. But without perverting the truth too indecently, Shaftesbury could, as he began to don the mantle of the Guardian of the Ancient Constitution, plausibly claim to be revolving back to the principles that had begun his political career: the Cromwellian polity sketched out in the Humble Petition and Advice of 1657 of a 'government of a single person and [a bicameral] parliament'. There was, after all, a rich historical tradition to draw on, stretching back even beyond the Provisions of Oxford and Magna Carta to the purported Saxon *witangemot*, which insisted that royal power had always rested on conciliar consent. What made the royal polity of England English, and especially un-French, was that it had always been a contract. This

61

is what the Stuarts, misled by councillors like Danby who hoped to swell their own fortunes on the back of an over-mighty sovereignty, failed to understand. Any subject expecting to be protected from the ever present Catholic-tyrannical menace across the Channel by Crown-engrossers such as Danby was deceived. For only under an authentically English mixed monarchy, one prepared to concede that sovereignty was shared among king, Lords and Commons, could the liberties of the people and the Protestant Church be truly safeguarded.

During the 1670s, precisely because Danby's domination of parliament was so successful and the royalist ideology of divine right and non-resistance so entrenched, those who begged to differ had to look elsewhere to broadcast their competing view of the constitution. So it was in the streets, coffee-houses, clubs, taverns and printing shops rather than at Westminster that in the 1670s the rough prototype of party politics was born. Clubs like Shaftesbury's Green Ribbon, meeting at the King's Head tavern in Chancery Lane, where like-minded members could convince themselves of the wickedness of the Crown party and the existence of a Catholic conspiracy, multiplied, so that by the time the Popish Plot broke there were no fewer than twenty-nine such clubs in London alone and the most successful produced provincial affiliates in towns like Taunton, Bristol and Oxford. London's rapidly multiplying coffee-houses offered, as one astonished visitor from Florence testified, snug alcoves where news could be thirstily digested, along with one's coffee or chocolate, quite free of official censure or intimidation. Some were famous hotbeds of gossip, among them Hooke's and Wren's favourite, Garway's in Change Alley, London (where tea was introduced to England along with constitutional radicalism), and Aubrey's Rainbow in Fleet Street. The clash of polemics during the 1670s had fuelled a phenomenal resurgence in the business of multiple-copied 'separates' and intelligences on politics that streamed out into the provinces from London, and that made exhilarating reading compared to the drearily official *Gazette*. Between 1679 and 1682 no fewer than seventeen new newspapers would be founded, most of them expressly to promote a party view. Other spectres of political life of the 1640s and 1650s returned to harass Charles II as they had Charles I and Cromwell. Petitioning movements, which had not been seen since the Commonwealth, began to be mobilized again, especially when some sort of Catholic bogey was the motivator. Apprentice gangs—the sons of men who had taken to the streets in the 1640s—now reappeared with all their old, violent energy. Satirical poems, squibs and broadsides, which had long been available to high-placed patrons, now put on their street dress: ballads and bawdy verse hawked in the taverns. The theatrical innuendo became an art form. The galleries waited for it, then lapped it up, hooted and brayed with pleasure. And none of the scribblers could complain that Charles II had failed to provide them with rich material.

None of this, it has been well said (though perhaps too often), yet amounted to anything like a world divided by recognizably *modern* party politics. Loyalties were still notoriously fickle, their protagonists quite capable of switching sides at the drop of a hat. None the less, the embattled ideologies—divine right kingship and the 'mixed' monarchy—did represent two genuinely and mutually incompatible visions of what the authentic political constitution of England had been and ought to be. Whigs, in particular, liked to reach back to medieval statutes to emphasize the continuity of a peculiar English tradition, Shaftesbury insisting that 'the parliament of England is that Supreme and absolute power which gives life and Motion to the English government', the patriotic mantra drummed home over and over. Conversely, each of them identified their opponents as embodying politics that were, literally as well as metaphorically, foreign to England. Which is why the aggressively and self-consciously English antagonists in this war of ideas reached for the most unsavoury foreign labels they could think of by which to demonize their opponents, namely something associated with either the Scots or the Irish. Thus (a few years later during the Exclusion crisis surrounding James's succession), the defenders of Crown supremacy took to name-calling those whom they accused of dragging the country back to a civil war as Scots-Presbyterian outlaws or 'Whiggamores', and the Whigs returned the compliment by claiming that behind the disingenuous arguments to stand by Church and throne, their adversaries were nothing more than Irish-Catholic rebels or 'Tories', from the Gaelic *toraighe*, meaning a bog-trotter or bandit.

During the 1670s something much more serious than traded abuse was going on in English politics. Positions were hardening and polemics flying. No one in 1678 was ready to predict, much less desire, a new civil war. But equally no one thought that some sort of fundamental crisis about the government of England, some sort of 'revolution' in fact (in the contemporary sense of the term), was likely to be averted, so long as the heir apparent remained the avowedly Catholic, suspiciously quasi-absolutist James, Duke of York. In 1677, before Titus Oates ever opened his mouth, the MP for Hull, the poet Andrew Marvell, neither the most credulous nor the most opportunist of Englishmen, who had come of age, politically, in the Protectorate, let it be known in print that 'There has now for divers Years, a Design been carried on, to change the Lawful Government of England into an Absolute Tyranny, and to Convert the Established Protestant Religion into down-right Popery.'

The fact that the kind of convictions expressed in Marvell's *Account of the Growth of Popery and Arbitrary Government in England* were so commonplace helps to explain the otherwise astoundingly hysterical response to Oates's 'revelations' of a plot, masterminded by the Jesuits, to murder the king (some of his 'informants' believed by the knife, others by poison), to replace him with the Duke of York and to institute a French-Catholic absolutist state supported by French troops. The allegations were, of course, a pack of ugly lies, but they were artfully concocted ugly lies. Titus Oates was a monster of malignant ingenuity, but he was no fool. His active homosexuality had ensured that in his twenty-nine years there was virtually no major English institution from which he had not been ejected: his

Cambridge college (Gonville and Caius); his Church of England ministry in Kent; the navy, where he had signed on as chaplain to avoid perjury charges incurred while a curate; and finally he had been thrown out of the Jesuit colleges Colegio de los Inglese Valladolid, in Spain, and St Omer, in France, where he had gone as a purported convert. All of these places, of course, had offered Oates both irresistible opportunities and draconian penalties. But in his relatively short scapegrace life Oates had already shown himself to be an accomplished predator who, even when found out, managed somehow to avoid the worst consequences of his malice.

He was clever enough, in fact, to turn the latest notoriety, expulsion by the Jesuits, into something like evidence of both knowledge and integrity! As Oates rolled off his fantastic whoppers, it does not seem to have occurred to anyone to wonder whether or not his rough treatment at the hands of the Jesuits (though not as rough as the navy) might not have been a motive for a campaign of personal revenge. Shamelessly, Oates claimed that he had only gone over to St Omer as a kind of spiritual double-agent, the better to plumb their nefarious designs on the liberties and Church of England. And to give this outlandish claim more credibility, Oates acted as though he was indeed some sort of self-appointed spy, keeping as many careful notes and records of conversations with the Jesuits and their hireling assassins, both at home and abroad, as Robert Hooke or John Evelyn made of their experiments and their gardens. Oates was, in his own repulsive way, a *virtuoso,* lavishing as much attention and care on the fabrication of truth as the natural philosophers paid to the acquiring of it. In fact, the first person to whom Oates confided his knowledge of the Plot, the London clergyman Israel Tonge, flattered himself with the reputation of a scholar (he did in fact have an authentic doctorate) and kept company with some of the most eminent of the Fellows of the Royal Society. This did not, however, make Tonge rational, since he subscribed to the popular fantasy that the Great Fire of London had been started by Catholic arsonists. And it was that conflagration that had destroyed Tonge's vicarage along with his library of natural philosophy—had, in fact, ruined his life.

It was because Tonge had such powerful connections that he managed to get Oates an audience with the king himself to hear the shocking substance of the forty-three articles of the conspiracy. Charles was, understandably, incredulous; but his initial amusement at the improbability of the whole story, not least the incrimination of the queen's doctor, gradually gave way to enough anxiety to send the matter on to Danby. In the last week of September 1678 Oates appeared before the full Privy Council, and his apparent mastery of minutiae convinced some of them at least that there might be something to the story, however fantastic it seemed at first.

Oates knew his public. He had mixed into his story exactly the kind of sensationalism the suggestibly anti-Catholic public loved to hear: arson, poison, criminal doctors, wicked queens, malevolent monks. And as details leaked out, the story took fire like lightning striking dry leaves. The high-ups fanned the flames. Whether he believed it or not (and there is no reason to suppose he did not believe it) Shaftesbury saw it as Danby's come-uppance and railed against the first minister, who, while pretending to keep the country safe from Catholic intrigue, had actually invited it. At this stage, sceptics were still attempting to keep the thin walls of common sense from collapsing altogether. But two pieces of unexpected good luck for Oates ensured the rout of reason. First, one of the innumerable figures named in his list of the wicked, the Duchess of York's secretary, Edward Coleman, had actually corresponded with Louis XIV's confessor about the chances of a Catholic restoration in England— not in itself an act of criminal treason, rather an act of criminal stupidity, since Coleman had failed to destroy the letters and left them to be easily decoded. Even better, on 17 October, the body of Sir Edmund Berry Godfrey was found on the grassy slopes of Primrose Hill. Godfrey just happened to be the magistrate who had first taken Oates's sworn deposition about the plot. Speculation that he might have committed suicide rapidly gave way to a verdict that Godfrey had been murdered. Only the most ingenious and desperate thought that the culprits had actually belonged to the *anti*-Catholic hue and cry, trying to provoke a violent reaction.

If that were in fact the case they had done their work very well, since Godfrey's body was publicly exhibited surrounded by candles, as if he had been martyred in the cause of saving Protestant England. Mania now took possession of the country. Conveniently, November was, thanks to Guy Fawkes, the month for anti-Catholic bonfires. Now the 5 November celebrations turned into massive

'Pope Burnings', some attended by thousands of people. More Pope Burnings took place on 17 November, the anniversary of the accession of Good Queen Bess who had stood strong and steadfast against the Romish threat. The public imagination was gripped by the vision of imaginary Catholic 'night riders' roaming the countryside, looking for Anglican clergymen or justices of the peace to murder. To guard against the threat, apprentice gangs armed themselves, some of them with the 'Edmund Berry Godfrey' daggers that were so popular that 3000 of them had been sold in a day. By the time that Oates appeared before the full House of Commons he was able to state quite categorically and without fear of contradiction that 'there has been and still is a damnable and hellish plot, contrived and carried on by Popish recusants for the assassinating and murdering of the King and for subverting the government and rooting out and destroying the Protestant religion.'

Seeing a genuinely popular movement boiling up from below like some volcanic discharge, Shaftesbury, who had his own paid agents, made sure to channel the energy to his own and his party's advantage. Enthusiastically and inventively perjured 'informants' and 'witnesses' were paraded before parliament, beginning with the swindler and thief, William Bedloe, who claimed to have direct knowledge that Jesuits had killed Godfrey and to have seen his body at the queen's palace at Somerset House. Accusations of treason and murder now moved from known Catholics and priests to alleged 'sympathizers', among them Samuel Pepys. A former servant testified that Pepys had all along been a secret Catholic; and, much more damagingly, another long-time crook, John Scott, swore that he personally knew Pepys to have favoured and advanced Catholic officers in the navy and to have given the French plans of fortifications and ships in preparation for their planned invasion. It was enough to send Pepys to the Tower of London, where John Evelyn dined with him and sympathized with his plight. But it was a back-handed tribute to the plausibility of Oates's conspiracy story that even Fellows of the Royal Society, who were supposed to have no difficulty in recognizing the truth when they saw it, differed among themselves. For poor Pepys, the whole thing was a tissue of villainy. Evelyn hated Oates no less, but found him regrettably credible. To his credit, Pepys was not prepared to let the infamy roll over him. He fought back by hiring his own investigator, one John Joyne, to ingratiate himself with Scott, follow his movements and produce evidence of his disreputable life—not, as it turned out, a hard task. Pepys survived, unlike the twenty-four innocents who lost their lives to the witch-hunt.

By the end of 1679, after a Pope Burning attended, it was said, by a crowd of 200,000, the ugly energy unleashed by the Plot was converted by Shaftesbury into a specific political programme. Danby's intimidated government had crumbled and he himself faced impeachment unless, Shaftesbury made it clear, a new election was called. Monster petitions were mobilized (again recalling the 1640s); one from London, Southwark and Westminster was 300 feet long and bore 16,000 names. The king conceded. The election—contested in an unprecedented number of boroughs—was fought, sometimes bitterly and violently, and duly produced exactly the overwhelming Whig majority in the Commons that Shaftesbury needed. It came to Westminster, moreover, hot for a specific political goal, Exclusion: the elimination of the Catholic Duke of York (and any heirs he might have with Mary of Modena) from the line of succession. On Charles's death, the crown was to pass instead to his eldest illegitimate son, the Duke of Monmouth. For that matter, so Shaftesbury's propaganda claimed, the Duke was actually no bastard at all but the legitimate heir, since Charles, unbeknownst to everyone at the time and since, had actually married his mistress Lucy Walter during their relationship in Paris.

It was an extraordinary crisis in the life of the British monarchy. At stake were not only the lives of countless hundreds victimized by the lies and hysteria but also the fate of the polity itself. To concede the Exclusion was to accept that parliament had the constitutional authority to judge the fitness or unfitness of a prince to succeed to or occupy the throne. And neither Charles II nor the Tories were about to make that concession. *Patriarcha,* a treatise actually written fifty years before by the Kentish gentleman philosopher Sir Robert Filmer, was now published. It argued that God had directly given earthly authority to Adam, from whom all kings were lineally descended—a direct line of succession that could never be broken by any kind of inferior intervention. Shaftesbury and the Whigs in their turn revived some of the most radical thought surviving from the Commonwealth that insisted on the contractual

71

nature of the monarchy—not least, of course, the first of John Locke's *Two Treatises on Government.* Much of this was too heady for most of the Whig rank and file in the Commons, who were easier with the familiar platitude (recycled, for example, by Denzil Holles, still very much in action) that in England monarchy had always been bound by the law, not least its obligation to uphold the coronation oaths, and that parliament most certainly did have a right, not only to judge the degree to which those obligations had been kept but also to 'bind, govern, limit, restrain and govern the descent and inheritance of the Crown'.

Shaftesbury, though, had left his days with Oliver Cromwell far behind. He was no Ireton, not even a Pym. Ultimately he shrank from pushing Exclusion to the point where he might be forced to mobilize a new civil war over it. And the more his side was actually accused by the Crown and the Tories of wanting exactly that outcome, the more Shaftesbury recoiled from it. It was prudence rather than political queasiness that brought him up short before committing the country to a conflict he was doubtful he could ever win.

He was right. But where did that fatal pessimism leave him? Since he was not prepared to contemplate another revolution for a kingless England, Shaftesbury was fatally dependent on the force of public opinion and intimidation persuading Charles II to capitulate voluntarily to Exclusion. But there was something about the extremity to which he had been put that drew from the languid old lecher a demonstration of such political toughness and finesse that it ran rings round Shaftesbury, supposedly the great master of strategy. First, Charles sent his deeply unpopular brother and his wife out of the country, thereby removing from the scene the person who provoked most hatred and fury. But having made a concession, Charles then proceeded to stamp his high heels on the principles that mattered. On the issue of the exclusively royal prerogative to rule in matters of succession, Charles was as adamant as Elizabeth had been a century before. If, as seemed all but certain, he died childless, James, Catholic or not, *would* succeed. But—and this was the critical manoeuvre—as long as James insisted on remaining a Catholic, his would have to be a reign with a difference. Whatever his private beliefs, they could not affect the solemn obligation embodied in the coronation oaths to defend and protect the established Protestant Church of England. And to allay the suspicions that had got his father into such irreversible trouble, the Catholic king would have to agree to abstain from making his own appointments to high ecclesiastical office and transfer control of military appointments to parliament.

It was an inspired circumnavigation of the conflict. The Church had surely been saved, without compromising the authority of the Crown in matters regarding succession. And Charles's 'expedient' seemed reasonable enough to begin turning public opinion back towards the king. But when a second Whig-dominated House of Commons was elected (after Charles had dissolved the first), Shaftesbury was too confident in his apparent triumph to notice the slight tremor in the ground under him until it became the gaping fault that swallowed him up. The Commons passed an

Exclusion Bill by a two-to-one majority, while the Lords defeated it by the same majority. The deadlock meant that Charles was in a position to call Shaftesbury's bluff, and he coolly proceeded to do so (after having taken the precautionary measure of pocketing another massive hand-out from Louis XIV). In 1681 a third parliament was summoned to Oxford, where the Crown and its enemies had tested their wills in 1258. All sweet reason, Charles tabled his 'expedient' once more, only to have it brushed aside, as he had calculated, by Shaftesbury's insistence on Exclusion. The only way forward now was a resolution by force. Indeed, some of the Whigs showed up at Oxford in arms, while others talked openly of a return to the Commonwealth—exactly the ammunition Charles needed to make his case that it was the Exclusionists, not the loyalists, who were pushing the country towards civil war. In the end, he knew that Shaftesbury just did not have the stomach for a true battle; and just in case he did, with Louis XIV's gold jingling in the royal treasure chest, Charles knew that this time, unlike in 1642, the Crown had the funds to mobilize in a hurry.

So what followed Oxford, as far as the Exclusionists were concerned, was—nothing. With nowhere to go, they divided into those who sharpened their sabres and those who shuffled back in anticlimactic gloom to their horses and houses. With the wind shifting smartly, the villains of the piece—the fantastic cast of con-men, cut-throats and repeat-perjurors who comprised the case for the Popish Plot—were the first to smell trouble and promptly turned king's evidence, confessing one by one to the pack of lies. During the trial of George

Wakeman, the queen's doctor, Chief Justice Scroggs launched the first attack on Titus Oates's veracity. What might have been a revolution now collapsed. Acquitted of high treason, Shaftesbury fled to Holland where he died in 1683. Oates was arrested in 1684—for cruising, of course—but the next year was tried for and convicted of perjury, for which he was savagely flogged, set in the pillory and then sent to prison. Never pinned down for long, though, he re-emerged in 1688 and died (what else?) a Baptist preacher.

Buried beneath the débâcle, Shaftesbury left something behind other than a reputation for breathtaking political cynicism, and characteristically the pieces of his legacy were at complete odds with each other. On the one hand, his willingness to patronize and make credible the political theory of John Locke and other exponents of a contract theory of government had given a new lease of life to genuinely radical ideas, which, it had been assumed, had perished for good in 1659. The notion that the government derived its legitimacy not just from its capacity to protect (as Hobbes had argued), nor simply from scriptural authority (as Filmer had insisted) but from the consent of the governed as well, who, when they entrusted it with power, had *not* thereby surrendered their natural rights of liberty and property, would have an extraordinary future ahead of it. The proposition that 'Every form of Government is of our Creation,' wrote Locke, 'and not God's and must comply with the safety of the people in all that it can' was still radical and even shocking. But it was no longer unusual or outlandish to read or hear it uttered. Nor was the allied axiom that in entrusting a government (or a monarch) with authority, those from whom it ultimately derived ought not to be assumed to be alienating their rights to call it to account, should it grossly exceed its lawful authority; should it, in fact, pass from authority to tyranny, or even flout the liberties it was appointed to protect. Perhaps these arguments may have stayed marginal to English politics for the best part of another century. But across the Atlantic, the refusal of southern New Englanders to truckle to what they saw as the 'arbitrary' power of the royal governor of all New England, Sir Edmund Andros, and instead to set out on a self-authorized exodus to Connecticut, already showed that the seeds sown in the rich but unsavoury soil of the Exclusion crisis could bear fruit.

Ironically, though, what the founding fathers of Connecticut were objecting to was precisely the aggressive manipulation of official authority that was *also* Shaftesbury's legacy. For during his brief period in power, he had out-Danbyed Danby by using every conceivable political lever—patronage, bribery, judicial intimidation and a massive print propaganda campaign in the now uncensored press—to build what he and the Whigs hoped would be an invincible political machine. And this was the machine that was conveniently handed over to Charles II and his new ministers—in particular Laurence Hyde, Earl of Rochester (Clarendon's son), and Robert Spencer, Earl of Sunderland—who used it to build massive ramparts around the restored authority of the monarchy. The years from 1683 to 1688 were years of packings and purges. Town corporations suspected of being unfriendly to the succession were required to turn over their charters, which were duly amended to produce more obliging local governments. Unhelpful judges were weeded out, zealous Tories rewarded with place and favour. It was all very carefully engineered, and with a veneer of legality; but between them Charles II and his last government managed to build a machine of state power the likes of which his father and grandfather (or for that matter Protector Cromwell) could scarcely have dreamed. But then they had lived in what now seemed an incomprehensibly remote age, driven by passions and clouded by pious prejudices. Men like Sunderland, though, were modern political animals, whose understanding of humanity presupposed the usefulness of the baser, regrettably universal instincts of greed, ambition and egotism. Shaftesbury, when all was said and done, had come from a generation of men who fancied themselves technicians of administration. Sunderland and his kind, on the other hand, were the first modern political managers for whom money was the lubricant of power.

They knew, moreover, all about the tactical deployment of half-truths and bogeymen. If there were any murmuring of protest from the shires about the high-handed and arbitrary interference in local affairs, all they had to do was to invoke the dreadful spectre of Cromwellian revolution and they could expect the gentry to shut up and pass the port. In 1683 a group of republicans—among them two aristocrats, Algernon Sidney and Lord William Russell, as well as the ex-Leveller John Wildman—frustrated and embittered by Shaftesbury's betrayal, turned to conspiracy instead in an attempt to put Monmouth on the throne. As soon as this Rye House Plot was discovered, the government realized that it was a gift, not a threat. The principals were beheaded for treason, Sidney heroically insisting, in a letter to the Sheriff of London written on the eve of his execution, that 'God had left Nations to the Liberty of setting up such Governments as best pleas'd themselves' and that 'Magistrates were set up for the good of Nations, not Nations for the honour of Magistrates'. Armed with such incendiary confessions, the government could defend its aggressive policy of interference in town charters, its packings and purgings, as a matter of state security.

But for the misfortune of having to leave the earthly world he had enjoyed only too visibly and too much, Charles II could die in February 1685 in the satisfying knowledge that he had made the realm safe for the monarchy. Evelyn's last sight of the king was, for him, a depressing spectacle, 'unexpressable luxury, & prophaneners gaming & all dissolution, and as it were total forgetfullnesse of God (it being Sunday Evening) . . . the King, sitting & toying with his Concubines Portsmouth [and] Cleveland . . . A French boy singing love songs, in that glorious Gallery, whilst about 20 of the greate Courtiers & other dissolute persons were at Basset round a large table, a bank of at least 2000 in Gold before them . . . a sense of utmost vanity.' There was always time, though, Charles must have reckoned, for repentance. At the last he accepted his brother's offer to be received back into the arms of the Mother Church, confessed his sins (or a necessarily abbreviated digest of them) and was duly granted the Catholic

78

rite of absolution. And Charles might have taken even the privacy of this last little ceremony as a happy instance of how the Stuart monarchy might survive within an Anglican kingdom. How wrong his mother had been and how well this boded for the prospects of his brother! All James had to do was to abide by the intelligently laid-out limits within which he was free to practise his confession; accept the fact of parliamentary elections without having to surrender his prerogative (in, for example, a choice of ministers) to them; defer to parliament in military and ecclesiastical appointments; and then sit back on a throne cushioned by common sense.

At first, it seemed that this was precisely what would happen. Although it suited later Whig history to argue that, from the very beginning, James II was an alien, un-English presence in the body politic, bound to end in expulsion, there was, in fact, nothing inevitable at all about what finally unfolded. (Indeed, even *after* William of Orange's landing at Torbay on 5 November 1688, James, had he behaved intelligently, might easily have kept his throne.) One of the new king's first acts was to promise to William Sancroft, Archbishop of Canterbury, that he would 'undertake nothing against the religion which is established by law', but adding, rather ominously 'unless you first break your word to me'. And it was evident, moreover, from the largely uncontested elections of 1685 and the favourable Tory-monarchist majority returned that James had inherited the continuing groundswell of public loyalty left by his brother. When the Duke of Monmouth attempted an insurrection in the West Country (at the same time as a rising led by the Duke of Argyll in Scotland) to make Exclusion a fact by force of arms, he was defeated as much by the massive indifference of the vast majority of the population as by his own military and political ineptness. Even the brutal 'Bloody Assizes', presided over by the enthusiastic hanging Judge George Jeffreys, remains more notorious in subsequent Whig history than at the time, when rows of gibbets were nothing special in the political culture.

Unreconciled Whigs could reassure themselves that in the end, Death, the Great Excluder, would win the battle for them. For James was fifty-two when he became king, middle-aged, if not actually rather elderly by the standards of the seventeenth century, and still without a son. His heirs were his two daughters by Anne Hyde, Mary and Anne, both of whom had ignored their father and remained Protestant. In 1677, Mary had been married off by Danby to none other than the Prince of Orange, soon to be William III, now cast (and for good reason) as the international hero of Protestant resistance to the aggressive Catholic expansionism of Louis XIV. William's story, moreover, was known in England through the brilliantly produced propaganda histories of the war of 1672, complete with graphic illustrations by the geniuses of Dutch history prints, Romeyn de Hooghe and Abraham de Wicquevoort. In these unforgettable images the French-Catholic troops of Louis XIV are depicted, much like the Spanish a century before, as subhuman marauders, revelling in rape and mutilation (impaled babies, eviscerated pregnant mothers, roughed-up grandpas—the usual thing), while the invariably fat, gloating friars sing masses in Protestant churches reconsecrated to Rome.

It was exactly this ominous sense of the resurrection of an international war of religion, and the unsettling sense that he had got himself marooned on the wrong side that were to be James's undoing. His brother had bequeathed him a state constructed from pragmatic ingenuity. But surely God had anointed him with the holy oil for purposes other than just lubricating the wheels and cogs of power? If, after all his family's troubles and travels, the Almighty had seen fit to set him on the throne, how could he turn aside from doing His will? And doing it urgently.

It was hard, at first, to take this intensity of mission seriously. For all his dark solemnity James seemed to behave, in crucially telling respects, precisely like his brother, sleeping with his mistress Catherine Sedley even while making a parade of openly going to Mass. Surely, then, this was a man, whatever his coarse humourlessness, who understood the arts of convenience, political as well as sexual. Why ruin a good thing? What was *wrong* with the 'arrangement' made by Charles II— that James would not be expected to enforce the penalties against Catholics so long as he made no attempt to repeal them?

But the temperamental difference between the two sons of Charles I *was* genuine and did have serious implications for the political fate of Britain. Hard-boiled though he could be, Charles II was by nature a pluralist, someone who was quite prepared to listen to people with whom he did not necessarily agree (other than Shaftesbury, that is). But if Charles accepted, to some extent, variety,

James was relentlessly single-minded. Not surprisingly, he was proud of inventing a 'Universal Sauce' made from parsley, dry toast and vinegar, and beaten in a mortar, which he thought equally suitable for dishes of fish, flesh and fowl. If they were ground fine enough, and with enough perseverance, he may have supposed he could make his own views of Church and state palatable to his people. He could not, in all conscience, remain content with the bounds set by his brother. From the beginning of his reign he chafed at them. James's goal was not, of course, to force England back to Rome overnight. The slightest historical acquaintance with the ill-starred reign of Mary Tudor made that course of action obviously undesirable. But he certainly meant to go beyond the timid attempt of his brother in 1672 to allow Catholics some relief from the penal laws and the practice of their religion within their own four walls. He made it clear to Sancroft and the bishops, as well as to his Tory ministers, that he would be satisfied with nothing less than free and open public worship. And he was not going to forget the humiliation of his own ejection from office as a result of the Test Act. It should either be repealed, or what he claimed to be the 'dispensing power' of his royal prerogative could be used to publish a Declaration in effect suspending it, along with the other penalties for Catholic and Nonconformist practice.

But that 'dispensing' power had already been judged illegal in both 1662 and 1672 when Charles II had advanced his much more cautious measures. So why James should have imagined that the High Church and Tory country gentlemen who had flocked to the Stuart cause against Shaftesbury and Monmouth should now change their minds was a mystery. Equally, James overrated the ease with which he could persuade his natural constituency that there was nothing untoward in reopening the formal relations with Rome, sundered since the 1530s, nor in re-establishing four Apostolic vicars-general for England, nor in appointing Catholic officers in the army and navy. And why did he imagine that he could make the English people, whose anti-Catholic prejudices had certainly not been leavened by the exposure of Oates's fraud, accept the overnight visibility of Catholic practice—monks and nuns in their habits, public processions on feast days, churches echoing again with the sounds of the Mass? But by 1687 James was no longer listening—at least with any degree of attentiveness—to the voices of reason. He was issuing warnings and veiled threats to the bishops that they had better not think about opposing his will, or 'I shall find a way to do my business without you.' James was listening to the voices in his head. And they were singing hosannas.

At which point a word of warning is in order. What then unfolded was not a simple struggle between the forces of reaction and progress, between benighted absolutism and constitutional liberalism. That was certainly the history of the 'Glorious Revolution' that the Whigs liked to tell. But the Whigs were only the principal and not the exclusive beneficiaries of that revolution (there was a large bloc of Tories in the post-revolution parliament), and they certainly did not bring it about. What made the difference between the fiasco of the Exclusion crisis and the victory of 1688 was the fact that *Tory* England—the bishops, the peers and the country gentry—was driven, despite its adherence to the doctrines of non-resistance, to resist. Among the famous 'Seven' who issued an invitation to William to come to England to secure a 'free parliament' and the Church of England was none other than that ultimate anti-Whig, Danby. For the Tory commitment to obey had never been unconditional. Obedience to *lawful* commands was their watchword. And by January 1688 they had become convinced that it was James who was the real revolutionary, who sought to overturn everything the Restoration had stood for, and who now had at all costs to be stopped. Even the staunchest Tory allowed that it might be possible for a king to unking *himself* (as Edward II had done), so sundering the bonds of loyalty tying subject to monarch.

Well, *was* James a revolutionary? To consider calmly and dispassionately what the two sides in the confrontation of 1687–8 actually stood for is to scramble all our conventional clichés about the good, the bad and the constitutional. Whatever else 1688–90 may have been it was certainly not, as Macaulay thought, a Manichaean struggle between the forces of light and darkness. Many of the things that are said about James are extrapolations from the received wisdom that he got what he deserved; that the long-nosed face (which actually was no more or less 'haughty' than any other portrait type of that period) betrays a man of incurably despotic temper. Not all of this image is wrong. James had obviously not graduated from the same charm school as his brother. But he was at least as intelligent as Charles, had shown himself more competent in naval battle and was, without question, a lot more conscientious in his attention to government. Much of the stereotype of the brutal autocrat is a projection backwards from the story written by the winners. There is no question whatsoever, of course, that James was indeed a divine-right absolutist who believed that parliament had the right to offer advice and criticism and even propose legislation, but that he had the right if he so chose to reject all of it and to have that be the end of the matter. But the *cause* for which James was apt to get stirred up was, after all, toleration, that 'liberty of conscience' that Cromwell had so often warbled about, only extended, unlike the Cromwellian state, to Catholics. No wonder, then, that some of James's warmest allies were not just Catholics, but dissenters like the Quaker William Penn the younger. And by no means all the men of science and reason were to be found in the camp of his enemies. Pepys, for one, James's Secretary of the Navy and the epitome of humane reasonableness, remained loyal to the bitter end. It is odd, in fact, that while in conventional histories the European 'enlightened despots' of the *eighteenth* century, like Frederick the Great and the Emperor Joseph II, get credit for *imposing* toleration on their subjects, the same benefit is not extended to James II. In Ireland, James was the first English king who actually made a strenuous and politically dangerous effort to reverse the brutal wars of colonization that had disfigured the country and dispossessed its native landowners since at least the reign of Elizabeth I. His cardinal sin, to Macaulay, was that he unaccountably appeared to favour the people whom the Victorian

85

historian called the 'aboriginals'. Conversely, those who opposed James were essentially held together in a classically Cromwellian alliance of bigotry, as the war of 1689–90 would make unequivocally clear.

But—as so often before in this story of the British wars of religion—having registered all these caveats, it is equally important to understand what the Whigs got *right*. Their suspicion that James's benevolence in extending toleration beyond Catholics to the 'fanatick' Nonconformist sects was a tactical rather than a wholehearted gesture was not unfounded. Suppose, those sceptics might have argued, the king's dispensation of the Test Act allowed full and open Catholic practice and teaching, so that the Roman Church would (as James made no secret of hoping) be in a position to reconvert England by persuasion; what would such an England actually look like? Was Louis XIV's France, for God's sake, internationally famous for its tolerant atmosphere? Was France a kingdom where all manner of Christians could peaceably profess their confession? All the sceptics had to do was to point to the most infamous act of Louis's reign, which took place in the same year as James's accession (and together with the usual French hand-out to the Stuarts): the uprooting and expulsion of the entire Huguenot community of France. This was not something that was seen in England as a remote and unimportant act. The saga of the cruelly treated Huguenots, together with their exodus to Protestant lands—especially the Netherlands—was an event which actually *defined* allegiances in the mid-1680s and that seemed to point towards the inevitability of another pan-European war. Among the places in which the Huguenot diaspora settled with its immense treasury of wealth, skill and talent was, of course, London. It was not just fellow Dissenters who made them welcome. Henry Compton, the Bishop of London—who incurred so much of James's displeasure that he had him removed from his diocese—was the foremost organizer of relief for the stricken refugees. And, of course, their story was told and retold over and over again in the pathetic images produced by the Dutch engravers and writers.

Not surprisingly, then, Nonconformists were not at all united in gratitude to James for his efforts on their behalf. Presbyterians in particular warned against accepting favours from the king who, in the end, was committed to a Church and an absolutist style of monarchy that was to its very marrow deeply intolerant. In Ireland, where he had a free hand politically, toleration of Protestant dissent was actually banned. And James's virtual declaration of war on the traditional English institutions that presumed to oppose his will—the universities, the bishops and the judiciary—and the ferocity with which he fulminated against them did not suggest a prince who was truly interested in a tolerant, spiritually pluralist commonwealth. 'Get you gone!' he told the Fellows of Magdalen College, when he expelled them from their fellowships after they had opposed his nomination of a Catholic to be their President. 'Know I am your King. I will be obeyed, and I command you to be gone. Go and admit the Bishop of Oxford, Head, Principal, what do you call it, of the College . . . I mean President of the College. Let them that refuse it look to it. They shall feel the weight of their sovereign's displeasure.'

There was a middle way open to James (as there had been for Charles I), and it was urged on him by William Penn. Settle for *de facto* toleration without insisting on the formal repeal of the Test Act, he pleaded, and all those whom you have dangerously alienated in Church and shires will return to their natural loyalty. But James II had, in effect, decided to ditch them in the belief that somehow a coalition of opposites—Catholics, ultra-monarchists and Dissenters—could see him through the crisis. He doubtless imagined that he was imitating his brother's firmness in 1680–81. In that instance, however, Charles had drawn to him the majority of the political country, while James was in the process of alienating it. It had been Shaftesbury who had boxed himself into an untenable corner through his inflexibility. Now it was James's turn to do the same, with equally calamitous results. In hindsight it seems incredible that the king could have seriously hoped to offset the enormous power of both the Whig and Tory gentry and aristocracy by so improbable an alliance of Catholics and Dissenters. But his trump card, he must have believed, was the potency of the royal mystique. By invoking the supreme authority of the Crown, which the Tories had for so long themselves trumpeted, James hoped at the very least to divide them and to take enough of them along with him to dispense with the Test Act, pass his new Declaration of Indulgence, without parliamentary approval if necessary, and agree to accept Catholic officers in the army. And, in fact, the idea was not so fabulously far-fetched. The

Marquis of Halifax had been dismissed in October 1685 for refusing to go along with the pro-Catholic plans, but Sunderland stayed. The tug of loyalty to the Stuarts for which so many old Cavalier families had fought and suffered was very strong, and had James exploited it with more cool intelligence and a modicum of flexibility he might yet have prevailed. But something told him, disastrously, that for all their belly-aching the Tories would in the end come round to his way of things. Where, after all, could they go?

The answer was, of course, to the Dutch Republic and to William. This was the critical difference between the failed revolt of 1680-85 and the success of 1688–9. All the Whigs had in play in the earlier crisis, as an alternative to the legitimate heir, was the conspicuously illegitimate Duke of Monmouth. But James's own daughter, Princess Mary, was another matter entirely. And her husband the Prince of Orange was by now legitimate in an entirely different sense: the symbolic figurehead of the European resistance to French domination. Not that it was in the mind of the 'Seven' who turned to William in 1688 to have Mary replace James on the throne. Had that been mooted, Tories like Danby would never have dreamed of going along with the plan, nor could they have carried the gentry with them. Rather, they wanted to bring William and his troops in to make James cease his unlawful behaviour. On just what constituted unlawful the Whigs and Tories had some measure of, but not complete, agreement. They could agree, for example, on the illegality of the dispensing power, on the need to force James to liquidate his standing army and its

Catholic officers. But while that, together with the retention of the Test Act, was good enough for the Tories, the Whigs wanted to have him accept the 'fundamental law' of parliamentary government: that parliament was an equal partner in government, not merely a disposable source of advice.

And what about William himself? What did he want? First and foremost, whatever was good for the Dutch Republic. Seen from the perspective of purely British history, the revolution of 1688 seems something spontaneously and indigenously generated. The Victorians, especially Macaulay, saw the event as one of those moments that expressed the glorious peculiarity of the English tradition of liberal parliamentarianism, as if somehow the island itself had choked on Catholic despotism, coughed it up and been returned to health, to normality, courtesy of William and Mary. But the truth is different and altogether more European. As so often in the past—in 1066 for example—a turning point in English history was decided by the forces of international, not national, history. It took an immense foreign armada of possibly 600 vessels, carrying perhaps 15,000 Dutch and German troops, to bring about the fall of James. And even this would not have been decisive without the victory at the battle of the Boyne in Ireland two years later. What happened there was essentially the Irish theatre of a huge international conflict. It was fought mainly between non-English Europeans—the French under the Duc de Lauzun on one side, and on the other a force of 36,000, two-thirds of whom were Dutch, German and Danes, and were commanded successively by Field

Marshal Schömburg and, when he fell, by King William. The only actor in this military drama who had any decisive effect and who was indisputably English was John Churchill, whose defection in November 1688 from King James to Prince William was crucial, and whose violent destruction of Irish resistance two years later was even more decisive. So it was not surprising that, ennobled as the Duke of Marlborough, he would succeed William as the great commander of the European war against Louis XIV.

The critical event of 1688 is better described as the invasion it undoubtedly was, rather than as a 'revolution'. It had been contemplated by William in the Netherlands long before he had an official invitation. William was shrewd enough to know that it would be a gamble. But by the spring of 1688 he had come to believe that it would be worse *not* to embark on it. The controlling imperatives were all Dutch. The *rampjaar* or year of disaster in 1672 had been the unforgettable moment that defined William's identity as it had scarred for ever the memory of Dutch history. The republic had come close to being wiped off the face of Europe as an independent power through an encircling alliance of France and England, and whatever it took to prevent that from recurring William would do. His marriage to Princess Mary had seemed to militate against a repetition of the Treaty of Dover. But although her father was now on the English throne, William was not so sure. James was, of course, on the take from Louis XIV just as his brother had been. And if he were unable to get his way with the relief of Catholics, it was all but certain that he would look to French military as well as financial aid. Moreover, William was well aware that, as far as ruining the Dutch Republic was concerned, Louis XIV knew that there was more than one way to skin a cat. The Dutch could be struck at through economic and systematic (though undeclared) naval actions, preying on their colonial trade. Massively dependent on imports of grain and timber from the Baltic, they were critically vulnerable to a concerted attack from both French and English ships. So during the mid-1680s Louis XIV and his more bellicose ministers repudiated their agreements signed at the Treaty of Nijmegen in 1679 and began to let privateers loose. Either way, Louis must have reckoned, he couldn't lose. Either the arrogant Dutch commercial empire would piece by piece fall apart, or else the republic would be forced back into a war that once again it would have to fight on two fronts.

William was perfectly aware of this and, resigned to the coming conflict, set about putting the republic in the best possible position to fight it. The campaign in the field had to be preceded by a campaign of persuasion, and that too had to be fought on two fronts. At home he needed to convince the previously peace-inclined commercial cities, especially Amsterdam, that unless they accepted his war policy they would suffer irreversible harm from French economic and maritime aggression. Then William went on a diplomatic offensive among the German princes, and especially with the Holy Roman Emperor in Vienna, emphasizing that the incorrigible expansionism of Louis XIV represented so paramount a threat to the stability of Europe that it cut across old lines of confessional allegiance.

There was, of course, yet a third front for William in the public-relations war that had to be won before his military plans could be made operational, and that was the domestic crisis in England itself. Here, his best ally was James II. For by the beginning of 1688 James had committed himself to a collision course with all the good and great who had stood by his brother and himself a decade before. Brushing aside any moderate advice, and dismissing any ministers who had the temerity to offer it, James was reinforced in his own myopic obstinacy by men like Sunderland, who saw in grovelling loyalty a way to make themselves arbiters of power and were prepared, if necessary, to publicize their own conversion to the Catholic Church. Persuasion was abandoned for intimidation. The size of the standing army available to James was almost doubled, much of it drawn from Irish troops commanded by Catholic officers. In April, the king ordered his Declaration of Indulgence to be read on successive Sundays from the pulpit. When a group of bishops, including Sancroft, attempted to explain their refusal to authorize the readings, James exploded in a storm of rage, declaring their objections to be 'a standard of rebellion'. All those who were not now unreservedly for him were, in effect, to be considered and treated like traitors. The most prominent of the objecting bishops were arrested and tried in what turned into a public-relations disaster for the beleaguered king. They were acquitted, but not before one of the justices had delivered his own stinging verdict on the manifest illegality of the dispensing power. The liberated bishops emerged from confinement to find themselves celebrated up and down the country as the champions of the country's liberties and the guardians of the Reformation. Bonfires were lit, and effigies of the Pope, and of James's confessor, Father Petre, fed to the flames.

None of this affront caused James to hesitate for a moment in his headlong sprint off the cliff. Let the bishops have their day, for he had something incomparably more powerful going for him: a Prince of Wales. For, after years of disappointments, Mary of Modena had actually been delivered on 10 June of a healthy baby boy, baptized with Roman rites as James Francis Edward Stuart. Predictably, and notwithstanding the queen's visible pregnancy over the previous months, the infant was immediately denounced by James's now innumerable enemies as a fraud: some other baby, perhaps produced by one of the royal mistresses, and now deposited in the royal crib to thwart the succession of Mary and her husband, Prince William. At any rate, the shock of the news immediately accelerated the timetable of the Dutch military operation. Just a week after the announcement of the royal birth, and doubtless prompted by the Dutch ambassador Dijkvelt, the 'Seven' sent their formal invitation to the Prince to come to England, not as conqueror but as the protector of Protestantism and liberty. It was exactly a century since the launching of the Spanish attack on Elizabeth's kingdom, a fact not lost on the defenders of the queen's legacy. But this would be the Good Armada, and the Protestant wind, this time, would be kind to its ships.

Looking on with increasing dismay and disbelief at what was happening in England, Louis XIV had in fact already offered James military help, but had been brushed off by the Stuart king's unfaltering sense of righteous invincibility. Now, when James could have used it, it was too late, for Louis had committed a sizeable army to the Rhineland where William had made sure the troops would be tied down. But, even at this critical juncture, James was held back from switching his own military resources from domestic intimidation to a posture of national defence. He could still not bring himself to believe that his daughter Mary would allow her husband to launch a full-scale invasion against her own father. And though this seems, in hindsight, a pathetically naïve delusion, the family ties winding about the two chief protagonists of this great drama did, in fact, bind them closely together. James was not just William's father-in-law, he was also his uncle. His sister (also called Mary) had been married to William's father (also called William). And despite the historical divide, which would, after 1688, always separate them, they had much in common beside shared blood. Both were orphans of political upheavals. A year after Charles I had been executed, William's father, the Stadholder William II, had marched on Amsterdam to bend the city to his will—a tactic right out of the Stuart manual on political persuasion. Not long after this *coup* William II died, just before the birth of his son. His political enemies seized the opportunity to revenge themselves and, to preclude any further attempt at Orangist aggrandizement, made William III a ward of state and proceeded to abolish the Stadholderate. The prince had grown up as both pupil and captive of his political enemy Jan De Witt who attempted to turn him into a good republican, in much the same way that there had been talk during the Protectorate of making the youngest Stuart, the Duke of Gloucester, a 'safe' king.

Both James and William, then, had gone through the experience of loss and humiliation. Both had leaned on surrogate fathers—De Witt and Clarendon—about whom they felt at best ambivalent. Both ended up leading guarded, somewhat secretive lives, hardening themselves against adversity. As Duke of York, of course, James had had an incomparably easier time of it than William III in the Stadholder-less republic. But his position was not so strong that it could protect him against ejection from office as a result of the Test Act or from being sent out of England during the Exclusion crisis (to Scotland, where he inflicted as much damage as possible on the Presbyterians). The two of them ended up as taciturn, habitually suspicious personalities, despising courtly banter and putting little faith in political negotiation unless backed up by the hard facts of military force.

In one respect, which would in the end prove critical in 1688, James and William differed radically: the value they placed on printed propaganda. Here, their backgrounds told. Although he had come to power over the bodies of the De Witts and was restored as Captain and Admiral General, William still had to contend, over sixteen years, with the complicated, interlocking, highly decentralized institutions of the Dutch Republic. It was no good simply blustering and bullying his way to leadership, because in the last resort money, not princely mystique, spoke loudest in a country that was the prototype of a modern polity, a place where decentralization rather than the concentration of power worked best, where the marketplace of ideas as well as commodities required religious pluralism. Knowing the Dutch Republic's reputation for toleration, James actually tried to trade on it. When, during their many exchanges of correspondence, James tried to represent his own Declaration of Indulgence as a commitment to toleration, he was shocked to find William actually defending the Test Act as a regrettable necessity for Anglican peace of mind about the future of their Church establishment.

William's response suggests that in the summer of 1688 he and his Chief Minister, Grand Pensionary Gaspar Fagel, were paying as much attention to the public-relations end of their enterprise as to military planning. The manifesto, of which a massive 60,000 copies were printed both to herald the arrival of the Dutch army and to justify its presence, carefully avoided the slightest suggestion that William and Mary were coming as conquerors to set themselves up in James's place. The aim, repeated over and again, was a restoration, not a revolution: the restoration of Church, of orderly parliamentary government, of the rule of law, in fact the restoration of a true English monarchy instead of the Catholic 'tyranny', ruled by Jesuits, arbitrary courts and Irish troops that James was in the process of instituting.

As in 1066 and 1588, though, strategy was the prisoner of providence, otherwise known as the weather. It was three months before the enormous armada and its huge cargo of troops, many of them the cream of the Dutch army, were able to sail from Scheveningen. The chosen landing place, perhaps influenced by the most influential of the English sponsors, Danby, was the northeast coast (where Henry Bolingbroke had begun his campaign against Richard II), far enough from James's concentration of troops in the southeast to be able to establish some momentum before meeting the king's army. Danby had promised that a supportive rising would begin in his own county of Yorkshire. But while the Protestant winds of late October were kind enough to William's fleet, they blew him the wrong way, from the strait of Dover towards western rather than northeastern England. Eventually God stopped being coy and revealed himself to be a Protestant gentleman, for it was on the anniversary of the deliverance from the Gunpowder Treason, 5 November, that William made landfall near Torbay in Devon.

When he had taken in the full seriousness of his position, James II went from disbelief to consternation. In panic, he threw into reverse almost everything that had given offence. The Declaration of Indulgence was withdrawn; a new election was called, for which Roman Catholics were not to be eligible; the most senior officers of Church and state who had been dismissed were reinstated. But it was much, much too late. As far as the huge coalition of the disaffected was concerned—and especially the Tory gentry and the Church—only the presence of William's army and the prince himself could possibly guarantee that James would keep his word and neutralize his pet standing army. In fact, had he shown some presence of mind, James might still have been able to control the situation or at least contain the damage, for on paper at least his troop strength was easily twice that of the Prince of Orange. But those 40,000 men were dispersed around the country, and James had collapsed back into a realm of ancient nightmares in which nothing, especially not the physical safety of a royal family, could be taken for granted. So he kept at least half his available troops in the south back in London. It was far from certain, moreover, whether the rest of the army sent southwest towards Salisbury would fight when it came to it. Mutinies against Catholic officers were reported as commonplace. And then came another massive blow, which seemed to shock the king more than anything since hearing of the Dutch fleet passing the strait of Dover: his younger daughter, the Lady Anne, had disappeared, re-emerging as a defector in the camp of her brother-in-law.

James now led what was left of his army into Wiltshire. His own condition did not inspire confidence. Insomniac and suffering from chronic nose-bleeds, he seemed as disoriented by his predicament as his army, which lacked any kind of maps. Supposing he decided to tackle William head-on, no one had much idea of how to find him. And James was so nervous of having left the queen and the Prince of Wales behind in a capital depleted of troops that in the end he gave up looking for William and retreated from Salisbury back to London. Before he got there he learned of the defection of the general in whom he had placed most confidence, John Churchill. It was a betrayal he never forgave or forgot.

Free to advance, his army swelling daily, William played his hand with great care and subtlety. He would advance his army to no more than 40 miles west of London, he let it be known, it being understood that James would withdraw his troops a like distance east. In between, the parliament could deliberate on the fate of the kingdom, free of any kind of intimidation. The moderation of these demands was, in fact, deceptive. As the royal position disintegrated, the Whigs could hardly refrain from the opportunity, not just to disadvantage James but be rid of him altogether. And it was equally impossible for William not to be tempted by his amazing run of luck into seeing himself as something more than an arbitrator. But to keep the Tories in the camp meant making at least a show of sweet reason and hoping that James, true to form, would spurn it. James's only ploy at this point was to call William's bluff and accept the terms. But in the first week of December he was haunted by memories of his father falling into the hands of the enemy, losing all freedom of action and, inevitably, his life. James was, if anything, even more anxious about the Prince of Wales's safety, for in the person of the baby boy lay the eventual redemption of his cause. So he prevaricated just long enough to see the queen and the Prince of Wales safely off to France. A few hours after he had told a meeting of lords that he would remain and continue negotiations with William, James himself made his escape. It was 3 a.m. on 11 December 1688. Burning with furious chagrin at his plight, driven by absurd passions, he enacted one last childish gesture of malice. The writs for the new free parliament were brought to him along with the Great Seal. The writs were promptly burned, the Great Seal dropped into the Thames as he crossed to the south bank. He might just as well have lowered his throne into the muddy water.

For the Whigs, of course, this completely unanticipated turn of events was better than anything they could have imagined in their wildest dreams. Initially, the Tories were appalled, for throughout the campaign they had been in denial that they were in the business of dislodging James from his throne; rather, merely making him heed the law. Before long, however, the most thoughtful Tories realized that the abrupt exit of the king had actually let them off the hook of their own conscience. It remained abhorrent to think of themselves as in insurrection against their anointed monarch. But what if the throne could be said to have been vacated—opening a void that nature and the state abhorred? The argument had been used before, speciously, in 1399 when Richard II's vacation had been spent mostly in the Tower. But this time James had indeed gone on his travels. If they did not want—heaven forbid—England to relapse into a Commonwealth, a royal solution had better be found, and quickly.

For a moment, all these calculations were thrown into disarray by the improbable return of James to London. When he was almost on board ship, he had been recognized (though as a fleeing priest, not as a king), searched and physically harassed. In fact, such was his pathetic condition that it actually inspired sympathy from the London populace for the first time in years. Fortunately for William and the Whigs, James was not listening to the cheers. His only thought was to get out of the country again as quickly as possible, and in this, of

101

course, his captors were only too delighted to assist. This time he did not come back.

With the throne now well and truly vacant, the second Convention Parliament in thirty years debated the future of the realm. Despite the fact that both Whigs and Tories (the latter returned as a minority but a substantial one) and the country thought of the assembly as a free parliament, it actually met under the conditions of a foreign occupation, with Dutch troops patrolling Westminster, Whitehall and most of the City of London. And, needless to say, William's ambitions had grown and hardened as his military position in England had become unchallengeable. James's presence in France had altered the dynamic of their conflict in ways that no longer allowed for sentimental niceties. For James was there, not just as a guest, but as an ally in an international war that had already ignited across Europe. So some sort of half-baked provisional arrangement—of the kind that parliament presented to him—might not be enough security for the kind of test he would imminently face. In fact, the Convention had divided. The Whig majority in the Commons was all for William and Mary becoming monarchs right away, and doing so on the grounds that James had demonstrably violated his coronation oath and had dethroned himself by breaking his contract with the people. The Tory majority in the House of Lords, however, refused to acknowledge any such contract and instead took refuge in the 'vacancy' argument, by which the throne must needs be filled without altering its divine-right sovereignty. The compromise was that William and Mary would be made regents until the death of James, at which point they could ascend the throne as his already designated lawful heirs. No mention was made by either side, of course, of the inconvenient existence of the Prince of Wales.

But it was precisely the fact of the Prince of Wales—and the possibility that as time went on his legitimacy would seem more, not less, credible—that made William realize, with his peerless sense of timing, that if he failed to seize the moment, he would squander an advantage that might never return. So, with the Dutch Blues on the streets, he simply rejected every overture short of the crown itself. He knew, of course, that in the last resort the Tories had no alternative. Veiled threats that if the matter were not settled he would depart forthwith sent them into a tizzy of anxiety. On 6 February, the House of Lords capitulated.

A week later, on 13 February 1689, William and Mary were declared king and queen. At their coronation on 11 April, before the crowns were set on their heads a reading took place of the Declaration of Rights, passed by the Convention. The moment was not just ceremonial, but profoundly significant for the future of the monarchy in Britain. For it solemnized the Crown's commitment to the reforms of the Long Parliament and the Protectorate as a condition of its authority. No more standing armies; no dispensing power; no resort to extra-parliamentary taxation; no resurrection of special courts and tribunals, ecclesiastical or civil; freedom to petition guaranteed; free elections; annual parliaments. Later in the spring an Act of Toleration was passed. It fell a long way short of the promise of its billing, not extending to all Christian sects (those, for example, who denied the Trinity). But, as John Locke wrote to a friend in the Dutch Republic, 'Toleration has now at last been established by law in our country. Not perhaps so wide in scope as might be wished for by you and those like you who are true Christians and free from ambition or envy. Still, it is something to have progressed so far. I hope that, with these beginnings, the foundations have been laid of that liberty and peace, in which the Church of Christ is one day to be established.'

Whatever else it was, the English state of 1700 was unquestionably not the Stuart monarchy of 1603 or 1660. But William's government did have a true predecessor—and that was the Protectorate of Oliver Cromwell. For the regime that had been all too briefly established in 1657—of a 'single person and [a bicameral] parliament' guaranteeing regular elections and limited toleration—looks like the authentic blueprint of what actually came to pass after 1688. In this sense, at least, the real 'Interregnum' might be seen as 1659–87! Just as the government sketched out in the Humble Petition and Advice had corresponded to what a majority of the country's ruling landed elites wanted then, so the Williamite government corresponded to it a generation later.

This was not what old Edmund Ludlow, the last of the regicide republicans, had foreseen when, at the age of seventy-one, he left his Swiss exile on Lac Leman for England to see first-hand if William was indeed, as he hoped, the new 'Gideon'. Ludlow took with him bitter memories of comrades assassinated in Lausanne, or dying sad and poor in exile, or of soldiers of the 'Good Old Cause', such as Algernon Sidney in England, betrayed and hanged. But Ludlow fondly imagined that the issue in 1689 was the same as it had been forty years before, namely 'whether the king should govern as a god by his will and the nation be governed by beasts, or whether the people should be governed by themselves, by their own consent'. Once in London, though, aside from congenial evenings spent with the survivors of countless republican débâcles, such as John Wildman, Ludlow was doomed to disenchantment. William had no interest whatsoever in encouraging a government based on popular consent. He was neither a crowned republican nor Gideon. He was, for Ludlow, the worst of all reincarnations: a second Cromwell. It was not long before indignant noises were made in the Commons about the presence of so notorious a regicide as Edmund Ludlow— indignation endorsed by the new king. Before worse could happen, Ludlow returned his old bones to the limbo from whence they came.

Future Ludlows would have to travel a little further in search of their elusive Promised Land: across the Atlantic, in fact, where many of those seeking a truly new world, such as William Penn the younger, could find space to make it. The 'Revolutionary Settlement' turned out to be neither. But that, paradoxically, was its greatest strength and accomplishment. The unsettlement of 1689—and with it the creation of a polity within which mutually conflicting views on what had happened and why could be sustained—was a measure not of failure but success. For a kingdom of debate had been created, in which it was possible for fierce arguments about the constitution and government of the state to be conducted without necessitating outright civil war.

Thomas Hobbes—who had survived to see the Popish Plot—had insisted that the containment of argument was impossible short of the surrender of liberties to an omnipotent adjudicator, the Leviathan. But if William were indeed powerful, he was certainly not omnipotent. It was a back-handed compliment to the rough-house ebullience of party politics that the king was so shocked and vexed by it. He had imagined he would lead a grateful and united nation into the European war, which he assumed to be as much in English as Dutch interests. Instead, he discovered that what he had effected had developed a political momentum that refused to march in lock-step with military obedience. The more he pressured, the more trouble he got. In the 1690s, with the country at war, the first parliamentary Committee of Account, to which government officials were obliged to report, was established. And the Triennial Act (another revival of 1657) ensured that parliamentary oversight would be a permanent, not an intermittent, feature of the English political system. However irksome for the king, William would learn to live with these inconveniences. For it turned out that what the country needed was not, after all, a Leviathan, but a Chairman of the Board.

Nothing like this peculiar regime, in which viable government co-existed with party polemics, existed anywhere else in Europe. However puffed up with self-congratulation, Macaulay was justified at the end of volume III of his great *History of England* in seeing the implanting of a genuine parliamentary system as the precondition for avoiding the later fates of absolute monarchies, destroyed by much fiercer revolutions: 'For the authority of law, for the security of property, for the peace of our streets, for the happiness of our homes, our gratitude is due, under him who pulls down nations at his pleasure, to the Long Parliament, to the Convention and to William of Orange.'

But who, exactly, were laying flowers on the bier of William of Orange? The English, naturally. For Macaulay neglected to add in this anthem that English liberty was won over Irish and Highland-Scottish corpses. That if 1689 were a triumph for England, it was a tragedy for Britain. And that outside England, lawlessness, insecurity of property, war in the streets and bitter domestic sorrow were as much the enduring legacy of what Cromwell and his reincarnation, William, wrought as any of the glories of the Glorious Revolution.

For although Ireland may be at the western edge of Europe geographically, it can never escape the inexorable effects of the Continent's wars. Not for the first or last time, it found itself fighting a European war by proxy and paying, as a result, a terrible price. When William set out on the enterprise of England he knew very well that his campaigns were unlikely to stop at the Tweed or the Irish Sea. His pessimism served him well. In March 1689, a month before William and Mary were crowned, James arrived in Ireland, supported by 20,000 French troops under the command of the Duc de Lauzun. Tens of thousands of Irish Catholics streamed to volunteer for his army. In May in Dublin, James and the 'Patriot Parliament' rescinded Cromwell's Land Settlement (perpetuated by his brother Charles), restored confiscated lands to their original owners and brought Catholics back into every branch of government. For the first time since the wars against Elizabeth, Ireland was in the hands of native Irish (Macaulay's 'aboriginals'). Unfortunately it was also in the hands of James II and the French, neither of whom were especially interested in what the Irish wanted except as a stepping stone to the reconquest of England and the re-establishment of an authoritarian Stuart monarchy there. James formally anathematized the constitutional settlement in England as 'contrary to the law of God, nature and the nation'. In return, the Irish parliament produced a reassertion of divine-right kingship categorical enough even for James, who in 1692 would candidly instruct his son that his only proper recourse was to a Catholic court, guarded by a Catholic army. 'Your Majesty's right to your Imperial Crown is, originally, by nature and descent of blood, from God alone by whom kings reign and not from your people, not by virtue of any contract made with them or any act of your estates on their behalf . . . neither the peers nor the people, collective or representatively have or ought to have any coercive power over the persons of the kings of this realm.'

The armies that faced each other twenty miles north of Dublin on the last day of June 1690 were divided, then, by more than the river Boyne. They also stood for utterly different historical destinies for Britain. Neither offered a particularly happy outcome. But perhaps the measurement of felicity is beside the point. The point is that they represented contrasting visions of power. In

108

James's tents between the walls of Dublin and the river were encamped the servants of a cult: the mystery of the godlike king, the obedience of the Christian flock, the unquestioning service of the faithful. William, on the other hand, was the chief engineer of a war machine. His grandfather Maurice had led the first armies to use printed drill manuals. When William looked out across the river at the French–Irish lines he did so through the most accurately lensed telescope that Dutch instrument-makers could devise (though he was looking the wrong way when an opportunistically fired cannonball nearly took his head off on the eve of battle). His army was truly international, containing Danes and Germans as well as Dutch, Huguenots and English, as befitted the king of a multinational corporate state. And it was funded, of course, by international finance—Portuguese Jews and Huguenots, precisely the kind of people for whom the absolutist monarchies found no place.

In the end, it's true, machinery was not what decided the battle but, rather, intelligent and daring strategy, accomplished by horses, riders and shooters. William sent a division of his army down river to ford it and outflank the defenders while his own troops rode straight across in a headlong attack. Surrounded as the French and Irish were on three sides, panic inevitably ensued, with James himself not especially keen to fight to the bitter end. After a night spent in Dublin, he made one of the hasty departures, at which by now he was well practised, and settled down to end his political career, as he had begun it, as a guest of the king of France.

To many, then and since, it looked like the end of a chapter. And so it was, if the book is a history of England. But if the book is a history of Britain, the Boyne was just the turning of another bloody page.

CHAPTER FIVE

BRITANNIA INCORPORATED

In Williamite Britain, showing up late could get you killed. William III came from a culture that set great store by good timing. In 1688, his own carefully maintained and calibrated political clock (as well as the luck of the Protestant winds) had made the difference between a throne and a débâcle. The Dutch king expected men, money, armies to move like clockwork, with reassuring predictability. Although the kingdom he now governed fell far short of those ideals of regular movement, the winding of a spring, the greasing of a wheel might yet make the machine keep proper time and motion.

There were some places within his new realms, though, that seemed regrettably indifferent to punctiliousness, nowhere more than the Scottish Highlands. There, where a third of Scotland's population lived, loyalty seemed still to be governed by codes of honour and bonds of kinship that appeared timeless, impervious to the quickening of modernity. Although from Edinburgh or London such places, with their predilection for cattle stealing, evidently seemed backward, they could still muster crude force enough to do damage to the fragile machinery of power that William and his Scottish allies were putting in place. At the river gorge of Killiecrankie, in the southeast Grampians, on 27 July 1689, John Graham, first Viscount Dundee, obstinately and sentimentally loyal to

King James, threw 2000 Highland warriors, some of them barefoot, down the hillside against 4000 musketeers and dragoons. In ten minutes 600 Highlanders, including Dundee, died under a hail of well-drilled fire. But in the same ten minutes they had sliced to pieces as many of the enemy, caught fumbling with the muzzles of their muskets as the claymores came brightly at their heads.

Ultimately, it would not matter. In the spring of 1689 James VII (James II of England), the last in the line of Stuart kings who had been on the throne of Scotland since 1371, was formally deposed. But William ruled securely only south of the Forth. The shock of Killiecrankie, and continuing resistance in the ungovernable Highlands, made William's allies in Scotland, especially the Campbells, determined to bring the clans to heel. The means would be moderation where that worked, coercion and slaughter where that seemed to be needed. In the summer of 1690 a warship sent from Ulster sailed through the Hebrides, burning down Jacobite villages and killing those unlucky enough to be found there. On the island of Eigg, all the adult men were away fighting on the mainland, so the women were raped before being put to the sword.

In August 1691 the principal leader of the campaign, the Earl of Breadalbane, published an order stipulating 1 January 1692 as the deadline for making a formal act of submission to King William. Perhaps this was too *much* time to get the intended result. For while there were some clan chiefs who did indeed make a pledge of allegiance, urged on by the Governor of Fort William, Colonel Sir John Hill, there were others who held out as long as they could, hoping for some military miracle from

112

France or Ireland, or perhaps just wrestling with their consciences. One such clan was the MacIains of Glencoe, a branch of the fervently Jacobite Clanranalds. Their chief, the twelfth Chief of Glencoe, Alasdair Macdonald, who had fought at Killiecrankie, procrastinated—fatally, as it turned out, and long enough to get selected by Breadalbane for an exemplary killing. A glance at the map made it all seem foolproof. Eight hundred soldiers from the new, palisaded Fort William on Loch Linnhe would be sent to torch Glencoe, about 8 miles (13 km) south, where 600 mostly unarmed villagers lived in groups of crofts scattered through the valley. Blood would of course have to be shed if the exercise in terror were to have its proper effect. But no one would hear about it because the troops could block off the mountain passes leading into the steeply walled valley.

Things began to go wrong with these careful calculations when Alasdair Macdonald belatedly decided to make his submission. He had waited until the last possible moment in the hope of obtaining permission from the Jacobite court in France to relinquish his old oath of loyalty to James. When no word came, and the clock was ticking ominously down to the New Year, he finally made the journey over the old Highland Way to the west of Ben Nevis and down to Fort William on 31 December to make his pledge to the new king. But he was told by Colonel Hill that he was in the wrong place and was sent off again through the deep snows, south across the western Highlands of Argyll to Inveraray on Loch Fyne. Detained en route, Macdonald finally appeared at Inveraray on

113

2 January, one day late. Hill had given him a letter to take to the Sheriff of Argyll, Sir Colin of Ardkinglas, in the hope that the submission of 'the great lost sheep Glencoe' would be acceptable even if late. But the sheriff was away and heard Macdonald out only on 6 January, warning ominously that it would be for the Privy Council in Edinburgh to make a final determination on the lawfulness of the submission. A day later, John Dalrymple, the 'Master of Stair', William's counsellor on Scotland, wrote to the commander-in-chief with orders confirming that the lands of the chiefs who had failed to submit would be ravaged: 'Glencoe hath not taken the oath at which I rejoice. It will be a proper vindication of the public justice to extirpate that den of thieves . . . It were a great advantage to the nation that thieving tribes were rooted out and cut off. It must be quietly done, otherwise they will make shift for both men and their cattle . . . Let it be secret and sudden.' On the 16th Breadalbane signed the order for a killing.

The soldiers arrived at Glencoe on the first day of February. Their officer, Captain Robert Glenlyon, was a Campbell, but distantly related to the MacIains, as were many of his men. Tradition required that hospitality be offered, and for ten days 120 officers and soldiers were lodged, warmed and fed against the bitter Highland winter. On the 12th an order arrived commanding Glenlyon 'to fall upon the rebels, the Macdonalds of Glencoe, and put all to the sword under seventy'. At five in the morning, in the icy darkness, the troops butchered at least thirty-five of their hosts. The elderly chief, Iain MacIain, was shot in the back

114

while he was rising from his bed to dress, his widow robbed of her rings and stripped naked. Unlike many other women (also stripped) and children, who died of exposure, she was rescued by her sons. At Inverrigan, Glenlyon had nine men shot and reserved for himself the *coup de grâce* with a bayonet. Attacked by a sudden fit of conscience he attempted to prevent the killing of a small boy, but the soldier shot him anyway, commenting that to spare a nit was to ensure the growth of a louse. Corpses were defiled with dung, cattle driven into the hills. But far more villagers escaped than perished—enough, since the troops had failed to seal the passes at either end of the valley, to make sure the story got out.

There was an immediate outbreak of hand-fluttering and pious professions of regret in London and Edinburgh, especially by those who, directly or indirectly, had actually been responsible for what was now called 'slaughter under trust'. The obligatory inquiry was instituted at Holyroodhouse. The Scottish parliament formally expressed its horror. Breadalbane and the Master of Stair became the scapegoats for what had been an entirely premeditated act of official murder.

For all the mistimed cues and fatal stumbles, the dawn massacre in the heather floor of Glencoe, the 'weeping valley', anticipated the standard operating practices of the British Empire, to be repeated countless times, over the next two centuries, in America, Asia and Africa. 'Backward peoples' were to be given the opportunity to collaborate and, if they accepted, would be welcomed to a proper share of the spoils and to a partnership in the modernizing enterprise.

Rejection—invariably characterized as unreasonable —would invite annihilation. In the 1690s the two opposed worlds ought not to be thought of simply as English and Scots, with the anti-Jacobite Scots cast as unscrupulous cronies of the colonial power to the south. For the crucial conflict was taking place *within* Scotland, between two cultures: one based on the ancient obligations of honour and kinship, the other on the aggressive pursuit of interest and profit. That some sort of climactic battle between those societies would take place in the century about to dawn might have been predicted by the prescient. But what could never have been anticipated was the transformation that actually followed, so complete and so breathtaking that it turned Scotland from a victim of the English state into the bulwark of the British Empire, from the hard-luck case of Britannia into its most dynamic and aggressive working partner.

In 1700, that future was virtually unimaginable. The Highland clan was governed by the regularity of tradition and an immemorial calendar of work and tribal play—the seasonal obligations of pasture and hunting and the family rituals of celebration and mourning. Clan loyalty was built on the assumption of a common tribal ancestor. Even though this was, more often than not, a myth, it created a genuine bond, which extended all the way from the chief through his bigger tenants, the tacksmen, to the simple crofter. If the grandest lairds were beginning to develop a preference for Bordeaux over ale and whisky and an ear for the viola da gamba as well as the pipes, the Highland tacksman was still close to the crofters. Like them he still wore the plaid and spoke Gaelic, ate herring

116

and oatmeal and blood pudding, and kept his sword at the ready to answer the call of honour. Like them he lived by contracts dictated by custom, and sworn by word of mouth.

South of the Forth, in urban, commercial, Lowland-Protestant Scotland, as well as in metropolitan England, contracts were made with money and law, written on paper, signed in ink and sealed in hard wax. In that world the bonds of family were more and more a matter of business and property: the maximization of estates; the capitalization of farms; production for urban markets on both sides of the border of the Tweed. With more to sell, the appetite for buying grew. Silverware and pottery dishes began to be common in Lowland farmhouses along with linen sheets and grand bedsteads with turned posts. It was a society that had not yet turned the corner into modernity, but it had craned its neck and seen what it was like.

In the years after Glencoe, both Scotlands (but especially the south) endured the misery of what became known as the 'ill years'. For several summers in a row the sun refused to appear. Torrential rain deluged the country and continued into the autumn, turning the stunted crops of barley and wheat into sodden slurry and making any kind of harvesting impossible. Occasional years of respite suffered from the seed deficits of their predecessors. Cattle and sheep developed murrain and footrot. The first (and mercifully last) great famine in living memory dug its talons into Scotland. At least 5 per cent of Scotland's one and a quarter million population died of hunger. Patrick Walker, a pedlar in the Highlands, claimed to have seen women in distress after all the meal had been sold, 'clapping their hands and tearing the clothes off their heads crying, "How shall we go home and see our children die in hunger?"' Sir Robert Sibbald, the first Professor of Medicine at the University of Edinburgh and author of *Provision for the Poor in the Time of Dearth and Scarcity* (1699) catalogued the wild herbs and grasses that might be digestible and recommended that cats be eaten if there were no other kinds of meat. The highways were full of destitute, disbanded soldiers, vagrants of all kinds. Plainly, it was a time to steal or starve.

In all this darkness, though, there were some Scots who believed they could see the light. It shone from a plan that they were convinced would raise Scotland virtually overnight from impotence and misery into a global power, rich beyond the dreams of any Glasgow counting-house. A New Caledonia was to be planted across the Atlantic athwart the trading routes of the world at the isthmus of Darien, just south of Panama. There amid the palms, fortunes would be made that would seed a Scottish prosperity the like of which had never been seen.

The scheme was not as lunatic as it might at first sound. The 'free port' was to be created about 150 miles (240 km) away from where the Panama Canal now cuts between the Pacific and Atlantic oceans, and with very much the same commercial logic behind it. Its most eloquent advocate, William Paterson, a Scot who had made money in the West Indies and had been a founder of the Bank of England, argued persuasively that what was holding back the expansion of Asian–European trade was the ruinously lengthy and dangerous choice of journeys, around either the African Cape of Good Hope or the South American Cape Horn. If the Company of Scotland could realize its dream, all this would change. Ships from China and Japan could sail east and at New Edinburgh exchange cargoes with ships sailing west from Europe. With freight costs slashed, the goods thus shipped would become more cheaply available in their respective domestic markets. Demand would soar correspondingly, and the volume of trade increase exponentially. And sitting on top of the world's newest and most prosperous exchange and mart would be the Scots, taking portage, marketing and banking charges off the top and waiting for the next great fleets to sail in from the Pacific and Atlantic.

The Darien projectors were not, in fact, proposing anything more outlandish than the kind of services that had been offered for centuries in Amsterdam. This may, indeed, have been the very reason why the circle of Dutch money men around William III felt so threatened by the scheme. But the project also struck at the reigning economic orthodoxy of the time, which conceived of international trade as a zero-sum game, playing for shares of a fixed amount of goods and gold. To maximize that share meant using the power of the state—militarily if necessary—to lock up exclusive sources of colonial supply, and to enforce a monopoly of shipment and marketing for the home country's vessels and ports. Pepper, tea, silk or sugar were to be carried *only* in the ships of officially licensed and chartered companies.

But Paterson's 'Company of Scotland Trading to Africa and the Indies' was something else again:

a shameless commercial maverick disrupting orderly procedures of mercantilism. Its first—its only—great project would be the creation of a tropical free zone, where sellers and buyers from who knows where could come together on the little neck of land between the oceans to haggle and clinch deals at mutually agreed prices. No wonder everyone in London—other than Paterson's circles of Scots and well-wishers like Daniel Defoe— wanted it to fail. Lobbying hard against it in the English parliament, the Royal African Company predicted that if this unregulated monstrosity were allowed to establish itself, there would be a mass migration of England's merchants and seamen across the Tweed and 'our commerce will be utterly lost'. In one week the stock of the other pillar of English colonial trade, the East India Company, fell from 72 to 50 pence.

If the reaction in London to a Scottish –American hypermart verged on the hysterical, the Scots themselves made no secret of the fact that they thought of the Darien venture as a break-out from the economic stranglehold of English power. One of the Company's most fervent supporters, Andrew Fletcher of Saltoun, wrote that all his countrymen's 'thoughts and inclinations as if united and directed by Higher Power seemed to have turned to trade . . . the only means to recover us from our present miserable and despicable condition'. No one in Edinburgh in the summer of 1695 could possibly have missed the significance of the moment. At one end of Holyroodhouse the Glencoe inquiry was under way, at the other end a debate on the new trading company—Scotland's past and Scotland's future weighed together.

So when the first fleet of three ships sailed out from the Firth of Forth in July 1698 flying the blue-and-white saltire, and the company flag of llamas, Indians and an optimistically rising sun, it was carrying more than the 1200 men, women and children selected to be the first colonists. It was carrying the hopes of the entire country. And much of its money. The response to an English prohibition on capital investment in existing enterprises had been an outpouring of investment in the Company of Scotland. Fourteen hundred subscribers had anted up £400,000 of working capital needed to float the first voyages to Panama, and since some of those subscribers were institutions, the actual number of individual investors was much bigger. The true believers went all the way through Scottish society and could be found in the north as well as the south of the country, from dukes and countesses to advocates, from surgeons and preachers to small shopkeepers, tanners and gunsmiths, from Glasgow and Edinburgh to Selkirk, Inverness and Aberdeen. To look at the Company's ledger book is to see entrepreneurial Scotland attempting to get under way, sailing for better times.

It was not a good sign that on the first days of the journey the fleet got separated in a dense fog off Orkney. But this would not be the worst or the last of its problems. In a much more serious sense, the Darien expedition had no idea where it was going. Its main source of intelligence, not only about the sea route but also about the conditions likely to face the fleet when and if it arrived, was a surgeon called Lionel Wafer who had served with the pirate Henry Morgan in the Caribbean. Wafer was impressively detailed with his information. Darien, he assured the projectors, was a paradise. The water was fresh; the game plentiful; the fish virtually jumped into the waiting pan. The climate was benign, the soil rich; corn grew thick and tall. The natives, governed by their grand 'Emperor', were friendly and peaceful and so vain that they spent much of their day combing their long dark hair. The Company swallowed the whole story. Together with the rest of their cargo, 10,000 combs were loaded on to the ships: wooden for the simple people, horn for the middling sort, pearl-inlaid for the Emperor and his courtiers. What else would be needed in New Caledonia? Some 2808 Presbyterian catechisms to convert the pagans and 380 Bibles for the settlers; 1440 good Scottish hats and a copious supply of wigs, without which no respectable Darienite could think of emigrating. They had, after all, been promised 50 cultivable acres (0.2 sq km) of paradise and inside three years a house built at the Company's expense. Gentility was waiting in the balmy tropics. In no time at all they would be the lairds of the lagoon.

Even before the expedition got anywhere near Darien the dream had turned into a nightmare. The ships were either becalmed or battered by violent storms on the eight-week journey across the Atlantic and south through the Caribbean. Crew and passengers died at the rate of five per week from the usual dysenteric diseases. When the settlers reached the 'Golden Island' pinpointed by Wafer as their ideal haven, their New Edinburgh, they discovered it was mostly a mosquito-infested swamp. And the natives apparently were not desperately awaiting their shipload of combs, or in fact anything else the Scots had to offer. There was no Emperor, no court, no realm: just feral pigs and spear fishermen. Aware they might be attacked at any minute by the Spanish, who evidently did not share the Scots' view that Darien was 'vacant' land, those who had survived dysenteric fevers and had not gone down with malaria spent their time and energy in the sweltering, rain-soaked forest hacking out a primitive palisaded stockade and lugging enormous cannon into their bravely christened Fort St Andrew.

By spring 1699, they were dying at the rate of ten a day. Though they had brought 14,000 needles, their clothes were hanging off them in stinking, mildewed rags. There was no ripe fruit hanging on the trees begging to be picked. The 'game' was elusive and the remains of their shipped supplies were alive with maggots. A handful of dried peas was shared out between five. The peas would then be skimmed for worms when boiled up. The beef, one of them wrote, 'was as black as the sole of my foot and as rotten as the stump of a rotten boot'.

Ten months after they had left Scotland, all they had to show for the great plan to build a New Caledonian free-trade fortune was a ditch 20 feet deep and 25 feet wide (6 x 8 m), still called by the Panamanians 'Punta des Escoces', Scotchmen's Point. But there was no bustling New Edinburgh, no colony of thrifty, self-supporting farms; no tidy little harbour ready to welcome the incoming fleets, no portage industry set to haul chests across the neck of the isthmus; nothing in fact except a miserable collection of sodden, rat-infested grass huts, a dilapidated fort and 400 graves.

Those who could summon the energy and the will left the hell-hole of Darien and limped home. A few weeks later a Spanish raiding party, thoughtfully encouraged by the English, burnt the huts and destroyed Fort St Andrew. So when a second expedition, oblivious of the fate of its predecessor, arrived in the winter of 1699 all it found were ruins, rapidly being repossessed by the rainforest. 'Expecting to meet with our friends and countrymen,' one of the new arrivals wrote, 'we found nothing but a howling wilderness, the Colony deserted and gone, their huts all burnt, their fort for most part ruined, the ground which they had cleared adjoining the fort all overgrown with weeds, and we looked for Peace but no good came, and for a time of health and comfort, but beheld Trouble.'

Back in Scotland, when the full extent of the disaster at Darien sank in, it assumed the magnitude of a national trauma. The futile venture had eaten up a full quarter of Scotland's liquid capital. But the most serious casualty of the fiasco was the last best hope of a national regeneration. That hope—of Scotland going it alone and outflanking the English trading empire—disappeared in the morass of Darien. Self-reproach for any naïveté about the expedition disappeared in an immediate wave of intense anger and hatred against the bullying English who had doomed it to disaster. The Governor of Jamaica, it was known, had issued a proclamation actually forbidding English colonists, merchants or seamen from giving any assistance to the beleaguered Darienites, however desperate their plight. Direct collusion with the Spanish was suspected. In the inflamed

124

atmosphere, counter-actions were taken in the economic war, allowing Scots to trade with an enemy of England in time of war. When the *Worcester*, a ship believed to have harassed the Darienites, was caught in port at Leith, its captain and two of its crew were summarily tried as 'pirates' and hanged, to rejoicing in the streets.

But revenge was not a viable strategy for the future. Scotland had come to an obvious fork in the road ahead, and the serious day when it had to choose could not be postponed much longer. It could slog on, becoming ever more impoverished and isolated, even perhaps defying England by calling back the Stuart child born in 1688 to reign as James VIII of Scotland. But this would be tantamount to a declaration of war, and there was no guarantee that the French would prove any more reliable or more powerful an ally than they had been in the past. The new war that had broken out in Europe suggested that the armies of Louis XIV were less invincible than the ceiling murals in the Hall of Mirrors at Versailles would suggest. The alternative, however bleak for those cherishing Scotland's independence, was union. By no means all of the governing class or even the people were uniformly hostile to it. A proposal had been tabled in 1689 but had been rejected by the English Convention Parliament. After the Darien fiasco, however, a large section of the nobility, especially those with cross-border economic interests and property, and many of the commercial and professional classes of the Lowlands, had come to accept that some sort of closer association was needed and even desirable. The best option would be a federation, the two kingdoms retaining their separate political identities. But by the middle of the first decade of the eighteenth century, the Scots were not going to be allowed the luxury of prolonged consideration.

For war and the succession had made Scotland's allegiance a critical issue for the English government. In 1702 William III had died after being thrown from his horse when it stumbled over a molehill. His sister-in-law, Anne, optimistically celebrated as 'the teeming princess of Denmark', had not, alas, made good on the promise. For Anne came to the throne after five infant deaths, at least thirteen miscarriages and two episodes of pseudocyesis. The chances of her producing a surviving heir were assessed pessimistically. Her last surviving son, Prince William Henry of Gloucester, had died in 1700 at the age of eleven. Threatened with the undoing of 1688 and the jeopardizing of a Protestant succession, with the Act of Settlement of 1701 the Whig defenders of the Revolution had gone as far afield as Sophia, Electress of Hanover, daughter of Charles I's sister, to pre-empt the much more obvious Catholic James Edward Stuart (not to mention 56 other Catholic heirs). A sign of their determination to avoid a Jacobite restoration was the passage in 1706 of the Regency Act, establishing an emergency Council of State following the queen's death and pending the arrival of the Hanoverian successor. So with England at war with James's patron and protector, Louis XIV, it now became even more imperative for the security of the realm that Scotland be made to sign on to the Hanoverian succession. Chivvied along, the Scottish parliament at first demurred, insisting on

126

making its own separate arrangements for the throne of Scotland. An ugly economic war looked likely, perhaps a prelude to the real thing. In 1705, an Alien Act was passed in Westminster, shutting down most of the cross-border trade and deeming any Scots in England to be foreign subjects.

The blackmail worked. In 1706 commissioners from the two parliaments, not just the English but (in response to an astonishing proposal by the Duke of Hamilton) also the Scots chosen by Queen Anne's government, met in separate rooms to consider a union of realms. The two sides never confronted each other face to face, communicating only through messengers. In the streets of Edinburgh and Glasgow there were riots. Daniel Defoe, ex-bankrupt, who had got out of prison by volunteering his services to Robert Harley as a spy and (in various guises—a 'fish merchant' in Glasgow, a 'wool manufacturer' in Aberdeen) a propagandist for union, became alarmed in Edinburgh in October 1706. 'I had not been Long There,' he wrote back to Harley, 'but I heard a Great Noise and looking Out Saw a Terrible Multitude Come up the High Street with a Drum at the head of them shouting and swearing and Cryeing Out all Scotland would stand together. No Union. No Union. English Dogs . . . and the like. I Can not say to you I had no apprehensions.' The crowd broke down the doors of one of the treaty commissioners, Sir Patrick Johnson, with a sledgehammer, terrorizing him and his wife until 'the lady in despair and fright came to the window with two candles' calling for the Town Guard.

Defoe may have been a paid secret agent of the English government, but there is no doubt that he was sincerely committed to his mission of persuasion. His *Six Essays at Removing National Prejudices Against a Union with Scotland*, published in 1706–7, scornfully satirized those in both countries who liked to boast of the purity of their race, when in fact, Defoe argued, the history of Britain was a history of happy mongrelism and had been all the better for it. Paterson, the Scots founder of the Bank of England and the Darien projector, was one of his close friends, and Defoe's vision of a British future was of a free and natural movement of men, goods and ideas across the borders of the old enemy kingdoms. The new Great Britain was supposed to end, once and for all, the endless history of sorrow and bloodshed that had come between England and Scotland. These kinds of sentiments, however well meaning, probably converted very few. Palms needed to be greased before the deed could be done, though on what scale remains difficult to determine. Sums of money were certainly distributed to secure the necessary votes for passage of the Union Bill through the Scottish parliament, and promises of landed estates were certainly dangled before obliging Scottish peers. But in the currency of early eighteenth-century politics, no decisions got taken without these kinds of lures, and some of the cash clearly went to Scotsmen who continued to vote *against* the union. As far as enthusiasts like Defoe were concerned, the biggest sweetener of all was above board and public. To make the union of the two National Debts more palatable, the English parliament had voted to offer £398,085. 10s.—the precise 'Equivalent' of all the losses incurred on the Darien expedition. For those still suffering the disastrous consequences of their unfortunate investment, this was not a trivial compensation.

In the winter of 1706 it needed just six weeks for the Act of Union to go through Westminster, ten for Holyrood. There were still hold-outs against it, unable to bear the loss of Scottish independence, however grim the alternatives and however improved the economic outlook. Andrew Fletcher of Saltoun, for one, bitterly opposed the union as a conspiracy to defraud Scotland of its liberty; and before the juggernaut rolled over him, John Hamilton, second Baron Belhaven, delivered in parliament on 2 November 1706 a Shakespearean lament for his country: 'Like Caesar sitting in the midst of our Senate attending the final blow . . . looking about her covering herself with her royal garment and breathing her last'. Like other pro-unionists, Defoe mocked the melodrama uttered by the 'rough, fat, black, noisy man more like a butcher than a lord'. But he was honest enough to admit (in private) that 'a firmer union of policy with less union of affection has hardly been known in the whole world'. And he would eventually sympathize with Belhaven's sadness, visit him in prison, befriend and console him.

Brutal and peremptory though the process may have been, the union was not a crude annexation. The Scottish Kirk retained its own identity and governance, the two systems of law were largely kept separate, and no changes were made to Scotland's universities, burghs and hereditary criminal jurisdictions. The parliament at Holyrood was to be done away with, by voting for its own abolition, but Scotland was to have 45 members in the Commons and 16 elected, so-called representative peers. The first set of MPs was elected by the Scottish parliament in 1707, but from 1708 general elections were held in the Scottish constituencies. To the dismay of some, the number of MPs had dropped dramatically from 157 to 45, but this might seem less of an outrage against a representative system when one considers that for much of the eighteenth century the entire Scottish electorate numbered only some 2600 in a population of one and a quarter of a million. What Scotland lost in 1707 was certainly not a democracy. But still it had been a true political nation, a place in the world. And now as the Chancellor of Scotland, James Ogilvy, Earl of Seafield, said as he signed the Act of Union, 'There's ane end of ane auld sang.'

If one of those new Scottish members of parliament wanted a heartening vision of the Britain to which he had become attached—with whatever measure of reluctance or enthusiasm—all he had to do was take himself down-river to Greenwich to the handsome new Royal Naval Hospital. Christopher Wren's twin, colonnaded pavilions could not help but put the traveller in mind of the Cour Royale, the grandiose approach to Versailles. But at Greenwich the approach was by way of the Thames, and the vista, as befitted an institution of charity, was public and not blocked off by grandiose screens and grilles. Inside the Great Hall facing the chapel, the invidious contrasts with French autocracy continued in the ceiling allegory painted by James Thornhill: the first great visual manifesto of the post-1688 monarchy. The allusions to the most famous allegories of the baroque monarchies—Rubens' apotheosis of James I at Whitehall and Le Brun's fawning celebration of the Sun King, Louis XIV, at Versailles—were glaring, the better to mark the differences between despots and constitutional monarchs. On Thornhill's ceiling, Apollo had changed sides from the vainglorious absolutist to William and Mary, the champions of Protestant freedom. Louis had taken things from the peoples of Europe: territories, cities, farms. But William was a giver, restoring to a duly grateful continent the cap of Liberty, while the arch-enemy (thinly disguised as Arbitrary Power) lies trampled beneath his feet. The invidious comparisons are trumpeted throughout the allegory. Over there, the curses of serfdom, popery and blind superstition. Over here, the wisdom of the arts and sciences to guide the omniscient, benevolent king. Over there, the Jesuits, over here, Newton. It would be these milder but sterling virtues that would make Britain great: Prudence, Temperance and Charity.

The blessings of charity are personified in the apparently venerable presence of the most senior pensioner in the Hospital, the reputedly ninety-seven-year-old John Wall (who in fact was constantly in trouble with the authorities for his filthy language and incorrigible drunkenness). But then it is vain to look to allegories to tell the truth. The image of the new Great Britain—peacefully devoted to toleration and freedom—was at odds with the historical reality of a state transformed by nearly three decades of war into an immense and formidable military machine. During the Restoration, the English army seldom consisted of more than 15,000 men. By the end of the War of the Spanish Succession in 1713, there were over 90,000 men in the army and more than 40,000 in the navy (although by 1715 this had dropped to a peace-time force of 32,000). Military spending—more than £5 million a year during the Nine Years' War, 1689–97 and over £7 million a year during the War of the Spanish Succession—had almost doubled, rising from £36 million to £65 million. By 1710, military spending had swallowed up almost 10 per cent of Britain's entire national income. To build a single first-rate ship would cost between £30,000 and £40,000. Keeping soldiers in the field and ships on the high seas, and supplying them with adequate victuals and munitions had added £40 million to the National Debt and created another kind of army—which would not be demobilized once the fighting had stopped: bond-holders, tax-assessors and accountants; customs-and-excise men, thousands upon thousands of them. By the end of the wars, Britons were being taxed twice as heavily, per capita, as their French counterparts, a burden that would only get heavier as the relentlessly martial eighteenth century rumbled on.

Bureaucratic, militarized and heavily taxed though post-revolution Britain was, there was one feature of the Greenwich myth that was true. While Louis XIV could simply decide how much money was needed for his campaigns and then decree the funds into the treasury, in Britain the monarch and his ministers had to ask for it. So whether he liked it or not—and assuredly William did not—he and his successors had no choice but to go to parliament to fund their wars.

Virtually everywhere else in Europe, if not the world—from Ming China to Mughal India to

Romanov Russia to Hohenzollern Prussia—the more militarized the state, the stronger the king. But in Britain, the longer the wars went on, the stronger *parliament* became, as the purse whose strings it controlled so tightly became bigger and bigger. Apart from the States General and provincial estates of the Dutch Republic, Britain was the only major European power where senior military men—generals like Marlborough—also sat in parliament and assumed a role as power-brokers, not to subvert parliamentary government but to reinforce it.

In one of the greatest ironies of British history, positions traditionally taken by monarchists and parliamentarians were now reversed. The Whigs, who in the reigns of Charles II and James II had insisted on limited monarchy, now found themselves to be running the war, while the Tory champions of unlimited monarchy were mistrustful of it, not least because nearly a quarter of all money voted in 1702–13 for expenditure on the army was going to foreign (especially Dutch) subsidies! The Tories also began to present themselves to the electors of the counties as the champions of the over-taxed landed classes, held to ransom by men whose commitment to the war was driven as much by profit as principle. It was a turnaround worthy of Dean Swift's most biting satires on the squabbles of Big Enders and Little Enders, but it had an entirely serious effect on British politics. For as long as the little-king party ran the war government, and the big-king party was more often than not in opposition, the role reversal dictated a benevolent equilibrium and ruled out the possibility of military autocracy.

Better yet, the Tories—who in the reign of Charles II had been content to see a single parliament renewed for more than fifteen years— now wanted more, not fewer, elections. Their most articulate spokesman, Henry St John, Viscount Bolingbroke, who cast himself as the guardian of ancient English liberties, even went so far as insisting that frequent revolutions were a sign of political vigour. The Whigs, of course, felt that 1688 had been all the revolution the country needed, but since the revolutionary settlement had guaranteed triennial elections it was all but impossible for them to avoid regular political upheaval. And, for better or worse, the politics was the kind of combative partisanship that, without any anachronism, we can recognize as prototypically modern. The two parties were at each other's throats, not just on the specific policies of the day (the corruption of ministers, the propriety and expense of the war, the profiteering of contractors) but also in their reading of the Revolution of 1688 and the character of the political nation that had been created—or reaffirmed—as a result of it. Paradoxically, neither of the parties was especially eager to represent what had happened as a historical rupture with the past. As the principal beneficiaries of the change, the Whigs were not about to endorse a view of opposition that seemed to license resistance to the king's ministers. So they portrayed themselves as the real conservatives and James II as a renegade, like his father before him, bent on violating the fundamental tenets of the 'ancient constitution'— the rule of law, the Protestant settlement and the proper restraints imposed by parliamentary government. The 'revolution' that deposed him had been, then, an act of lawful resistance, the restoration of the authentic constitutional monarchy under which the nation now lived. 'The tyrant conspired to enslave free-born Englishmen into SLAVES,' a typical Whig polemic shouted, 'the CREATURES of Popery and Tyranny! He would have had Papist Irishmen in your houses . . . quartered on your wives and daughters; he would have made TORQUEMADAS of your judges. He had broken his sworn CONTRACT with his people and Resistance to his despotism was a sacred duty, the calling of patriots.'

The Tories remained adamant that the Whigs had usurped the title of defenders of the monarchy, while deforming its character. That monarchy remained what it had been before 1688: a divinely appointed office. Their own participation in 1688 had not in any way altered or compromised the sacrosanct nature of the institution, but had merely been an *ad hominem* act filling the vacancy that James had unfortunately created. There had been a change of personnel, not a change of constitution:

> RESISTANCE which is nothing but foul HYDRA-HEADED REBELLION is a very MONSTROSITY, an abomination unto God to whom alone it is reserved to decide the fate of His Anointed . . . King James was not cast out—Truly he resigned his throne and this being vacant Prince William was invited hither. But he has been captive to wicked counsellors, has dragged the country into wars so that his minions could line their pockets with our TAXES. Not content with

plundering your purse they conspire at the DESTRUCTION of the true Church of England by a most disingenuous allowance of OCCASIONAL CONFORMITY (which is nothing other than the pernicious TOLERATION of Dissenters), his minions, the SEEDS OF CROMWELL, are even now encompassing the MURDER OF TRUE, Divinely-Appointed MONARCHY.

The abuse could get ugly and personal. William III, his bitterest enemies put it about, was not only foreign and corrupt but a homosexual eunuch too, which explained his difficulty in begetting heirs. A typical serenade of the period went:

He has gotten in PART the shape of a man
But more of a monkey, deny it who can
He's the tread of a goose, the legs of a swan
A DAINTY FINE KING indeed!
He is not qualified for his wife
Because of the cruel midwife's knife
Yet BUGGERING BENTINCK does please to the life
A DAINTY FINE KING indeed!

The differences between Whigs and Tories, then, were not just the petty quibbles of gentlemen who, once the political name-calling was done, could get together over a glass of wine or a tankard of ale. These differences cut to the bone. They went to rival coffee-houses (the Whigs to Old Slaughter's, the Tories to the Cocoa Tree) and different clubs (the Whigs to the Kit Cat, the Tories to the Honourable Board of Brotherhood from 1709, or Edward Harley's Board from 1720). They were two armed camps, bent on mutual destruction, and contested elections were fought with everything the combatants could get their hands on: money, drink, entertainment, shameless promises of jobs, juicy libel and, in the last resort, either the threat or the reality of a serious brawl.

From the poll-books kept by many constituencies we know that, even though the electors were for the most part the social inferiors of the candidate, they were anything but docile or easily impressionable. The voters of the fiercely contested counties were freeholders: literate, opinionated, informed by the newspapers and journals that mushroomed after the abandonment of the Licensing Act, and predictably bloody-minded about the hot-button issues of the day like toleration of Dissenters or Catholics and the imposition of new excises. By the standards of the time, the size of the electorate was surprisingly large: a quarter of a million adult males or 15 per cent of that population. And it was divided right down the middle, county by county, village by village. The poll-books of even the most modest hamlets show electors voting their party choice, irrespective of the opinion of the local squire—and switching that choice from election to election.

The battle for power was so intense and so vicious that politicians and their respective camp followers—placemen and pen-pushers, hacks and roughnecks—were not inclined to be magnanimous in victory. As Queen Anne got older, and the anxiety about the succession became more acute, the temptation to make a pre-emptive strike on the enemy was virtually irresistible. Politicians on the losing end of elections were now faced with losing, not only their jobs along with the little barony of dependent supporters they had accumulated but their liberty too. Being out of power and out of place could now also entail impeachment, imprisonment, total personal and political ruin. To allow a floored antagonist to get up off the mat was to court destruction. Equally, to fail to nip a potent, scurrilous campaign in the bud while it was still an irritation rather than a threat was to show fatal weakness.

So, with an eye to their future after the aged Queen Anne had gone, the Whigs decided to pluck out the most annoying thorn in their flesh: the ultra-Tory, High-Church preacher Dr Henry Sacheverell. In 1709, thirsty for confrontation, Sacheverell had, in his own words, 'hung out the bloody banner of defiance' and on 5 November had preached a violent sermon in St Paul's before the Corporation of London, condemning the Glorious Revolution of 1688 as a transgression against God's anointed and accusing the Whigs of putting the Church of England in danger by its *de facto* policy of tolerating Dissenters. For Sacheverell, both crimes were tantamount to bringing back the evil days of the Commonwealth, an overturning of everything that England truly was. To make sure that his alarm bell would be heard, he had 100,000 copies of the sermon printed and distributed. By 1710, the campaign to discredit the Whigs as the destroyers of the true Church had become ubiquitous and vocal. The government—unpopular through the prolongation of the war in Europe and the high costs in excises it placed on the people— either had to brazen out the shouting or stamp on Sacheverell before he became a real menace.

In 1710 Sacheverell was impeached in the

House of Lords. The trial was a public-relations fiasco for the government. Henry Sacheverell became a hero of the streets of London, and Dissenter meeting-houses and chapels, including those of the Huguenot community who had settled around Spitalfields after their expulsion from France, were ransacked and burned to the ground. Sacheverell was escorted to his trial each day by a guard of myrmidon butchers and mobbed wherever he was sighted by delirious crowds yelling his name and issuing death threats against the Whig ministers. Inside parliament Sacheverell upended the onus of guilt, prosecuting not only the government but also the entire Whig version of the history of 1688 and especially their claim to lawful resistance, which he dismissed as a wicked oxymoron. Pro-Sacheverell riots broke out in virtually every major town in the southwest and Midlands and, faced with a breakdown of order and insufficient troops to repress it, the government decided to cut its losses, whatever the embarrassment. Sacheverell was given a transparently trivial sentence—suspended from preaching for three years and the offending sermon to be burned by the public hangman. The news was greeted with bonfires and bells around the country, reminiscent of scenes at the Restoration of 1660, as well as another round of chapel-breaking. In the next election, the Tories swept to power.

When the Queen died in August 1714, the political nation held its breath. Anything and everything was on the cards, including another round of civil war. Street violence between party gangs became commonplace, the 'Mughouse' vigilantes paid by the Whig John Holles, first Duke of Newcastle, taking it to the High Tory and Jacobite mobs that had ruled the alleys since the Sacheverell riots. Rumours took wing. Before she died, it was said, Queen Anne had let it be known that she wished her Catholic half-brother James Edward Stuart to succeed her, not the Elector of Hanover, and had even signed a will to make her intentions clear. But however hard they searched, no one could come up with the document that would get in the way of the succession of the uncharismatic middle-aged Elector George. The Jacobite press ridiculed him mercilessly as a lecherous dolt, with not a word of English at his command, sporting two mistresses, one fat, one thin, both ugly, who had not scrupled to have one of his own wife's former lovers murdered. His coronation was greeted with another wave of rioting in at least twenty English towns. Predictably enough, it was even worse in Scotland. At Inverness the proclamation of George's accession was interrupted by the town magistrates and 'God save the King' shouted down by cries of 'God damn them and their king'.

Not surprisingly, George took it personally and blamed the Tories for encouraging if not actually engineering the hostile demonstrations. As much of a soldier-king as William III, George also disapproved of the unseemly hastiness with which they had sought peace with France and the poor terms on which the Treaty of Utrecht had been settled in 1713. He wanted them out of power. Purges were conducted on office-holders and money taken from the civil list for the 1715 election, which duly produced the enormous Whig majority the king desired. Faced with the prospect of years in the wilderness and a permanently unsympathetic king, the Tory leaders, the Duke of Ormonde, and Bolingbroke, panicked and took a flyer on the alternative—James Edward Stuart. In hindsight it seems like an unbelievably foolhardy, if not insane, gamble. But after Sacheverell, Jacobitism had got into the bloodstream of English politics to a degree that would have been unthinkable ten years before. Even so, the problem —and it was a huge one—was that a King James III/VIII was only going to be a possibility courtesy of a French invasion. And after decades of interminable war, an emptied treasury, desperate impoverishment, near famine conditions and partial occupation, France, if not Louis XIV, was utterly exhausted. Besides, an attempt had been made to land James Edward in Scotland seven years before, in 1708, which, although triggering a panic at Westminster and the passage of the Treason Act, ended in an ignominious débâcle. The ostensible leader of the rebellion, the Duke of Hamilton, had swiftly disappeared to Lancashire at the critical moment. A flotilla of English warships had barred the entrance to the Firth of Forth, while James's face erupted in an unkingly flowering of measles. The would-be James VIII never landed.

Without a better planned and better executed French military action in 1715, the only hope that the Tories and Jacobites had was for an uprising to begin in Britain itself—starting, of course, in Scotland. And this was very much on the cards. The glowing vision of mutual prosperity and pan-Britannic harmony sketched by boosters of the union like Daniel Defoe had, of course, failed to materialize. Arguably Scotland, even Highland

141

Scotland, was no worse off than it had been before 1707, but new taxes on linen, malt and salt had been introduced, and no bonanza in Scottish exports to England had opened up. After the failure of the 1708 Jacobite plan the English law of treason was put into effect along the border, with fresh hardship for all those living in that region. The most obvious beneficiaries of the union had been those who were already among the richest and most powerful Scots, like the Duke of Argyll. There were other nobles, in particular the Earl of Mar, Secretary of Scotland from 1713 to 1714, who had served in the Tory governments of Anne, who saw 1715 as the coming of a long Whig winter— and then acted to guarantee it.

On the assumption that James would arrive with the French in force, and that there would also be an English uprising in the old Catholic region of Northumbria, Mar raised his standard at the ancestral stag-hunt at Braemar in September. In the northeast Lowlands other disaffected nobles rallied to him, and in the west some (though not all) of the clans began to rally their Highland followers. Throughout Scotland, in fact, not just in the Highlands, support for the Hanoverian regime melted away alarmingly. Defensive trenches were dug in front of Edinburgh Castle. Perspiration flowed freely in London. Already in July, plans had been made for a hasty exit to Holland for George I.

But even though it may have had more going for it in 1715 than 1745, the Jacobite rebellion never came close to overthrowing the union and its German king. At Sherriffmuir, on 13 November, Mar's 4000 Jacobites fought a much smaller force of around 1000 under Argyll to a draw but still failed to take either Glasgow or Edinburgh. Reduced to futile marches and counter-marches, while waiting for a French invasion that seemed mysteriously postponed, the rebels found the momentum draining away from the rising. The English and Scottish components of a joint army had no sooner come together than they fell out and became reduced (as so many times before) to a raiding and wrecking force until finally cornered in Lancashire.

The *coup de grâce* actually took place a long way from the Tweed and the Tay at Versailles. Just a few days before Mar came out for the Stuarts, their greatest patron, Louis XIV, had died, leaving an infant great-grandson as his successor. Any chance that the Regent, Orléans, had of stabilizing his country and relieving it of the crushing burden of taxation depended on a peace policy. There would be no invasion. Just over six weeks after he had arrived in Scotland on 22 December 1714, James was back on board returning to France. Not long afterwards, the whole Jacobite ménage—3000 Irish, Scots and English—which for years had camped at St Germain on Louis XIV's long-suffering generosity, was removed to the less grandiose milieu of Bar-le-Duc in Lorraine. Their cause was still gallantly flattered. But the truth was that they had become an expensive nuisance.

In England the Whig government and the king could breathe just a little more easily. The northern earls were, in the ancient style, beheaded for their treason (as their predecessors had been in 1569), allowing the Earl of Derwentwater to make a magnificently histrionic speech, on 24 February 1716, from the scaffold at Tower Hill, custom-ordered for Jacobite hagiographers. But even if, in hindsight, the rising of 1715 might look like a storm in a teacup, and even though successive Whig governments cynically conjured up the Jacobite bogey whenever they wanted an excuse to intimidate or incarcerate their political opponents, the threat had in fact been serious. And it didn't go away. In March 1719 a mini-armada of 29 Spanish ships and 5000 troops, with arms for another 30,000, set sail from Cadiz for Scotland, although the Protestant wind intervened as close as Coruña, dispersing it and stranding the Pretender.

Britain, though, was not yet becalmed. If anyone in 1715, or even 1720, had predicted that the next two decades would see an astonishing drop in the wind-speed of politics in Britain, they would have been written off as hopelessly deluded. But from being a political nation notorious for its feverish hyperactivity and infuriated partisanship, early Hanoverian Britain became—almost— sedate. And the man who administered the sedative was Sir Robert Walpole.

It was Walpole's intuition (as much as his calculation) to present himself as the soul of common sense. But much as he cultivated the impression that his bottom-heavy 'soundness' and common-sense pragmatism rose naturally from his roots among the Norfolk gentry, 'Squire Walpole' resembled the typical country gentleman about as closely as King George III would approximate to the average farmer. And although he would never have made a profession of it, Walpole's approach to politics arguably owed much to John Locke— not the Locke of the two *Treatises on Government* but the Locke of the *Essay concerning Human*

Understanding, first published in 1690 and already run through several editions by the time Walpole was in his political apprenticeship. Of course Walpole was uninterested in the finer points of Locke's epistemology—the science of how we acquire dependable knowledge. But in common with many of his contemporaries he surely took on board Locke's flat denial of truths grounded in revelation rather than experience. If attachment to mutually intolerant beliefs, of the kind that had so bitterly divided the political nation, had not been brought about by some irrefutable epiphany but rather had been the product of particular historical happenstance, then perhaps another kind of historical happenstance could make them go away.

So Walpole set out to preside over a politics of reasonableness rather than righteousness. His management style was meant to make room for the realization of the non-political life, a principle abhorrent to the classical tradition that had dominated the seventeenth century, in which life was political or nothing. Walpole had the modern instinct that the pursuit of material satisfactions could take the edge off mutually destructive ideologies, so he did his best to massage the inflamed body politic with the ointment of epicureanism. Property, tranquillity and pleasure were to replace intransigence, intolerance and anathema as the sovereign instincts of public as well as private life. For the gentleman, the panelled library and the well-stocked deer park would do better than the venomous libel and the reckless conspiracy. For the common sort, honest toil and the satisfaction of simple wants would do better than drunken uproar and riot. Of course there was a huge element of self-interest in the propagation of this pastoral view of political quiet. Walpole wanted to de-fang English politics principally to ensure that his enemies remained toothless. But there is also no doubt that he tapped into a genuine sense of exhaustion at the factional bitterness that had disfigured public life since the death of Charles II. Richard Addison, the editor of the *Spectator*, spoke for many when he wrote that 'there cannot a greater judgement befall a country than such a dreadful spirit of division that rends a government into two distinct people and makes them greater strangers to one another than if they were different nations . . . a furious party spirit which rages in its full violence . . . fills a nation with spleen and rancour and extinguishes all the seeds of good nature, compassion and humanity.'

The antidote, administered by Walpole, was what his generation called 'politeness'—not just in the modern sense of good manners (although that was not unimportant), but rather a civilized self-restraint. The polite man, unlike the passionate man, wanted to strengthen the social bonds between men rather than sunder them; to give society an appreciation of the interdependence of its parts rather than the inevitability of its conflicts and incompatibilities. So the great project of Walpolean pragmatism was an attempt to change the subject of British politics—away from conviction and towards the practical business of making a fortune. The pursuit of self-interest, he might have said, ought not to be confused with aggressive selfishness; for instead of dividing the nation into so many discrete individuals, it actually tied them together in mutually compatible and fruitful enterprises. From such pursuits would come the greater good of the country. Which would *you* prefer, he might have asked, the unsparing attack of principles that led to incessant war and chaos, or what he had to offer: peace, which in turn would relieve the landed interest of the grievous burden of land taxes they were always complaining about, and political stability, all the desirable ingredients of what today might be classified as a healthy business environment?

From the beginning, Walpole had bet that the politics of the future would be more concerned with portfolio management than religious passion or legal debates. In 1712, at the height of the Tory ascendancy, he had been sent to prison for embezzlement, and the painful experience had taught him a lesson about the tight interconnection between political and financial fortunes. In 1720 he was able to put that precocious understanding to good use. He had been a minister in the Whig administrations of George I off and on for five years. Though there were still well over 200 Tories in the House of Commons by 1720, their Jacobite flirtation had, for the time being, broken them as a serious threat. But no sooner had the Whigs established their dominance than they themselves fractured into competing baronies and factions based on interest groups rather than ideologies. Driven by a ferocious ambition, Walpole was just one of a number of equally unscrupulous and intelligent sharks circling governments in Westminster, their nostrils sensitive for the slightest whiff of blood. It was only when the South Sea Bubble burst in 1720 that his reputation changed from one of shrewdness to indispensability, and this was a reputation largely of his own careful manufacture.

The plan, dreamed up by the South Sea Company, was going to make everyone happy, except perhaps the directors of the Bank of England. Its pet project was an idea that was simplicity itself: essentially the privatization of a large portion of the National Debt. As the government's wartime demands had become more urgent, so the interest rates payable on long-term obligations like annuities had become steeper— around 6 per cent. The Company, founded in 1711 and always more of a financial management organization than a commercial enterprise, offered to buy out that burden. Holders of long-term irredeemable bonds like annuities (on which interest was payable every year until the holder died) would be persuaded to trade them for company stock. The Company, now capitalized to the tune of some £40 million, would be given the monopoly to trade in 'The South Seas and West Indies'. A similar scheme, cooked up in France by the Scottish financier John Law, who had invented a 'Mississippi Company', seemed, for the moment, to have worked like a dream. But despite the vision of exotic riches, everyone understood that the South Sea Company was a shipless wonder, essentially a fund-management company. The only reason why a holder should want to make the trade of annuities against stock was a belief that the swift appreciation of South Sea stock would make him more money than he could ever dream of in a lifetime's receipt of annual interest payments.

The prophecy was self-fulfilling. Between January and June 1720, South Sea stock rose from

128 to 950 and peaked at 1050 on 24 June. Annuity holders climbed over each other in the crush to get their hands on certificates, sending the price through the roof. Rents soared. New shell companies sprang up overnight with equally spurious commercial rationales: companies formed to trade in human hair or woad or coral fishing. On 23 May the government auditor, Harley, wrote to his brother Sir Robert, now Earl of Oxford, 'The madness of stockjobbing is inconceivable.' It must have seemed, as booms always do, that it must go on for ever; a perfect instance of the fit between public interest and private profit. Until, that is, some prominent stockholders decided enough was enough, took their profit and departed. Isaac Newton made £7000; Thomas Guy, founder of the London hospital of that name, £180,000. The rhythm of selling began to accelerate, and the stock suddenly started to dip, then tumble, and finally, as panic took hold, it went into free-fall: between 1 September and 1 October, its value collapsed from 725 to 290. Countless investors who had dreamed of making overnight fortunes were now left with neither their old dependable annuities nor stock of any serious value. Lord Londonderry lost £50,000; many less exalted were wiped out. The country was left drowning in worthless paper, thrashing about looking for someone to blame.

There were plenty of choice targets: John Aislabie, Chancellor of the Exchequer from 1718 to 1728, and Walpole's principal rival, who had himself held £77,000-worth of South Sea Stock at almost 100 per cent profit; Charles Spencer, the third Earl of Sunderland, who had been one of the project's principal promoters. But Robert Walpole was certain it was not going to be him. He had muttered some lukewarm reservations about the Company that he now suggested had been deep and solemn second thoughts. But in fact Walpole had been lucky, not prescient. He had invested heavily himself, had sold some stock too early (unlike the canny Guy) and then, repenting, had tried to buy in again at the precise moment when it was poised to depreciate. Luckily for him, the bid had been held up by a delay in the mail. But Walpole did nothing to allay a wholly undeserved impression of clairvoyance. His real art, at this moment, was less financial wizardry than crisis management. He knew very well that the government itself was on a sound footing. Whatever the cost to individual stockholders, the Treasury had relieved itself of nearly 80 per cent of all its previous annuity holders. Fortunes had been lost. But others had been won. So the crisis was more psychological than fiscal. Like FDR in 1932 he understood that the first priority was to stop the self-seeding fear. Noises needed to be made about a rescue scheme for the Company, however vaguely defined and ambiguously guaranteed. Happily his own shrewd investment manager and banker, Robert Jacombe, came up with one, largely based on the reconsolidation of Company stock into solid Bank of England obligations.

It was not so much what he said as the way he said it. When Walpole spoke to the House of Commons with his effortless geniality and evenness of temper, the stricken calmed down and began to feel unaccountably better as though they had all had a glass or two of his best port. Better yet, when he read them balance sheets that would normally have had them perspiring with bewildered anxiety, they discovered—miracle of miracles—that they could actually understand what he was talking about. And it didn't seem, after all, the end of the world. The carriages and the hunting hounds could stay.

In short order Walpole became the rock to which apparently foundering fortunes, financial and political, anchored themselves. And for his ability to shield the culpable from the consequences of the disaster he also became known as the Skreen Master—the master, we would say, of spin. Everyone was in his debt, not least because he had his hands on explosive information as to who exactly had bribed whom to get the Company deal done. Aislabie would have to be sacrificed but Sunderland was spared. King George, whose own hands were not clean (nor were those of his mistresses), was agog with admiration and gratitude. Walpole's ministerial colleagues, especially Sunderland, who had sniped at his presumptuous ambition, grovelled before his apparently arcane mastery of the spreadsheets, not to mention the discreet success with which he kept them out of prison. The serried ranks of the Whigs on the benches of the Commons loved him for deflecting popular anger. Even the more independently minded country gentry at least appreciated him making good his promise to keep the country out of the foreign wars that would raise their tax rates.

Walpole repaid their appreciation by departing from tradition and remaining in the Commons on becoming 'First Lord of the Treasury', not so much Prime Minister as Prime Manager. Part of the decision was a matter of prudence. Apart from the solid core of Tories there was also a sizeable group of independent members, and those two non-government factions needed to be kept apart for his own ministry to maintain its domination. So no pains were too great in his careful cultivation of loyalty in the House. 'So great was Walpole's love of the Commons,' wrote the Earl of Chesterfield, 'that when going to face the House he dressed as carefully as a lover going to see a mistress.' In keeping with Walpole's belief in the bonds of mutual interest over the alignments of ideology, he built a barony of connections and obligations. And they began with small, telling gestures. Rival politicians like the Whig specialists in firebrand 'patriot' oratory, William Pulteney and John Carteret, could always outshine him. But they could never outdine him. Walpole made a point of ensuring that every new Whig member of the Commons dined with him *tête-à-tête*. With a glass of his best claret in your hand, a juicy haunch of mutton oozing on the trencher and Cock Robin's glittering eyes twinkling benevolently in your direction as if the life of the party, the state of the nation depended on *you*, how could you possibly not swear undying devotion and loyalty to his interest?

And then, to be sure, there was the matter of jobs. Walpole sat at the heart of a vast empire of patronage. There had, of course, been first ministers before him who had made it their business to dispense offices to their followers or to strip them from the unobliging. But the expansion of the British state during the long decades of war had resulted in a massive multiplication of posts, especially in the strategically lucrative departments of revenue enhancement—customs, excise, land-tax assessment—and this gave Walpole an unprecedented bonanza of jobs to distribute. Some of them might be pure sinecures requiring nothing more of the holder than to sit back and collect, and these were especially useful assets in securing votes in the Commons. Many others were appointments that required real effort and even a modicum of integrity. But they conferred status as well as cash on the holder and could make a somebody out of a nobody, especially in their native county or town.

In retrospect it is possible to see that what Walpole built was Britain's (in fact the world's) first party-political machine. He owned the placemen in parliament primed to vote as directed. And since the passage of the Septennial Act in 1716 (the pretext of which was to keep dangerous Jacobitism at bay) elections now came just once every seven years, extending the life of members' offices that much longer. Walpole had the hacks scribbling away to persuade the country that he was working assiduously in its best interests (as he quite sincerely believed he was). He had George I eating out of the palm of his hand, especially when his managerial skills produced the civil-list money needed to keep the king and queen in decent style. And lest anyone imagine they could break ranks from his parliamentary coalition of office-holders, placemen and Whig loyalists, he had the necessary information to make them think twice about such rashness.

Perhaps the most breathtaking evidence of Walpole's sense of invulnerability was the house he built for himself in Norfolk, the most incautiously palatial building made for a non-aristocrat since Cardinal Wolsey made the mistake of creating Hampton Court. Houghton Hall was the Whig Xanadu: the last word in opulence. Anything that riches could buy Walpole bought—marble in cartloads, figured damasks and watered silks, furniture designed by the painter and architect William Kent and made from exceptionally expensive mahogany, antique busts, extraordinary masterpieces of Renaissance and baroque art— Titian, Rubens, Poussin, Holbein, Murillo—all shipped to the East Anglian pleasure dome, some of them by strategically placed ambassadors and consuls in Rome or Madrid. Walpole's son, Horace, who was to become a compulsive connoisseur of painting and an acute critic, undoubtedly had his eye educated by his father's collection and grew up there, dressed in clothes made of French silk, attended on by his own retinue of footmen. But Houghton was not just an eye-popping demonstration of the good life that Walpole promised to the landed classes. It was also a statement of grandeur meant to stun the sceptics into acknowledging that only someone securely in command of the destinies (and money) of the nation could possibly afford something on that scale of conspicuous waste.

His entertainment was Lucullan. In one year alone, and to one of his six wine merchants alone, Walpole returned some 500 dozen empty bottles. To those who had sampled the Haut Brion and the Lafite at one of the 'Norfolk Congresses', as the parties were called, it went without saying that, if King George had the throne, it was Cock Robin who had the palace.

Walpole's critics, like Edward Harley, may have sneered at the vulgarity of Houghton, exhibiting 'very great expense without either judgement or taste'. But there is no doubt that its owner's shameless appeal to enlightened self-interest was infectious. With the glittering prizes dangled before their noses, the governing caste of the country—some 180 peers and 1500 country gentry—lined up to trade party passion for Palladian architecture. They stopped shouting and started building. And what they built were sanctuaries from social unsightliness. Just as Walpole's political management was designed to choke off the din of political belligerence, so the building style recommended to the Whig oligarchs was meant to insulate them from any contact with the grubby irregularity of the material world. The managed state would be complemented by the edited landscape, both in the interests of the most advertised virtue of Walpolean England: harmony. In the treatises of architectural virtuosi like Richard Boyle, third Earl of Burlington (who seems to have been a covert Jacobite), the agreement of parts was a matter of geometry, as it had been for the ancients. But the cohesion and grace of the Hanoverian country house was a contrivance: the appearance of harmony through the manipulation of reality; continuous spaces and sightlines achieved through acts of separation and obliteration.

Earlier generations of country houses had most often been fronted by a road connecting them with a neighbouring village and parish. Now, however, status was measured by the distance separating the rustics from the lord, so the grander the house, the

155

more deeply enclosed it was within its encircling park. At Houghton, a stone column marks the place where the local village once stood. Its proximity to Walpole's great house became an inconvenience, so he had it demolished and moved further away, beyond the gates. Once through those grandiose iron-grille barriers, bearing (as at Versailles or Blenheim) the coat of arms or monogram of the owner, the visitor would approach the house via a long avenue of elms or plane trees, which also served to demarcate a barrier between the managed property and the wild wood. The breadth of the avenue would be optically calculated to frame vistas of the great house, standing on its raised platform of grass like a throne upon a dais. Instead of rustics straying about the environs of the house, there would be choice domestic animals: a carefully selected herd of ornamental sheep or cattle. But this too was an illusion. It was, in fact, especially inappropriate to invoke the Palladian aesthetic since a prime principle of Andrea Palladio's revival of the Roman villa in the Veneto was to re-create the closeness between landowner and his working farm. At the Villa Barbaro in Maser, Italy, for example, farm buildings, with room for animals, are linked to the main house by an arcaded loggia. At Houghton and houses like it, any whiff of the barnyard was banished well beyond the precincts, and the old clutter of stables, kitchen gardens or duckpond removed from the close vicinity of the house. Although, from the windows of the house, terrace, gardens and manicured pasture on which the glossy beasts grazed would appear to be a single unbroken space, it was in fact cut in two by the intervention of the ha-ha, a deep but narrow trench effectively preventing the animals from wandering towards the house.

The inventor of the ha-ha was Walpole's landscape designer at Houghton, Charles Bridgeman, and the conceit was also pure Walpole in that it converted a military trench into an ornamental effect. Discreetly defended pleasure, the appearance of inclusiveness through the policing of exclusion might have been the watchword of the regime. The grazing animals— especially deer and their woodland habitat—were protected by the most ferocious anti-poaching laws enacted in England since the Angevins. In 1723 Walpole's parliament put no fewer than fifty capital offences on the statute book, most of them dealing with poaching, the cutting of trees (or even tree limbs) and the robbing of fishponds. In enacting the savage code of penalties, the government was responding to a sudden crime wave in Waltham Forest in Essex, committed by gangs with blackened faces. For those who have argued that Walpole was merely using a disingenuously concocted Jacobite scare to impose a judicial terror on the countryside on behalf of the landed oligarchy, the Waltham Blacks have been described as heroes of the poor: Hanoverian Robin Hoods liberating the rich man's venison, or men on the margin of subsistence just attempting to keep body and soul together. In this particular case, though, there seems little doubt that for once Walpole's low threshold of paranoia was perfectly justified since the most recent research makes it incontrovertibly clear that the Waltham Blacks were, in fact, part of a well-organized Jacobite underground.

Justified or not, however, when the Whig government made it possible for a man to be hanged for taking a sheep, it was completing the security arrangements deemed necessary to protect the investment that the oligarchs had made in their property. Walpole made good his promises to use the institutions of government to look after the interests of the landed classes. Land taxes were kept low, and enclosure acts got rid of the scattered strips that had supported families for centuries, replacing them with consolidated, rationally planned, profit-yielding farms. Smallholders who had kept the odd pig or goose and grown a few crops on their strips now had their land taken away for paltry compensation or sometimes none at all. Reduced to living entirely off wage labour, they could hang on in their village or trudge off to somewhere else in hopes of better prospects. The stewards who had seen them off remained quite dry-eyed. It was a shame, no doubt, but agriculture was no longer a matter of sentiment, much less a charity. Like virtually everything else in Hanoverian England, it was strictly business.

If landowners needed to treat their country property as a money-pump it was because, increasingly, they also needed to keep up appearances in town. And while it was possible to cut something of a figure in a provincial town, especially those like Bristol or Glasgow where money came pouring in from the colonial trade, anyone of real ambition had to be seen in London. Walpole may have liked to play the country magnate at Houghton, but his house in Chelsea was just as important as a headquarters for political strategy.

For London, arguably, was the one empire of men and money that escaped from Walpole's managerial control. No one political boss, not even someone of Walpole's inexhaustible, omniscient talents, could manage a city of some 700,000 souls—easily the biggest urban concentration in all of Europe. One in ten of the population of England lived there and one in six had spent some time working there, and every day the country wagons and carriages would disgorge yet more hundreds looking to cash in on the dazzling fortune they imagined the city to promise. As a headache for political management London was a special source of aggravation, since it acted as a magnet for some of the most creative and independent men of talent, and had generated a market for their ideas independent of anything the Crown could adequately control. As a centre of patronage the court had already begun to atrophy somewhat under the later Stuarts, and the much more parsimonious and philistine Hanoverians completed the process of shifting the centre of attraction from court to city. By the 1730s there were in London some 550 coffee-houses and scores of clubs, all with ardent, literate clienteles for whom irreverence, often of a brutally malicious tenor, was as much a necessary daily diet as mutton pies and ale. And the likes of Steele and Addison, Swift and Pope, whose *Dunciad* (1728) railed against the scandalous scoundrel time of the pax Walpoleana, were more than ready to supply them.

And London was also a great, and potentially subversive, dissolvent of rank. Foreigners, accustomed to more rigorously policed separation of the social orders, were horrified by the promiscuous jostle of the city as well as its gut-packing greediness and roistering, drunken violence, and especially by the indiscriminate mingling of classes in the pleasure gardens. Paris could not yet boast anything like Ranelagh or Vauxhall where, since all the men carried swords and all the ladies arrived in painted finery, many of both in masquerade, it was quite impossible to distinguish between the genteel and the common.

The same was true of the great pleasure hubs of the city. The only marker of esteem, the only necessity for gratification in a place like Covent Garden, was money (or at least credit). And there was so very much to buy. Every kind of prostitute for a start, from fake-virginal to fake French to 'singers and dancers'. If you were after something more specialized, then Harris' *New Atlantis* or *The Whoremongers' Guide to London* could help find cross-dressers, flagellants, gay 'molly-houses' or posture girls who would dance naked over a silver reflecting dish. And if all this parade of vice sickened, more innocent pastimes were also available—like the hunchback Robert Powell's puppet show in Covent Garden, or the coffee-house of the retired actor and murderer Charles Macklin who had stabbed a colleague in a fit of rage and who kept his own private theatre of oratory where he gave voice on issues of the day. As the morning dawned, Covent Garden would fill with other kinds of vendors: pie-men and sellers of dried and fresh fruit and vegetables, dolls and toys, hats and canes.

It became a commonplace of moralists to deplore the seductions of display, the knowing arrangement, designed to prick the appetite. But there was no stopping it with clucking against iniquity. Shops—and there were, it was estimated, 20,000 of them in London—were increasingly fitted with glass windows, bowed in front to expand the area of effective display. Streets were better lit, so that the rituals of inspection became part of the experience of what, for the first time, can be described without anachronism as shopping. The mistress and master of the household as well as their servants might now take themselves to ogle exotica newly arrived on the market, like oriental goldfish, blue macaws or warbling finches. Previously inaccessible luxuries were now manufactured and priced to find a market among the middling sort of people: Delft blue-and-white pottery somewhat resembling Ming china, from which to sip your tea or chocolate; glass stemware in the shape of bells or bugles for cordials and wines; pewter or silver tankards for ale. And if drink led to the indulgence of other vices you could arm yourself (as contemporaries put it) against sexual diseases with the first commercially produced condoms: lambskins in packets of eight tied with silk for the well-to-do, linen soaked in brine for the not so well-off.

The city as a great Bartholomew's Fair—a gorgeous, chaotic theatre of eye-popping spectacle and greedy consumption—helped the oligarchs as much as it threatened them, since from Walpole's view it all acted as a political opiate, or at least a distraction. Better that energy be driven by the gratification of the senses than committed to the revival of partisan and religious wars. But for precisely that same reason, the increasing number of Walpole's critics in the late 1720s and 1730s saw the gilded web inducing a vicious stupor: robbing the deluded of the innocence of their bodies, the soundness of their minds and the integrity of their souls. London, they said, took free men and women and made them slaves.

The works of William Hogarth and Henry Fielding are full of victims of the Mephistophelian city, arriving dewy-fresh from the country, falling for scoundrelly promises of easily gotten fortune and descending swiftly into a bottomless pit of iniquity, disease, madness and death. But the credit trap could make short work of even the most urbane and socially sophisticated, and the drop from fashion to incarceration (for a debt as small as £2) was a descent into hell. Robert Castell, whose beautiful folio on Roman villas, *The Villas of the Ancients: Illustrated* (1728), was on the shelves of every country gentleman who fancied himself a new Pliny or Horace, found himself in the Fleet in 1728 at the mercy of his gaoler, Thomas Bambridge. Unable to pay the costs of his imprisonment Castell was thrown into a local spongeing house full of smallpox victims, effectively a sentence of death that duly overtook the unfortunate author.

Prison was one of the most robust growth sectors of Britannia Inc. Accordingly, the going rate for a wardenship rose steadily in the Macheath years of Walpole's prime. The sum of £5000 was what John Huggins paid for the wardenship of the Fleet, and he scaled his tariff of residential charges to the inmates to ensure that he got a decent return on his investment. Just £5 would get you your very own cell, a few shillings more something approximating food and (a hot-ticket item for purveyor and customer alike) regular rounds of beer or prison-distilled gin. If these rates were beyond your reach, you took your chances in the packed common prisons, sleeping on the filthy straw with no air, light or sanitation.

And that was the *basic* service, before Huggins began a programme of cost-cutting to minimize his outgoings: ignoring clogged drains; shoving ever more bodies into ever smaller spaces; raising the fee prisoners were charged for their own shackles. As for the utterly destitute, they were using up valuable customer space, so Huggins did whatever it took to move them along to a Better Place. Sometimes they were inconsiderate enough to refuse to go. One morning a group of visitors to the prison chapel were surprised to see a completely naked, breathtakingly filthy man, covered only with a half-shredded mattress, burst in upon their meditations, feathers stuck to him with his own excrement, looking, one of them thought, like a demented chicken. As soon as the visitors had made a hasty exit, Huggins had the pathetic figure thrown right back into the freezing shed from which he had somehow escaped. He died soon afterwards.

Word of such horrors got out—especially when they involved gentlemen like Sir William Rich, put in a room full of unburied corpses for daring to strike the warden. A parliamentary committee was established to investigate the state of prisons and published a report documenting conditions of unimaginable degradation. Hogarth, whose own father had done time for debt, painted the committee—for some reason in their own chamber rather than in the prison offices where they actually conducted their interviews. In one crucial respect, though, Hogarth's vision is accurate. The manacled, trussed-up prisoner—actually a Portuguese Jew— has become a martyr, almost Michelangelesque in his torment, while the gaoler, shifty and sinister, is made to appear the real malefactor.

In the late 1720s, the cry of 'Who are the *real* criminals?' became common in the news-sheets and coffee-houses of London. Everywhere the line between the lawbreakers and the law-enforcers seemed arbitrary. In 1725 the Lord Chancellor, the Earl of Macclesfield, was himself convicted of embezzling £80,000 during the South Sea Bubble. Conversely, when he was executed at Tyburn the same year, the most famous of all England's criminals, Jonathan Wild, was recognized by observers like Lord Chesterfield as having the distinctive quality of a 'man of parts' who, had circumstances been different, might have been 'rather born for a ribbon round his shoulders than a rope about his neck'.

Wild's career had begun, like that of so many others, as a pimp running a 'buttock and file' racket, stealing from the clients of whores while they were busy in bed. But like the upwardly mobile apprentices of the legitimate trades, Wild aspired to a better kind of business and found his true vocation as a master-receiver. Presiding over an enormous emporium of stolen goods, Wild made himself indispensable to both the robbers and the robbed. The thieves needed him to fence their loot and keep quiet about where he had got it; the householders needed him as the only sure way to get it back, there being no police force to do it for them. It was a perfect entrepreneurial loop.

Making sure there was no evidence to connect him to the crimes, Wild made no secret that he was actually running the gangs of highwaymen, housebreakers and cutpurses whom he was purporting to nail. Occasionally, for the sake of keeping up appearances as the 'Thieftaker General', he would in fact give one up to the magistrates—a regrettable sacrifice for the sake of business credibility. And he was not above complaining that the sums offered for the retrieval of stolen goods hardly compensated for all the onerous expenses incurred in organizing highway robbery. There were the horses to stable, the feed, the lanterns.

Twelve days before Wild was hanged the shrewdest and most honest of all writers on the freebooting English economy, Bernard de Mandeville (who scandalized moralists by acknowledging the correlation between consumer extravagance and the general accumulation of wealth), saw this master-criminal's true significance as having transformed petty larceny into a genuine industry, complete with regulated hours and places of work, and strict books kept on turnover and profits. He expressed his amazement at the hypocrisy of magistrates who 'not only know and see this but . . . continue to make use of such a person for . . . evidence and in manner own that they are beholden to him in the administration of justice'. Wild's authentic impersonation of the entrepreneur was capped, posthumously, by having Daniel Defoe ghost his gallows confession—which, needless to say, became an immediate best-seller.

It was the genius of John Gay to take the coffee-house truism that the lawbreakers and the law-makers were interchangeable and turn it into the greatest hit of the eighteenth century: his 'Newgate Pastoral', *The Beggar's Opera* (1728). The audiences who roared abuse at Peachum the Thieftaker of course recognized him as Jonathan Wild, just as they cheered Macheath the highwayman as a stand-in for Jack Sheppard the housebreaker, who had gone to the gallows a year before Wild and had become a street hero for escaping from prison no fewer than four times. But although there was a minor figure in Gay's show called 'Bob Booty', it was just as obvious that Peachum, the extortionist and swaggering man of parts, the man who pretended to civic virtue while bleeding everyone white, was also a thinly veiled caricature of Walpole himself.

So when *The Beggar's Opera* took London and then the provinces by storm it took anti-Walpole satire out of the pages of opposition journals and into the taverns, coffee-houses and theatres. Perhaps it stung to be depicted as the Gangster-in-Office, but Walpole had a hide like an elephant and was certainly not about to fold his tent and depart at the behest of John Gay. He also comforted himself with the knowledge that much of the wave of opposition fury stemmed from their consternation that the new king, George II, whose hatred of his father had led them to believe he would inaugurate his reign by disposing of his prime minister, had instead succumbed to Walpole's inexplicable spell. But although the newly aggressive tide of criticism did not for the moment do much to disturb his stranglehold on power, it did bear witness to a rising tide of revulsion at the world of which Walpole complacently boasted: a

166

sense that beneath the platitudes about peace and stability lay brutality, corruption and misery. Dig beneath the dross, the moralists said, and you will find disease and death.

A walk through the seamier areas of London, through the rookeries and alleys, was a walk over bodies. The supply of very potent, very cheap gin had created an entire sub-culture of dependency and violence in the city comparable only to the crack-houses of the 1980s. Hogarth's famous graphic nightmare of a world in deathly auto-destruction was, of course, a polemical exaggeration. But not altogether, since we know of at least one mother, Judith Dufour, who became notorious for strangling her own baby daughter and selling every stitch of her own clothing to satisfy her craving for a dram. There came a point, though, when someone got tired of stepping over half-dead babies in the gutter or infant corpses thrown into the Fleet Ditch along with the 'blood, guts and dung' that, according to Pope, one expected to find there.

Thomas Coram had made his fortune in Massachusetts from the Atlantic timber trade. All that he wanted was to settle down to a quiet life in Rotherhithe where he could see the Thames and the tides. But the sight of the tiny abandoned corpses in the streets would not let him alone, and he also knew that the mortality rate for infants born in the poor house and sent out to wet nurse was close to a 100 per cent. Opulent London was a hecatomb for babies. So Coram determined to tap some of the city's fortune to establish a foundling hospital, a place where infants, legitimate or illegitimate, could be deposited, no questions

167

asked, and would be given a decent chance of survival. For almost twenty years he made himself a nuisance to his friends, lobbying the great and the good and going so far as to petition the king, until the necessary funds were raised.

He also had to beat back accusations that a place to deposit bastards would reward depravity with impunity and thus further encourage it. Working with Hogarth, Coram had a fund-raising letterhead shamelessly designed to milk every kind of sympathy. In the drawing on the letterhead, Coram himself appears as a saintly patriarch leading his happy and smiling charges towards a better future. The campaign worked. George II— seldom a pushover for hard-luck stories—melted, along with the queen, and after that the Quality lined up to donate.

The hospital opened its doors in 1741 to its first children. The governors trooped into their council room where they looked at art that had a bearing on their newly discovered mission—Francis Hayman's *The Finding of the Infant Moses in the Bullrushes* (1746), for instance. But the most arresting sight would have been the enormous, full-length portrait of old Captain Coram himself, set against the kind of classical column usually reserved for princes, aristocrats or military heroes. The portrait was as close as Hogarth ever got to a revolutionary act, for it audaciously transferred to this bluff old fellow the customary attributes of royalty; the royal charter, for example, with its seal lay in his hands. The world and its oceans—the orb made literal—was seen as the source of Coram's virtuous fortune. Even the hat by his right foot was significant, for it was meant to remind spectators of another of the tireless Coram's campaigns—to protect British hatters from foreign competition. Needless to say, he had requested that his only remuneration for that advocacy be one of their hats. In other words Coram, in Hogarth's grand depiction (as well as in reality), was everything Walpole and his cronies were not: selfless, philanthropic, modest in his appearance and imbued with civic religion. He was a free man. He was a patriot.

Virtue and good intentions, though, would not alone guarantee the realization of Coram's vision. The hospital was so overwhelmed with demand when it opened that it needed a lottery to decide admission. Anxious mothers lined up to draw coloured balls from a bag. Draw a white ball and your baby was in; draw a red ball for the waiting list; a black ball would send mother and baby back to the streets.

But acceptance brought with it its own kind of poignancy. Inside a cabinet, still kept at the Foundling Hospital, are preserved some of the saddest things left to us from the eighteenth century: the keepsake tokens given to babies by their mothers on the point of abandoning them to the hospital. Although some social historians assume that the appallingly high rates of infant mortality would have inured these mothers to loss, the whole history of response to the Foundling Hospital, not to mention the care and affection given to ensuring that some sort of memento would survive, says otherwise. Though all the objects record a kind of emotional desperation, not all of them speak of destitution. A mother-of-pearl heart with the initials of the infant engraved on it was

169

expensive enough to have been made for a mother from a relatively well-off family, doubtless being protected from disgrace. In many other cases, however, the extreme simplicity of the pieces does suggest hardship. Often they were nothing more than objects that the mothers happened to have in their possession at the moment of parting: a hazelnut drilled through for a string, to be worn as a pendant or amulet against misfortune; a thimble; a homely sewn heart; or just a flimsy piece of ribbon to be transferred from a mother's hair to a baby's wrist.

History can be a heartbreaker. For the reason we know about these objects, the reason we still have them, is that they never reached their intended recipients. Those responsible for the children's welfare, for better or worse, had decided it would not be in their best interests to give them a reminder of the shame of their origins. Yet, somehow, neither could they bring themselves to destroy them. Instead they went to that most eighteenth-century of limbos: a cabinet of curiosities.

The Foundling Hospital could not create an asylum of health and good cheer overnight. Close to 40 per cent of the first generation of infants died within its walls, although even that was an enormous improvement over the rate of the orphaned or abandoned. And the cause of Coram's Hospital had another kind of effect too: the creation of a new kind of culture, self-consciously apart from the country of aristocratic estates and county hunts—the middle-class parish at work, well-off but busily charitable, interested in virtue rather than fashion, redemption rather than wit. There had been public philanthropy before, of

170

course—organized by the trade guilds as well as Crown, nobility and the established Church. But this was the first time that men and women who belonged to the world of the commercial economy—tradesmen, merchants and bankers—came together with well-known writers, artists and sculptors in a campaign of conscience to attack a notorious social evil.

They were also committed, not just to correcting ills but to a constructive vocation too—and what they wanted to construct were patriots. If the children deposited in the Foundling Hospital survived they were to be turned into model Britons of the future: not the gin-soaked delinquents of the alleys or little criminals on their way to a date with Tyburn's tree, but hard-working, God-fearing, industrious and enterprising model citizens. 'Patriotism' was on the lips of the men and women who launched these little crusades of moral and civic reform in the commercial and port towns of Britain, and increasingly it meant not just a sense of native pride but a commitment to social and political virtue as well. Patriotism, in fact, described itself as everything the Walpole political machine was not: modest in display; disinterested in conviction; impervious to corruption; jealous in the defence of the 'liberties of free-born Britons'; hostile to arbitrary power. Though the anti-'Robinocracy' opposition was made up of very different political types—Tories and Jacobites, independent Whigs, lobbyists for colonial trade and the aggressive expansion of maritime power—they all felt that if there were indeed a new Great Britain, it was they, not Walpole and his creatures, who embodied it. They attacked his devotion to the excise as a way of keeping the land taxes low, and especially the powers given to the collectors who could search warehouses and shops, locking up alleged malefactors without showing due cause. In 1733, when Walpole attempted to expand the powers of search and seizure still further, he was met with a coalition of resistance, not least from meetings of merchants and tradesmen throughout the country who demanded that their MPs vote against the bill as a violation of Magna Carta. When Walpole was heard to refer to a group of them lobbying against the bill at the door of the House of Commons as 'sturdy beggars', the news, relayed quickly through the press, triggered a storm of public indignation: 'Would not every FREE BRITON think the promoter of it [the Excise Bill] An ENEMY to his country? Would he not justly incur the Censure of the Roman Senate and deserve to have that sentence denounced against him "Curse on the Man who owes his greatness to his COUNTRY'S RUIN."'

When the offending bill was withdrawn, the cities, towns and boroughs of England were jubilant. Effigies of Walpole were burned; parades and processions marched through the streets trumpeting the imminent end of the Great Corrupter and the Robinocrats. As it turned out, the celebrations were premature. But the writing was on the wall, not least because, over the years that followed, the opposition press succeeded in painting a picture of Walpole's government as more committed to its own selfish interest than to the interest of the country, especially when it came to standing up for the rights of merchants on the high seas. In 1737 a print called 'The British

Hercules' depicted a bare-footed jack-tar, modelled heroically in the manner of the Farnese Hercules in Rome, holding a paper inscribed 'I wait for orders' in front of a prostrate lion and an idle fleet at Spithead. Xenophobic propaganda drummed up the cause of captains whose ships had been boarded by Spanish coastguards. When one of Captain Jenkins' ears had been sliced off, it was claimed, by a Spanish cutlass, and introduced to the House of Commons by 'Patriot' opposition leaders, like William Beckford, as a victim of dastardly papist brutality on the high seas, prints were published showing captured British seamen starving in Spanish dungeons. More than forty addresses and petitions were sent to parliament from the port cities—Bristol and Liverpool—as well as London and Edinburgh. Walpole's way, as ever, was management: a negotiated 'Convention' with Spain, which, because it kept the right of Spanish coastguards to search for contraband, triggered another outpouring of bellicose indignation. A young MP, William Pitt, aired his precocious oratory by attacking the Convention as 'nothing but a stipulation for national ignominy ... the complaints of your despairing merchants, the voice of England, has condemned it'. The pressure for war, both inside and outside parliament, was becoming irresistible. It would happen with or without Walpole. The Spanish saved him by obtusely refusing to ratify the Convention, thus giving Walpole a belated *casus belli*.

In 1739, the new maritime patriotism got its first *bona fide* popular celebrity: Vice Admiral Edward Vernon. With just six ships Vernon had managed to capture the Spanish Caribbean depot of Porto Bello in the isthmus of Panama, the principal base for coastguards, in November 1739, and overnight he became the toast of the taverns, the clubs and the streets. Inns were renamed for him, and Porto Bello roads and streets sprang up not just in London but all over the country. Villages were renamed Porto Bello in Staffordshire, Sussex and Durham. In Fleet Street, a pageant featured a painted pasteboard showing Porto Bello, in front of which a kneeling Spaniard surrendered to a triumphant Vernon. Silver tankards, Staffordshire stoneware mugs, engraved glass goblets, snuff boxes and teapots bore Vernon's likeness, the icon of his little fleet and the universally echoed slogan 'six ships'. In the spring of 1741, the Vernon bandwagon took to the hustings at Westminster and five other constituencies in an organized campaign to throw out Walpole's placemen and elect the naval hero as a public thorn in his side. At Westminster, on the very doorstep of parliament, and where the public street campaign was especially rowdy, troops were used to close the polls early to avoid humiliation.

The Vernon clamour could embarrass the Walpolean regime, but it could not win the war. After Porto Bello came the anticlimax of a botched attack on Cuba. Armed with accusations that he had, once again, betrayed the true cause of the nation, Walpole's opponents combined in a concerted attack, and this time had the parliamentary numbers to make it count. Before he could be pushed, Walpole chose to walk in February 1742. With him went peace. In decade after decade following Walpole's fall Britain would be at war, and whatever the coalition of enemies the country faced, at the heart of them would be the arch-competitor on land and sea, France. Just as in the sixteenth century England's national identity had been beaten out on the anvil of fear and hatred of Catholic Rome and Habsburg Spain, so British identity was forged in the fires of fear and hatred against Catholic, absolutist France. In 1744 an invasion panic struck southern England. George II was off in Germany leading his troops (as he had insisted) beneath the standard of the Electorate of Hanover. Garrisons had been emptied to supply the war on the continent. Britannia had to fend for itself. Only the Channel separated Britain from the frightening spectre of Jesuit inquisitions, wooden shoes, slavish prostration before the Bourbon despot, the end of good ale and the beginning of barbarous food. The ever dependable Protestant wind came between the French fleet and a landing. But both government and people knew that this was only a respite and not a victory. It did not take a strategic genius to predict that, sooner or later, the government of Louis XV would play the Jacobite card, in either Ireland or Scotland, or both.

The failure of the rising of 1715 had set back the Jacobite cause, but it had done nothing to rob it of its burning sense of righteousness and of the inevitable triumph of Stuart legitimacy over the usurping Hanoverians and their lackeys in parliament. The Jacobites still had their court-in-exile in France and a network of agents and diplomats throughout Europe that promised a rising, not only in Scotland but in England too. A war fought against the British, not only in Europe but in America, the Caribbean and southern India, would, at the very least, put an enormous strain on

175

its military manpower, giving the Jacobites their best chance of success in many years.

All the same, when on 19 August 1745 Prince Charles Edward Louis John Cazymyr Sylvester Severino Maria Stuart, the son of the elderly James VIII and III and the grandson of James II, stood in his plaid at the head of the loch in Glenfinnan, watched his standard being raised and told the assembled clansmen that he had come to make Scotland happy, he was putting a brave, bold face on what was already proving to be an unlikely gamble. He had arrived at Glenfinnan from the Hebridean island of Eriskay with the 'seven men' of folklore, as well as a chaplain, valet, pilot and clerk. And he had nearly not made it at all. The two French vessels carrying the Prince and his party across the Irish Sea had run into a British warship, the *Lion,* 100 miles west of the Lizard. Although the Prince's ship, the *Doutelle,* lay safely out of range of British fire, the *Elizabeth* was badly damaged. In a long and murderous exchange of broadsides with the *Lion*, the two ships smashed each other to pieces so comprehensively that the *Elizabeth* had to heave to and offload some 1500 muskets and 1800 broadswords intended for the Jacobite campaign. So Charles Edward had little to give the 200-odd clansmen other than hope and the undoubtedly glamorous charisma of his personality. What turned the day from quixotic adventurism into something more serious was the arrival, later that afternoon, of another 800 men led by Cameron of Lochiel.

It says something about the complicated allegiances in what was, in effect, another round of a Scottish civil war that had been going on for nearly two centuries that Cameron of Lochiel was not the epitome of the stag-chasing backwoods primitive clan chief. If anything, he was like an increasing number of Highlanders, more obviously part of the new than the old Scotland: a hard-headed businessman who capitalized on harvesting timber from his estates. As someone with a foot in the new economy as well as his heart in the old cult of honour, Cameron had mixed feelings about the arrival of the Prince. Before he would entertain the idea of committing his followers he asked the Prince for an insurance policy—not the sign of reckless patriotism. Should the entire enterprise come to grief, could the Prince promise that he would be reimbursed for all the sacrifices that would undoubtedly be asked of him? By the end of the afternoon, though, romance had defeated prudence; the tug of loyalty had triumphed over business acumen. Cameron pledged himself and his men to the Prince, and the Rubicon was crossed.

A thousand men did not a Restoration make. For although Scotland was the entry-way, the prize for the Stuarts was always meant to be Britain. And for there to be any chance of success, three interlocking strategies had to click together at exactly the right time. It went without saying that most of Scotland needed to come out in open revolt. But as the unhappy precedent of 1715 had shown, that would be of no avail unless Jacobites in England rose in the numbers their spies had promised. And, not least, a French invasion force of not fewer than 10,000 men had to be landed somewhere to complete the pincer effect and disperse Hanoverian attempts at repression. To the pessimists who observed that such invasions had a long history of failure, the Stuarts might well have ground their teeth a little and invoked one wholly successful invasion: from the Netherlands in 1688!

For some weeks the government in Westminster was unsure whom or what to believe about the rumours that the Prince had landed and begun a march south through Scotland. It divided between complacency and panic. The complacent view was that Charles Edward would waste his minuscule force attempting to besiege the impregnable Highland forts William and Augustus, by which time his untrained Highlanders could be picked off by the regular soldiers of Lieutenant-General Sir John Cope. But there were some in the government who had a much gloomier diagnosis of what was in store, believing it to be inconceivable that a landing of any kind would have been made without the assurance of a prompt French or Spanish invasion to follow soon afterwards. 'The undertaking,' one of these pessimists wrote, 'in its present appearance seems (as it is the fashion to call it) rash and desperate. But I cannot think it is altogether to be despised. We are so naked of troops that if a body of men was to be flung over no-one can say what may be the consequences.' The gloomy truth, Henry Pelham wrote, was that in England there were hardly enough soldiers to stand guard at the royal palaces or put down a smugglers' riot, much less resist an invasion of any strength.

The collapse was much faster and much more shocking than anyone in London could possibly have imagined in their worst nightmares. Charles Edward had sensibly bypassed the fool's target at Fort William and moved directly to take towns like Perth, where he knew he had the edge in numbers over local defences. Nervous that all he could put in the field was 1500 troops against the (wrongly) reported Jacobite army of 5000, General Cope made a tactical retreat all the way north to Inverness, leaving the Scottish Lowlands virtually undefended. On 17 September the Prince took Edinburgh. Dazzling though the prize seemed to be, it was a long way from being a complete triumph. The Provost and his council had decided against resistance. But their prudent decision was not at all the same as enthusiastic endorsement of the Prince's cause. Should the military balance of power change, they could as easily revert to Hanoverian loyalism. There were, in fact, still two well-supplied regiments of dragoons holed up in Edinburgh Castle, defying all attempts to winkle or starve them out. Most of these soldiers were Scots, and their continued loyalism was not atypical of many of the Lowland population. Even in the Highlands only about half the clans rallied to the Prince, so that through most of the '45 there were probably more Scotsmen fighting against Bonnie Prince Charlie than for him.

Increasingly, business got in the way of sentimental allegiance. Running short of money to pay their troops, the Jacobite officers were informed that the necessary funds were locked up in the castle along with the dragoons. None the less, they thought it worthwhile inquiring whether —at reasonable rates of interest—some of the cash might be made available to stop their men taking their desperation out on the city. It must have seemed like a reasonable proposition, since it met with a favourable response. Money was delivered from the castle to the Jacobites so that the two camps could carry on pretending to fire at each other.

Freshly supplied and financed, morale high and bellies full, on 21 September 1745, the Jacobite army marched out to meet General Cope's troops at Prestonpans, 8 miles east of Edinburgh, each army some 2500 strong. What ensued was one of the most notorious fiascos in British military history. Cope had managed to station his soldiers between the river and a bog, but, informed by a deserter about the Hanoverian positions, the Jacobites used a track through the mire to march to their rear and caught them literally napping before dawn. In the rout 300 British soldiers were quickly killed. The only professional loyalist army in Scotland had been destroyed. Needless to say, in London the disaster was blamed not on the incompetence of the officers but on the cowardice of the rank and file.

The almost unexpected completeness of their success forced the Jacobite army to consider what it was they were truly supposed to be: the liberators of Scotland or the restorers of the Stuart dynasty to all of Britain? The issue was thrashed out on 30 October at Holyroodhouse, where the Prince had taken up residence in the palace of his royal ancestors. Charles Edward argued that, even tactically, the right decision was to take the campaign into England. He and his followers had enjoyed extraordinary success only because of the temporary absence of concentrations of Hanoverian troops in continental Europe, but the day could not be far off when numbers of those soldiers would return. A far more formidable threat would face them than the soldiers they had

180

surprised at Prestonpans. The question was: where would be the best place to confront it? The Prince insisted that the other two pieces of Jacobite strategy all pointed to the necessity of a march through England. Without a campaign there, catching the enemy while he was still weak, the English uprising was unlikely to be at all successful—and without that rising the French invasion might not happen at all. It was imperative to be able to demonstrate to Versailles that this was not to be a repetition of 1715, that they were in earnest.

Lord George Murray, the ablest of the Jacobite generals, was much more cautious; still nervous about their position in Scotland, much less in Britain overall, wanting to consolidate a position in the Highlands where the war could be fought on their own terms, systematically breaking down the pro-Hanoverian clans, making the Stuarts the impregnable masters of the north and daring the English to come after them and risk more defeats like Prestonpans.

The differences aired at the council of war at Holyroodhouse were not just about military strategy. They went to the heart of why everyone in the Jacobite war was risking their neck. Was it, as Murray and the Highland soldiers believed, for Scotland, to restore the old world before the union and to recover a free and independent Scotland? Or was it, as the Prince imagined, a crusade to undo 1688: to throw the Hanoverians off the throne of Britain, to restore not just James VIII but James III?

After intense debate, the Prince won the argument—at least about strategy—by a single vote. The Jacobites marched south, moving at such a brisk pace that General Wade, based at Newcastle, who had expected to bar their way, instead found himself constantly outpaced. In rapid succession Carlisle, Lancaster, Preston and Manchester all fell to the Prince's army, virtually without a shot being fired in their defence. Each time Wade's troops attempted an interception by crossing the Pennines terrible weather held them up, and by the time they reached their destination on the western side of the mountains the Jacobites had moved on. It was the British, not the Jacobite, soldiers who were suffering the worst privations. On 19 November James Cholmondeley, the colonel of the 34th Foot, wrote to his brother, the earl, about one of the worst of those marches across the Dales. They had, he said, endured 'miserable roads, terrible frost and snow. We did not get to our grounds till eight and as my quarters were five miles off I did not get there till eleven, almost starved to death with cold and hunger but revived by a pipe and little good wine. Next morning we found some poor fellows frozen to death for they could get nothing to eat after marching thirteen miles.'

By the beginning of December the Jacobites were closing in on Derby. The predicted mass uprisings in the English cities had not yet materialized, but nor could it be said that northern populations in the path of the march had risen as a man to defend the house of Hanover. Instead there were reports of merchants, landowners and bankers in Northumberland, Yorkshire and Lancashire taking to the highways along with their movable wealth and families. As the sense of an unstoppable momentum became more ominous, London caught a violent attack of the jitters. There was the usual run on the Bank of England, and the usual atrocity stories to feed the hysteria, featuring children tied to the walls of Carlisle Castle so that, if royal troops attempted to take it, they would be obliged first to massacre the lambs. But there were also the first stirrings of some patriotic resistance and Scottophobia. 'God Save the King', which in an earlier form had actually been a Stuart song, was now sung for the first time as a national anthem in the theatres of Covent Garden and Drury Lane. Volunteer associations in some sixty counties had produced men willing to serve in the militia.

On 10 December, three regiments of infantry and one of horse guards were ordered out to a camp at Finchley, which the commander of the army, George II's son, the Duke of Cumberland, had established 'just in case', he said, the Jacobites whom he meant to engage at Northampton should give him the slip, as they had done so many times to Wade. Four years later Hogarth painted the scene along the Tottenham Court Road, and although he had the luxury of hindsight, his teeming, riotous picture—a huge and profitable success when it sold as a print from 1751—does say something about England at its chaotic moment of truth. No wonder, when George II saw the painting, he erupted in fury: 'What, does the fellow mean to make fun of my guards?' For the soldiers in the picture (and everyone else for that matter) are not exactly paragons of martial discipline. This England is less parade ground than fairground (Hogarth's preferred metaphor over and over again for its sprawling, unruly energy). Bare-knuckled prize-fighters go at it under the sign of the Garden of Eden like Cain and Abel. On the right hand the realm of vice assembles by the King's Head, featuring the likeness of Charles II and one of the late monarch's favourite pastimes, the whorehouse. A falling soldier spurns his Good Samaritan's water for what he really wants: a tipple of gin; a groper makes the milkmaid spill her milk while a crazed hag, probably meant to be Irish, with a cross on her cape, brandishes a Jacobite broadside. Opposite them are the *relatively* virtuous. The trees are in leaf. The courtyard in which the pugilists battle is the Nursery of 'Giles Gardiner'; a mother suckles her baby. And the forlorn mother-to-be clinging to the departing soldier's arm carries 'God Save the King' and a portrait of the Duke of Cumberland in her basket.

As a portrait of group energy this is distinctly a back-handed kind of flattery. Somehow, Hogarth asks us to believe that this disorderly rabble will compose itself into the disciplined troop seen in the background marching off towards Highgate Hill. But this is the miracle of England, patriot-style, strength from liberty. To spite the king, when he heard about his well-publicized objections Hogarth dedicated the engraved version to Frederick the Great, the King of Prussia, 'Encourager of Arts and Sciences' (in invidious contrast to the philistine Hanoverians). But perhaps there was a shade of irony there too, for his vision of bloody, bruising, riotous England was precisely the opposite of machine-tooled Prussia, the barrack-house kingdom.

Whether Hogarth's scratch army could pass the test of combat, few (other than Cumberland) were at all sure. Until Culloden in April 1746, the Hanoverian armies did not defeat the Jacobites in anything like a serious battle. At Falkirk, in January 1746, where 8000 soldiers had been committed on each side, much the biggest engagement of the war, the Jacobites had won the day but failed to press home their temporary advantage, wasting time, men and money until all three ran out in a futile siege of Stirling Castle at the end of the month. In the end, as in 1715, the Jacobites defeated themselves, and less on the battlefield than in the council room. At Exeter House in Derby, on 5 December 1745, five days before the march out to the Finchley camp, another critical debate had taken place on the future strategy of the campaign. Much the same arguments that had divided the Prince from Lord George Murray continued to exercise them. London is just 130 miles (200 km) off, said Charles Edward; a handful of militiamen and Finchley stands between us and a glorious Restoration. Move on the capital and the French will undoubtedly come. Our friends in England will declare themselves, and 1688 will seem a bad memory.

Murray was not to be moved. For months the Prince had been promising the imminent appearance of the French and they were still nowhere to be seen. The 3000 English Jacobites who were supposed to be rallying to the cause had proved equally elusive. All he could see was a pyrrhic victory: the Jacobite army trapped in London, its rear cut off by Cumberland, the reinforcements arriving daily from the Continent. It was time, he insisted, to cut their losses, to make a stand in the heartland of their cause: in Scotland.

185

The very force of his argument betrayed a fundamental insecurity about the viability of the whole enterprise. For in the last resort, successful as he had been, Murray was uncertain whether armed Jacobitism could survive anywhere other than Scotland, north of the Firth of Forth; or at least he wanted to pitch his tents as close as possible to a safe refuge should the balance of military power turn ugly. Perhaps folk memories of his ancestor Andrew Murray and of Robert the Bruce may yet have played over in his mind? Whether the cult of honour could survive in the new Britain of cash contracts and the drilled bayonet was increasingly moot. At any rate, this time he had the better of the debate. The Jacobite army, with the Prince sulking on his horse, turned about and retreated north. Needless to say, they had barely begun their long tramp home when Louis XV and his ministers were finally impressed enough by the progress of the Jacobites into England to send the long-awaited invasion fleet!

It was much too late. Battered by heavy winds and by the hero of Porto Bello, Admiral Vernon, the French probably would have been of little help. As it was, the Jacobite march north turned into a prolonged nightmare. Slowed by snowstorms and harried by Cumberland's pursuing army, now much reinforced, the retreat became ever more ragged and desperate. Garrisons manned by their troops on the advance into England were now left to treat with Cumberland as best they could. At Carlisle the Duke refused to accept the surrender of the Scots garrison in the castle, freeing him from treating the prisoners according to the conventions governing prisoners of war. This was a rebellion, not a war between gentlemen. Any Englishmen believed to have cooperated with the Jacobites were summarily hanged, and hundreds of their soldiers were crammed into a tiny, suffocating space, without air, light or water. Subjected to inhuman suffering, they were reduced to licking the slimy cavities of the interior rock wall for drops of moisture.

By the time that winter turned to spring in the Highlands it was clear to the Jacobites that whatever its temporary successes—as at Falkirk—their campaign was lost. With every week that passed, the Hanoverian advantage in men and guns told. By the time the two armies faced each other at Culloden, some 6 miles east of Inverness, on 16 April, Cumberland's force, about 9000 strong, was almost twice the size of the Prince's army of some 5000. And, more important, it was armed with heavy cannon and the new, lethal combination of stabbing and firing machines—the bayonet. On a sodden piece of land his generals had begged the Prince not to make his battlefield, the Highlanders charged uphill, a northeaster blowing hard in their faces, and straight into the Hanoverian guns that tore holes through their ranks. The charge that had been so terrible at Killiecrankie turned into a stumble of survivors, carried along by their own fatal momentum and some desperate instinct of clan solidarity. An hour after the firing had started there were between 1000 and 1500 Jacobite Highlanders dead on the field and 700 more taken prisoner.

All things considered, it was better to be one of the dead and be spared the sight of the Hanoverian soldiers coming at the wounded to break their bones and further mutilate their bodies before finishing them off. As many as 1000 of the helplessly wounded may have perished in this gruesome manner. The cold-blooded slaughter of the wounded and the methodical hunt for those in flight was justified in England by orders, purportedly given by the Prince before Culloden, to give no quarter. But those orders were a pure invention of Hanoverian propaganda. In fact the march through England had been fastidiously careful to avoid alienating local populations and captured troops, who it was hoped, might yet be recruited to the cause of King James III. But Cumberland relied on the paranoid caricatures of the Highlanders as half-evolved primitives, the better to justify his own pitiless repression. And the bloodier he got, the better England liked it. Handel wrote *See the Conquering Hero Comes*, first performed in 1746, to celebrate his triumph. Medals and gifts poured in to express the gratitude of the boroughs and towns. In Newcastle, the Trinity House society of mariners and merchants presented him with an ornate gold box in appreciation for delivering them from the Scottish plague.

After Culloden it might still have been possible —as some of their leaders had always thought—for Jacobite resistance to continue in the fastness of the Highlands and islands, until they could at least extract some sort of amnesty out of the government. Only three-fifths of the Prince's army, after all, had been present at Culloden. But Charles Edward Stuart broke his cause with the same kind of carelessness with which he had made it, summarily declaring it irretrievably lost and ordering an every-man-for-themselves, going on the run himself until he could ship back to France.

Behind him he left a population prostrated before a systematic exercise in state terror inflicted by one part of Britain against the other. Some of it was accomplished by physical force—whole villages burned to the ground without much close inquiry as to the sympathies of the local population. Cattle were stolen; thousands of crofters were turned off their land. What violence began, legal coercion completed. Hereditary jurisdictions were abolished, thus destroying at a blow the patriarchal authority of the clan chiefs and the entire chain of loyalty that depended on them. Speaking Gaelic was forbidden, as was wearing the plaid *unless* serving with the royal army (in which case, in a stroke of psychological cunning, it was positively encouraged). Everything about the ancient Highland culture of tribal honour was uprooted and the broken remnants flattened into submission.

In London the trial and execution of Jacobite lords became public entertainment, just another of the shows for the diversion-hungry city. The drama, after all, beat anything to be seen at Drury Lane. King George reprieved George Mackenzie, third Earl of Cromarty, when his wife went sobbing before the king, falling to her knees and then fainting away in a pathetic swoon of grief and terror. Even a sovereign notorious for his indifference to the stage was shaken by the performance. William Boyd, fourth Earl of Kilmarnock, and Arthur Elfinstone, sixth Baron Balmerino, on the other hand, exited with heroic obstinacy, proclaiming their devotion to the divinely anointed Stuarts. The most colourful of the lot, Simon Fraser, twelfth Baron Lovat, had been found hiding in a hollowed-out tree-trunk in

189

western Scotland. He had been a wicked opportunist, swinging between the two allegiances, remaining faithful to the king in 1745 but sending his son off to fight with the Prince. Now that the Jacobites had lost he blamed his predicament on the boy. Hogarth went to see Lovat and made an unforgettable print of the cackling old monster counting the clans on his fingers. En route to his trial, according to Horace Walpole, a woman stared into his coach and shouted, 'You ugly old dog, don't you think you will have that frightful head cut off?' To which Lovat replied without missing a beat, 'You damned ugly old bitch, I believe I shall.' He was right. So many people packed the site of his execution at Tower Hill, on 9 April 1747, that a specially built viewing stand collapsed (in yet another Hogarthian scene of downfall), killing seven, rather more than Lovat had ever dispatched in his life.

The London Scots looked on these terrible spectacles of retribution and humiliation (as well as what they heard of the miseries in the north) with a mixture of horror, pathos and rage. Tobias Smollett heard news of Culloden while drinking in a tavern and was so mortified by the raucous celebrations it set off among the English drinkers that, though no Jacobite, he felt impelled to write a dirge for the catastrophe that had overwhelmed his country, 'The Tears of Scotland'.

Mourn, hapless Caledonia, mourn
Thy banished peace, thy laurel torn
Thy sons, for valour long renowned
Lie slaughtered on their native ground;
Thy hospitable roofs no more

Invite the stranger to the door;
In smoky ruins sunk they lie
The monuments of cruelty

With this wave of sorrow and self-pity washing over him Smollett must have asked himself, like so many of his compatriots in the aftermath of the '45, how it was possible, now, to be British. Some of them— a shrinking minority—would have answered flatly that it was not; that now they lived in a colony beneath the heel of the conqueror, with language, dress and customs outlawed. Henceforth, unrepentant Jacobites, the survivors of the cult of honour, had to live an occult life of relics and fetishes that could be hidden away and taken out for moments of furtive veneration: locks of Bonnie Prince Charlie's hair; torn fragments of his plaid; goblets painted with an indecipherable smudge of paint that only the initiated, equipped with the right reflecting base, could see the colours resolve themselves into an icon of the lost loved one, the boy born to be king, the saviour across the water. The memorabilia remained hallowed while the real Charlie went horribly profane in Rome. Too many mistresses, far too much drink, years of tedious, sentimental prattle over the port about what-might-have-been made him bloated, prematurely decrepit and squalid, living off the charity of the gullible. Staring at the cracked masonry of the Forum he became himself a ruin, draped in the mossy weeds of his own bathos.

But except as romantic entertainment the Prince had become irrelevant to the real future of Scotland, which in the decades after Culloden did not surrender to sentimental grief but turned itself instead into the most dynamically modernizing society in Europe. In 1749, four years after the battle, Dr John Roebuck and Samuel Garbett accomplished a different kind of victory at Prestonpans, opening their plant making sulphuric acid. Even before the '45, the old Highland way of life was being altered by the capitalization of land, the change from customary communities to productive investments. Villagers were cleared off smallholdings they had occupied and farmed for centuries to make way for blackface and Cheviot sheep or Highland cattle, both supplying the burgeoning markets of the Lowland and English towns. And the aggressive engineers of the clearances, both Highland and Lowland, like the Camerons of Lochiel, could just as easily be Jacobite as loyalist. What was left of the old way when clan chiefs violated what had been the first obligation to their tenants: guaranteeing them the security of their tenure?

At least there was somewhere for the displaced to go. The clansmen who had been unable to break Britannia were now given the option of joining it, and many took it. In the second half of the eighteenth century tens of thousands of Highlanders were recruited into the British army and saw action in its many theatres of war around the world from India to Canada. Some 70,000 were said to have served in British regiments during the revolutionary and Napoleonic wars. And the annals of imperial government, as well as the barracks and the battlefield, are dominated to an extraordinary degree by famous Scottish names: Munros and Elfinstones, Murrays, Gordons and Grants. Even when some of the most obstinate Jacobites—like

Flora MacDonald and her husband, who had famously helped the Prince make his escape— emigrated to America, they declared themselves (in North Carolina) as resolutely patriotic British loyalists during the revolutionary wars.

Instead of being colonized by the British Empire, then, the Scots colonized it themselves. Nearly half of those leaving fortunes worth more than £1000 in Jamaica in the second half of the eighteenth century were Scots. Glasgow grew rich off the transatlantic tobacco trade, and the great merchant capitalists like John Glassford and Alexander Speirs became some of the most economically powerful men in Britain. Speirs is a perfect example of the new kind of 'North Briton' whom Defoe had in mind when he attempted to imagine a happier and more prosperous Scotland within the union. Speirs had been a merchant of modest means until he married into one of the older tobacco families, the Buchanans. After that there was no stopping him, and Speirs, Bowman and Co. became one of the meteors of the transatlantic trade, sending their own Clydeside-built ships (using a dry dock constructed in 1762) on sixteen voyages to Virginia and the Carolinas between 1757 and 1765. In America, Scottish agents had established company warehouses that dealt directly with the growers, cutting out middlemen. Cheaper costs of handling and shipping the crop and a booming market throughout Britain meant a doubled turnover between the middle and the end of the century, and higher profits. Those profits (interrupted for a while by the depression of the early 1770s and the War of American Independence) in turn capitalized other sectors of the economy in which Speirs and his fellow Glaswegian tobacco lairds made investments: glassmaking, sugar refining, linen weaving.

It was the vindication of Darien, and it was an improvement on Darien. Separate from England, the Scots who imagined a new kind of future for their country had been helpless to withstand the kind of political and military muscle that the English could bring to their economic intimidation. As an integral part of a united kingdom, they had been pulled into an increasingly indivisible economy that had transformed the entire country. The roads and bridges that had been built by General Wade and his teams of surveyors and engineers (including the artist Paul Sandby, who made a superlative record of the landscape), primarily for strategic purposes, now provided incomparably improved routes for the shippers of goods and the drovers of cattle and sheep. Highland products like kelp, slate, wool, whisky and even smoked fish (for there were hundreds of herring boats plying the waters of Loch Fyne alone) now found their way south to an English market. And the movement of men, merchandise and technology was genuinely two-way. James Watt, the Scot who provided a steam pump for the Greenock dry dock, teamed up with an Englishman, Matthew Boulton, to found Boulton & Watt, the Soho Engineering works near Birmingham; Coalbrookdale in the English Midlands sent its smelting technology north for the foundation of the Carron ironworks in Stirlingshire.

In the circumstances it cannot possibly be fortuitous that it was in Scotland, in the 'hotbeds of genius' that flowered in Edinburgh, Glasgow and Aberdeen, that the first theory of progress was systematically articulated. It was built, in the first place, on the denial of, or at the very least the sceptical indifference to, knowledge allegedly based on revelation, such as miracles. The kinds of miracles that the Scots were interested in were happening on Clydeside. Scotland, which had for so long been torn apart by confessional wars, was being healed by the cult of reason that flowered in the academies and reading clubs of these three cities. The culture that had been captive to nostalgia was rapidly turning into the empire of hard facts, the temple of the gospel of modernity. Both could be found housed in the extraordinary three-volume *Encyclopedia Britannica*, first printed and published in Edinburgh in 1768–71. Originally conceived by the Scottish printers Andrew Bull and Colin Macfarquar, it was edited chiefly by another Scot, the printer and antiquary William Smellie. The first revised and enlarged, ten-volume edition, 1776–84, was the brain-child of James Tytler, poet, printer, surgeon, chemist and hot-air balloonist, the very prototype of the new Scot. Just as English tourists were beginning to come north and ruminate soulfully on the Scottish tragedy on windswept moors and misty-shrouded lochs, Scottish writers and philosophers were brushing away the cobwebs of sentiment. First see with absolute clarity, argued David Hume, how it is we can know things for sure; and once sure of the solidity of our knowledge, make it work to make a society in which happiness might prosper. Happiness was what Bonnie Prince Charlie had promised his followers at Glenfinnan. But the chances of its realization, thought Hume and his fellow philosophers, depended exactly on the degree to which Britons liberated themselves from the old siren songs.

'This is the historical age and we are the historical people,' Hume announced. But for once he did not mean that Scotland, or for that matter the Britain for which he was an unapologetic champion, was history's fall-guy, doomed to the kind of repetitive cycles inscribed in the chronicles of antiquity. On the contrary, Hume, Adam Ferguson and Adam Smith looked at the epic of their own country and saw in one place the entire arc of human social development from hunting-gathering societies to nomadic herders, settled farmers and finally to true civilization: the beckoning world of commerce, science and industry, the world of the town. By the end of the century, no country in the world was urbanizing or industrializing more swiftly than Scotland.

The true Scotland was now to be discovered in the handsome squares and streets of the new Edinburgh and Glasgow. In 1767 James Craig, the nephew of the arch drum-beater for a united Britain and the lyricist of 'Rule Britannia', James Thomson, laid out the design for the New Town of Edinburgh. He inscribed on the plans some characteristic lines from his uncle's verse, comparing the edifices of the new Britain to a new Rome—in fact an improved Rome. Unlike Charles Edward Stuart, who was trapped in one kind of Roman reverie, the new Scots would return from the Grand Tour perhaps bringing with them plaster casts or antique medals supplied by the entrepreneur Gavin Hamilton, full of plans to make classicism commercial. And none brought off this apparently oxymoronic feat more triumphantly than 'Roman Bob', Robert Adam.

Thirteen years after Bonnie Prince Charlie brought the Jacobite army to its endgame at Derby, Robert Adam, the son of a successful Edinburgh architect, William Adam, came back to Derbyshire as a very different kind of invader, Britain's first invincible king of style. And in that capacity he took the country by storm. At Kedleston Adam was not shy about showing off his learning. The south front of the house is modelled on the Arch of Constantine and the domed salon on the Pantheon. But Kedleston was emphatically not a museum disguised as a country house. It was a brand-new style for a new kind of aristocrat. Its owner, Nathaniel Curzon, first Baron Scarsdale, had made his money and political power not just from land and political connections, the Walpolean way, but from the Derbyshire coal mines as well. And what he evidently wanted was a house in which wealth would not overpower the visitor with swaggering ostentation, but speak instead of noble, Ciceronian austerity, a temple of virtue and contemplation, cool, pure and benevolent.

Adam's triumph at Kedleston made him the most sought-after architect of his generation, an authentically British designer with offices in both London and Edinburgh, building in both countries. And part of the secret of his success was his ability to translate into building style the principle, articulated by Adam Smith, that what his generation called 'opulence' was not merely (as had been displayed at Houghton) a phenomenon of purely private accumulation; it was also a force for general happiness.

In 1746, while the last unfortunate survivors of Cumberland's terror were being tracked down, Adam Smith, the son of a customs officer on the north bank of the Firth of Forth, returned to his native country. He had turned his back on Oxford where, he wrote, the university had given up 'even the faintest pretence of learning'. But he also turned his back on the Scottish past for an exhilarating vision of what might be to come. The vision was based on Smith's rejection of guilt and sin, both the Catholic and Calvinist varieties. Instead, in *The Wealth of Nations*, written from 1766 to 1776, he laid out as a matter of historical fact man's instinctive and wholly natural drive towards self-betterment. That such an instinct was driven by motives of vanity and acquisitiveness was neither here nor there. Allowed to follow their natural urges, men would create, without even consciously willing it, a better world: a richer, more educated and freer society. And here Smith also turned away from the immense apparatus of Hanoverian state power. In the new world he was imagining it was no longer the enemy. It was simply an irrelevance. For no government was needed to legislate wealth; indeed, any that imagined it could was simply the victim of self-delusion. The best government was that which got out of the way and permitted the invisible hand of the market to do its work. The economic world, he wrote, was like a watch, the springs and wheels 'all admirably adjusted to the ends for which it was made'; so too the countless movements of industrious men would perfectly interconnect for the purposes for which God had made them.

That purpose was progress, material, moral and intellectual. And it was one of history's sweetest ironies that it fell to Scotland, bloodied, mutilated Scotland, to show Britannia the way ahead. If you want to see the future, the Scottish philosophers said, forget the vainglorious monuments of England's past, the dusty tombs and forbidding cathedrals. Come north, instead, to the new 'hotbeds of genius', to Glasgow and Edinburgh, and see what lies in store for Britain, perhaps for the world.

CHAPTER SIX

THE WRONG EMPIRE

The Scene: Represents a plain surrounded by woods. On one side a cottage, on the other flocks and herds—distant prospect. A hermit's cave in full view overhung with wild trees; wild and grotesque.

Enter: ALFRED with the Earl of Devon.

How long, O, ever gracious heavens, how long
Shall war thus desolate this prostrate land?

As our Anglo-Saxon hero, on the run from the Danes and flagging badly in energy and morale, was revealed by the candle-lights (in the usual tragick-antique costume of cuirass above, skirts below) bewailing his country's fate, the audience, we must assume, was putting on its own show of rapt attention. Anything less would have been not just impolite but imprudent too. For *Alfred. A Masque*, written in tandem by the Scottish poets James Thomson and David Mallett (*né* Malloch, but anglicized to improve his chances among the Sassenachs), with music by Thomas Arne, had been commissioned by the grandest of patrons, the hope of Free Britons: Frederick Louis, Prince of Wales. The performance at the prince's house, Cliveden in Buckinghamshire, was ostensibly private. But in every way that really mattered it was an occasion designed to advertise publicly, especially in the gossip-greedy press, the credentials of the prince and his supporters as True Patriots. The day, 1 August 1740, had been carefully chosen. It was the anniversary of the accession of his grandfather, George I, whom Frederick affected to respect in proportion to his public loathing for his own parents. It was also the day after the third birthday of his daughter, Princess Augusta, whose arrival had been made memorable by Frederick snatching away his wife, on the very point of delivery, from the king and queen and insisting she give birth instead in his house at St James's Palace. If Queen Caroline's verdict on her son, 'the greatest ass . . . the greatest liar . . . and the greatest beast in the world' might seem a little strong, especially when she made it no secret that to have him disappear from the world would not occasion waterfalls of grief, it was none the less understandable. But Frederick thought he had time on his side. His father, George II, was fifty-six; his unlamented mother had already departed three years before. He, on the other hand, was thirty-three and coming into his own.

Frederick would disappoint his followers by dying of a brain abscess in 1751. But on this summer night at Cliveden, with the Thames flowing sweetly by, it was possible to overlook his gambling and his women and his temper and see him instead as the cello-playing virtuous virtuoso, the epitome of the patriot prince, the guardian of liberty. Around him were gathered his political enthusiasts, erstwhile Walpole allies, but many of them had been turned out of office in 1737 when the tug-of-war over the prince's revenues was at its fiercest. Now they were bitter enemies of the government. In all likelihood there would have been George Bubb Dodington, the most recent reconversion to the prince's interest, swathed in brocaded silk beneath which his considerable bulk struggled, as Horace Walpole noted, to break free of its moorings. There too would have been Sir Richard Temple, Viscount Cobham (whom Walpole had not merely peremptorily dismissed but, unforgivably as far as Cobham was concerned, stripped of his command of the King's Own Horse regiment), with some of his own protégés, the 'Cobham cubs', his nephews the Grenville brothers, and William Pitt. There might also have been dissident Whigs like John Carteret. It is tempting, too, to include in the audience a particular ex-Tory politician for whom an Anglo-Saxon allegory would have had special significance: Henry St John, Viscount Bolingbroke.

Though Bolingbroke's disastrous flirtation with Jacobitism in 1714 was enough to bar him from the House of Lords, he was still an immensely influential figure. In 1738 he had published his *Patriot King* expressly as vocational guidance for the Prince of Wales. For Frederick, Bolingbroke had designed an improbably disinterested identity that would transcend selfish factionalism. As king, Frederick would ascend the throne sworn to purge the country of venality and oppression. But since Bolingbroke had also produced a history of medieval Britain purporting to see, from the very beginning, the forces of liberty and despotism locked in combat, Frederick's role would be to *restore* the ancient Anglo-Saxon spirit of freedom, which had its crowning glory in the reign of Alfred. It was Alfred, it was said (wrongly), who had originated trial by jury and who was habitually referred to as the 'Guardian of Liberty'. The prince's own ambition to be considered the Hanoverian Alfred had already been signalled in 1735 when he had commissioned a statue of the Anglo-Saxon hero king from the fashionable sculptor John Michael Rysbrack for the garden of his town house on Pall Mall.

Mallett and Thomson, the anti-Jacobite Scots, were nothing if not obliging, and what they produced for the prince and his circle that evening in 1740 was, in effect, Bolingbroke set to verse and music. Given the importance of the occasion, there could be no stinting on the performers. From Drury Lane, William Milward played Alfred while the great Kitty Clive took the part of the sympathetic shepherdess Emma. The musical attraction was the famous Covent Garden tenor Thomas Salway, who doubled as both the shepherd Corin and a bard whose solo rendition of a new song by Arne at the end of the masque was to be critical to the success of the entire evening. Before that cheering finale, though, the up-against-it king was roused to a fresh resolve to do battle with the alien forces of oppression by the spirits of three of his most glorious descendants, conjured up from the future by the clairvoyant hermit. The three royal phantoms—the Black Prince, Elizabeth I and William III—offer Alfred an inspirational glimpse of the imperial destiny awaiting his sea-girt realm (and unburden themselves of long, pull-yourself-together-for-Britannia homilies). But for the war-fevered audience of 1740 the last two would have had particular resonance, cast as they were as royal warriors for an expressly Protestant, anti-Spanish, Gallophobic nation. At that very moment the heir to the naval tradition, the universally acclaimed 'Free Briton', Vice-Admiral Edward Vernon, was busy fitting out a new fleet intended to attack the eastern end of Cuba.

His martial ardour duly rekindled, Alfred swears to rid the country of the foreign brutes: the cue for Salway to step out and celebrate the moment of patriotic reconsecration:

> The Muses, still with freedom found
> Shall to thy happy coast repair
> Blest isle! With matchless beauty crownd
> And manly hearts to guard thee.

At which point Arne's band would have struck up their fiddles, kettle-drums, oboes and brass, and taking centre stage, Salway (knowing a hit when he sang one) would have given the moment its all, his tenor lustily mounting the scale of the first verse like a sailor climbing to the crow's nest:

> When Britain fir- ir- ir- irst at HEAVEN's command
> A -ro- oh oh ohse from out the a-ay- zure main
> A -roh-oh -ohse from out the azure main
> THIS was the charter, the charter of the land
> And guardian ay-ay-ay-ay-ANGELS sung this . . .
>   strain.
> [pause, drum roll]
>
> *Chorus:* RULE, BRITANNIA . . . *Britannia rules the* *waves.*

Whether the applause was polite or deafening, the performance was not quite over. Back came the hermit (not to be confused with the bard) for a final oracle, prophesying British dominion of the seas. This, too, had already become a standard fixture of Alfredomania since on a reading of the *Anglo-Saxon Chronicle* he was credited (not completely without foundation) as the first native king to have built a formidable war-fleet. If *Alfred* kept to the tradition of the masque this would have been the moment for an allegorical dumb show with personifications of the oceans (the 'golden South', the 'Soft East', the 'stormy North' and the 'vast Atlantic surge'), each accompanied by appropriate music from Arne, entering to unload their respective tributes to Britannia.

> *Hermit:* Alfred! Go forth! Lead on the radiant
>   years . . .
> I see thy commerce, BRITAIN grasp the world
> All nations serve thee, every foreign flood pays
> its tribute to the Thames
> . . . Britons proceed, the subject deep command
> Awe with your navies every hostile land
> Vain are their threats, their armies all in vain
> They rule the world who rule the main.

And then (surely) yet another chorus with more trumpets and drums:

> Rule, Britannia, Britannia rules the waves.

Richard Temple, Viscount Cobham, at any rate was nobody's slave. Nor did he need tutorials from Bolingbroke on the antiquity or the posterity of British liberty. His entire career, he supposed, had been selflessly devoted to its preservation. A veteran of the wars against Louis XIV, he had fought for William and then for Queen Anne and Marlborough as colonel of a regiment of foot and had come to be known, for his passionate defence of the Glorious Revolution, as 'the greatest Whig in the army'. Cobham and his wife Anne, the daughter of a wealthy brewer, had no surviving children and instead had poured their affections into their nephews and nieces, the Grenvilles, and their money into one of the most beautiful if grandiose Palladian country houses in England: Stowe. It was, though, always meant to be more than a pleasure-palace, Cobham's Buckinghamshire retort to Walpole's Houghton. Stowe was supposed to stand for something: for the perpetuity of British freedom. James Thomson had written his ode 'Liberty' while staying there and probably read Bolingbroke's *Patriot King* in Cobham's library. The 'cubs' who congregated at the house—George Lyttelton, William Pitt and the Grenvilles—all saw themselves as very British lions, ready to roar.

It was in the park behind the house, though, that Cobham made his political sentiments unmistakably visible. Ironically, it was from the translated work of a French landscape architect, Dézalliers d'Argenville, that the designers of the inspirational garden had taken their cue. The lessons were all classical. The park was studded with little pavilions, domed and colonnaded like miniature versions of the Pantheon, and artfully sited atop knolls or at the end of pools of water which allowed the walker, following a carefully prescribed route, to pause, literally, for reflection. The fashion was self-consciously painterly, owing much to the enormous popularity of landscapes by Nicolas Poussin and Claude Lorrain among the English aristocracy. But in Cobham's case, the intended effect was deliberately historical and political. Between 1731 and 1735, he brought the architect William Kent to Stowe to design for the park a new set of structures, each of which was a piece of his own public philosophy. Opposite the Temple of Ancient Virtue (modelled loosely on the Temple of Vesta at Tivoli near Rome), Kent built a Temple of British Worthies. Though later also called a 'temple', the structure is not a solid pavilion at all, but an unroofed enclosure and terrace based on the classical exedra. Beneath a pyramid surmounted by Mercury (not just the usher to Elysium but the god of commerce), a sweeping, semicircular wall enclosed a row of niches, each with its own pediment, in which were placed the 'bustoes' (as the printed guides called them) of the worthies.

They were divided, right and left, into heroes of contemplation and heroes (and one heroine) of action. Both groups included inevitable and uncontroversially admirable figures—Shakespeare and Bacon among the thinkers (as well as Richard Gresham, the founder of the New Exchange); the Black Prince and Elizabeth I among the doers. But there were other personalities who were much more assertive embodiments of Cobham's conviction that patriotism was ever the enemy of 'slavishness': John Milton among the thinkers and John Hampden among the doers. It may be that, as a fellow Buckinghamshire gentleman of the opposition, Cobham flattered himself as a latter-day Hampden, a century on. For it was in the 1730s that not only Milton but Oliver Cromwell too was experiencing a revival of sympathy. Cromwell was being taken not just as another epitome of a Free

Briton but as one of the founders of the modern British Empire as well. And the 'bustoes' of the doers did, in fact, make up a procession of the creators of Anglo-British maritime and imperial power: Alfred, the 'creator' of the navy (sculpted again by Rysbrack, who must have been knocking them off on an Anglo-Saxon production line); Elizabeth; but also Sir Walter Raleigh and Sir Francis Drake who, the inscription read, 'through many perils was the First Briton that adventured to sail round the Globe and carried into . . . the Seas and Nations the knowledge and glory of the English Name'.

The connection between the championship of liberty at home and the creation of a maritime, commercial empire overseas was at the heart of the new, the first truly British, patriotism. Bolingbroke spoke for all the Patriots when he insisted that 'the Empire of the Seas is ours; we have been many Ages in Possession of it; we have had many Sea-Fights, at a vast effusion of Blood and Expense of Treasure to preserve it and preserve it we still must, at all Risks and Events if we have a Mind to preserve ourselves.' As the heirs to their heroes Drake and Raleigh, Cobham and his protégés believed that this empire would be something new in the world precisely because it would not suffer from Rome's fatal addiction to territorial conquest, a vice that had led to despotism at the heart of the empire and auto-destruction on its over-extended frontiers. The aristocratic 'boy Patriots' had seen for themselves on the Grand Tour (on which Thomson, for example, had travelled as a tutor) the eloquent ruins of that imperial hubris in Rome. Pompeo Batoni's paintings of themselves posed against the melancholy debris of the Palatine Hill, as well as Giovanni Battista Piranesi's extraordinary engravings, first published in the 1750s, acted as a salutory reminder of the history to be avoided. Four years later, during the wars against the French, Cobham had Kent build him a Gothic Temple of Liberty in tawny ironstone (a more ruggedly earthy material than the creamy oolitic limestone of the classical buildings), decorated inside with the imaginary heraldry of the Saxon kings. Over the door, an inscription from Pierre Corneille's *Horace* (1639) left no one in doubt: 'Je rends grâces aux dieux n'estre pas Romain'—'I thank the Gods that I am not a Roman'.

As the years went by and the history of the British Empire turned from fantasy to military reality, Stowe turned into a theme park of the Empire of Liberty. One of the Grenville boys, Thomas, killed in the naval battle off Cape Finisterre in May 1747, was memorialized by his own column. Another obelisk went up in 1759 to mourn (along with the rest of the nation) the most celebrated of all imperial martyrs, James Wolfe; yet another monument towards the end of the century commemorated James Cook. Significantly, Stowe became the first country house in Britain to open its park and gardens to the public, and to print inexpensive guides to go with the visit. By the early 1750s, prospective patriotic tourists had a choice of at least three (some as cheap as sixpence; others, with engraved views, two shillings and sixpence) to lead them round the patriotic landscape. At the Palladian Bridge they could ponder the bas-relief depicting 'The History of Commerce and the Four

Quarters of the World bringing their Productions to Britannia'. Inside the Temple of Friendship, in a gallery filled with the heads of Pitt, Cobham (passed on to his British elysium in 1749), Lyttelton and the rest, they could crane their necks at a painting of Britannia yet again enthroned in her glory and congratulate themselves on their good fortune to live in a country in which liberty and empire, usually mutually exclusive, were so harmoniously and so miraculously conjoined.

When they ritually invoked 'liberty', though, what did its champions actually mean? In the first instance, freedom from the 'slavery' of Roman Catholicism (which perhaps pained the Catholic composer of 'Rule, Britannia', Arne). But they were recalling a very specific historical tradition of seventeenth-century resistance to the efforts of 'despots' either to smuggle it in surreptitiously (in the case of Archbishop Laud and Charles I) or to impose it through a standing army (like James II). Liberty meant parliamentary consent to taxation; regular elections; and habeas corpus—all the virtues assumed to be absent from the slave states of Catholic Europe and that had been immemorially rooted in English (even Anglo-Saxon) nationhood. Liberty meant the constant reiteration of its historical epics—Magna Carta, the Petition of Right, and, most recently and therefore most hallowed, the Bill of Rights of 1689—and its heroes and martyrs: John Hampden, John Milton and Algernon Sydney. In the 1730s, the attacks on Walpole had added a modern inventory of despots: the Robinocrats, perhaps even worse than the Stuarts because of their hypocritical pretence to be defending the principles of 1688 that, by means of the Septennial Act of 1716 (elections every seven, rather than every three, years), parliamentary placemen and sinister armies of excise-men, they were in fact bent on corrupting and annihilating. In contrast to the grovelling hacks and the epicene toadies who lived off the leavings of the oligarchs were the honest sort of the country, men who sweated for a living: ordinary country gentlemen, merchants, decent artisans, men of commerce—the 'Heart Blood' of the nation. It was these men who believed themselves tyrannized by the arbitrary powers of Walpole's excisemen, and who looked to the promotion of blue-water empire to fulfil their partnership between trade and freedom. So when they spoke of liberty they meant, among other enterprises, the liberty to buy and sell slaves.

For one thing is certain about this generation: the kind of liberty they mouthed so freely was not for black Africans, whose welfare had definitely not been uppermost in the minds of those who had written Magna Carta or the Petition of Right. It seldom occurred to those who parroted nostrums about the empire of liberty that its prosperity depended on the enslavement of hundreds of thousands of Africans, since it would take another generation before 'natural' equality would join liberty in the radical canon. For an African to invoke the precepts of a Free Briton, these patriots supposed, was to make a mockery of their meaning. So while William Kent was erecting his memorial to the founding fathers of the empire of the free seventy-seven Akan-speaking Antiguan slaves, the leaders of an aborted rising intended to seize the island on the anniversary of George II's coronation

211

in October 1736 were being publicly burned alive. If the authorities on the island followed the Procedures described by Hans Sloane, later physician to George II, the slaves would have been nailed 'on the ground with crooked sticks on every Limb, and then applying the Fire by degrees from the Feet and Hands, burning them gradually up to the Head, whereby their pains are extravagant'. According to official records, five slaves were broken on the wheel, six gibbeted alive and seventy-seven burned—a total of eighty-eight executions in less than four months. Those less directly implicated in the plot might have got away with a castration, a mutilated hand or foot or a flogging 'till they are Raw, some put on their skins Pepper and salt to make them smart'.

The irony that an empire so noisily advertised as an empire of free Britons should depend on the most brutal coercion of enslaved Africans is not just an academic paradox. It was the *condition* of the empire's success, its original sin: a stain that no amount of righteous self-congratulation at its eventual abolition can altogether wash away.

And there were other twists of historical fate waiting just round the corner for the empire-builders—outcomes that they could never have foreseen in the bright prospectus of the foundation years. The blue-water character of the British Empire, the preference of its promoters for business opportunities over territorial conquest; and their instinct that military and commercial ventures should be mutually exclusive were supposed to immunize it from the evils notorious, not just in the empires of antiquity, but also in the imperial autocracies of the recent past—Ottoman and Catholic-Spanish. The British Empire was supposed to satisfy itself with just enough power, and just enough central regulation, to make the interlocking parts of its economic machinery work with well-oiled smoothness. Properly 'planted' and protected from foreign despoilers and interlopers, the colonies would furnish raw materials to the motherland, which in turn would send its manufactures and finished goods back. With a buoyant home market, the suppliers across the sea would make enough money to afford their imports and would plough some of the proceeds into making their plantations even more productive; this would lower costs, which in turn would make the goods more widely available to a bigger proportion of the population back in Britain. The rising tide of reciprocal good fortune would lift all boats, and, without the expense and distraction of vain conquests to protect, the empire of freedom and enterprise would knit the world together in an endlessly benevolent cycle of mutual improvement.

By the end of the eighteenth century it was apparent that this was not how things had worked out. Instead of an empire of farmers and traders the British Empire was, overwhelmingly, an empire of soldiers and slaves. The Americans who had taken the professions of liberty most seriously had flung them back in the teeth of Britain and gone their own way. And instead of an empire based on lightly garrisoned commercial stations around the world, Britain had somehow found itself responsible for nearly a million Caribbean slaves and at least 50 million inhabitants of the Indian subcontinent. The British had gone east to make a little money on the side and ended up, somehow, as the Raj. The footnote had become the main story. Look around the streets of urban Britain today, and you see that it still is.

So just how had Britain ended up with the wrong empire?

From the beginning the British Empire was habit-forming. The genial encouragement of addiction was its speciality: a quiet smoke, a nice cup of tea, a sweet tooth (and, a bit later, a pipe of opium)—exotic rarities converted into consumer cravings, exceptional wants turned into daily needs. Where profit beckoned, distaste could be overcome. King James I may have published tracts against the filthy weed *Nicotiana tabacum* ('good Countrey-men let us (I pray you) consider what honour or policy can move us to imitate the barbarous and beastly manners of the wild, godles and slavish Indians . . . in so vile and stinking a custom?'), but the first settlement the Virginia Company established to grow it still bore his name. Given the chance, the Jamestown settlers would have preferred to discover the gold and silver that seemed to have fallen into the lap of the Spanish empire of the south. But there was no gold in the Chesapeake Bay and the settlers had to make do with their dependably prolific flop-leaved plant. Many times, during the first half of the seventeenth century, the English tobacco colonies seemed close to obliteration: victims of disease, vicious wars with the Native Americans (in which the English, as well as the natives, slaughtered men, women and children) and their own profligate, unrealistic expectations. The climate, the insects and the unwelcome gifts they carried devoured men. Though 6000 immigrants had come between 1607 and 1625, in the latter year a census found the population of Virginia to be just 1200. Yet, as the tobacco habit became ingrained in European culture and Virginia leaf was established as the marker of quality, demand boomed, prices rose and the settlements in Lord Baltimore's Maryland and in Virginia hung on, consolidated and pushed inland. Attracted by the possibility of owning 'manors' of hundreds of acres, the younger sons of gentry and tradesmen arrived to become tobacco barons. Supplying the labour, alongside a limited number of African slaves, were boys—median age sixteen, seldom over nineteen; boys in their tens of thousands, out from the rookeries and tenements of London and Bristol, about 70 to 80 per cent 'indentured' (contractually committed) to work for three to five years for room and board before being freed to claim a small plot of promised land, to hire out their labour or set up shop.

This was how the colonial 'planting' was supposed to work: an anti-social no-hope population drained from the mother country and set to work with every prospect of 'improvement'; the land itself likewise kissed by amelioration; the mother country on the (carefully controlled) receiving end of a valuable raw commodity, busy turning out goods that it could ship back to the growing colony. And, unlike in Ireland where the obstreperous natives happened to be Christians (of a deluded, papistical sort) and could attract the support of mischievous foreign powers to make a nuisance of themselves, the American natives, who were evidently resistant to the Gospel, could now be shoved further and further up-river and into the trees and hills. Sir Francis Wyatt had spoken for the whole Anglo-American project in 1622 when he unblushingly declared that 'our first worke is expulsion of the Savages to gaine the free range of the countrey . . . for it is infinitely better to have no heathen among us, who at best were but thornes in our sides, than to be at peace and at league with them'.

But then it all went badly wrong. Beginning in the 1680s, tobacco prices began to decline and then went into free-fall, bankrupting the smaller planters, brokers and processors. The shock was not enough to abort the Chesapeake experiment altogether. There were upwards of 50,000 settlers in Maryland and Virginia, and they managed to find a more diversified range of crops to farm— indigo and wheat in particular. The colony would survive, and the tobacco market revive in the next century, but the bonanza was, for the time being, over.

Or, rather, it was elsewhere. For another kind of craving was sweeping through Europe in the second half of the seventeenth century, one that would transform the British Empire from a niche in the world economy to its star performer. The craze for hot, powerfully caffeinated beverages began with coffee, brought from the Islamic world via the janissaries of the Ottoman Empire as they moved further west into central Europe. Vienna would resist the Turkish siege, but it was defenceless against the coffee bean. The American cocoa bean, consumed as drinking chocolate, had been passed from Central American culture to their Spanish conquerors and refined and made marketable by the Dutch, always with their eye on the creation of new market openings. Both coffee and chocolate were widely available in the London coffee-houses by the third quarter of the seventeenth century.

But for some reason, which—as yet—no amount of anthropology, much less economic history, has managed to explain satisfactorily, it was the east Asian drink brewed from the leaves of *Camellia sinensis* that, right from the beginning, was the British favourite. When Thomas Garway sold 'China Tcha, Tay or Tee' in both leaf and brewed liquid form in his coffee-house in Exchange Alley in 1657, it was probably the choice green leaves of Hyson or Sing-lo grown in Anwei and Chekiang provinces. Anticipating some of the more miraculous claims made for green tea recently, Garway promoted it as a wonder drug: 'wholesome, preserving perfect health until extreme old age, good for clearing the sight'; it would pacify 'gripping of the guts, cold, dropsies and scurvies' and would 'make the body active and lusty'. But by the turn of the eighteenth century, when Tcha was being sold in at least 500 coffee-houses, black leaf, grown around the Bohea mountains of Fukien, on the southeastern coast, had conquered the market. The best of those teas, like Souchong, needed longer drying time, but enough of it could be processed and exported by the East India Company from Canton to lower the price and thus reach a wide market. Even more significantly, in the first decades of the eighteenth century Bohea made a crucial crossover from commercial drinking establishments into the domestic world, first in the houses of fashionable quality, but by the second decade among the trading and commercial classes and even artisans. It became, *par excellence*, the politely sociable drink, to be taken preferably at

217

home and with its little rituals and ceremonies more often than not in the hands of women. By the 1730s close to a million pounds of tea a year were being imported from China to Britain by the East India Company, which could sell it on the London market for four times what it had paid in China.

And although the evidence for its timing is necessarily anecdotal, it seems likely that from the beginning tea, like the more aggressively bitter coffee and chocolate, was thought to need sugar to make it palatable. When the first porcelain tea sets were being made, it would have been unthinkable not to have included, along with the teapot and milk jug, a sugar bowl. In 1715 Dr Frederick Slare, admittedly so shameless a booster of the miraculous qualities of sugar that he could recommend it not only as a cure for eye ailments but also as an ideal dentifrice, announced, in effect, the arrival of the modern British breakfast. 'Morning repasts called Break-fasts,' he wrote authoritatively, 'consist of bread, butter, milk, water and sugar', adding that tea, coffee and chocolate as the beverages of choice all had 'uncommon virtues'. The old early-morning meal of home-brewed small beer, bread and perhaps cheese or smoked fish was on its way out, at least in urban Britain. By the time that Hannah Glasse's *The Art of Cookery Made Plain and Easy*, the first cookbook directed at the middle classes, was published in 1747, its recipes assumed the wide availability and inexpensiveness of sugar. 'To make a rich cake' called for 3 lb. of 'double-refined sugar' to 4 lb. of flour; 'Everlasting Syllabub' used a pound of double-refined sugar to 2.5 pints of cream, 'Syrup of peach blossoms' (a wonderful idea) 2 pounds; and both Mrs Glasse's 'cheap' rice-puddings (baked as well as boiled) also used sugar as a basic ingredient. The British sweet tooth, gratified by tarts and puddings, flavoured creams and cheesecakes, jams, marmalades and jellies, had arrived with a vengeance in the national diet. It was an alteration of appetite that revolutionized the history, not just of Britain but of the world.

Sugar had been widely known and consumed in medieval Europe, but its high price and exotic origin meant that it was considered as either a spice or a drug. The most common sweetener, conveniently and locally produced, was honey. So when sugar shows up in the account books of grand aristocratic households like that of Simon de Montfort, the Earl of Leicester, at Kenilworth, it is rarely in amounts of more than a pound or two. It had reached Christian Europe via the Islamic world, and it had been a crusader dynasty, the Lusignans, sometime kings of Jerusalem, who had made the first attempt to domesticate it for production on Cyprus. But sugar cane is native to the tropical monsoon regions of southeast Asia from New Guinea to the Bay of Bengal, and to reach its mature height of 8 feet (2 metres) it needs the combination of drenching, daily rainfall and hot temperatures. It was precisely the difficulty of establishing it in the drier Mediterranean region, under optimal growing conditions, that kept yields relatively low and prices comparatively high. So for centuries sugar remained a drug or a spice, in both cases an exotic luxury rather than a daily commodity. But its Portuguese shippers and growers, abetted by Dutch and Jewish traders and refiners, were constantly moving west, out into the warmer Tropic of Cancer latitudes of the Atlantic, to Madeira and São Tomé, for example, in search of the perfect combination of heat and rain. Famously (although almost by accident when ships were blown southwards off course), they found what they were looking for in the former Portuguese colony of Brazil.

But there was something else that sugar cane needed if its golden juice was going to pay off, and that was intensive, highly concentrated, task-specific applications of manpower. For the cane was an unforgiving and volatile crop. It could not be farmed and harvested in a single growing year since it took at least fourteen months to ripen. But once it had reached maturity, the cumbersome grass needed to be harvested quickly to prevent the sugar going starchy. Once stripped and cut, the cane in its turn had to be speedily taken to the ox-powered vertical crushing rollers before the sucrose concentration of the juice self-degraded. Every subsequent stage of production—the boiling of the juice, the arrest of the boiling process at the precise moment for optimum crystallization, the partial refining in clay-stopped inverted cone moulds, the lengthy drying process—demanded the kind of strength, speed and stamina in tropical conditions that indentured white Europeans or captive Native Americans were ill equipped to provide. Both populations proved themselves hard to discipline, prone to drink and rebelliousness. They ran away a lot, and they died like flies from the stew of insect- and water-borne diseases that simmered away in the humid sunlight. But the Portuguese sugar lords and, more specifically, their Dutch and Jewish brokers knew it was worth persevering. All that the merchants of Pernambuco needed to solve in order to make a packet was the labour problem.

So, where to turn for a labour supply that was strong, disease-resistant but obedient, like the cattle that turned the crushers? Where else, of course, but where the Portuguese were already making money from the commerce in ivory, gold and humans—West and Central Africa.

It was a truly Faustian moment. And there *were* those who recognized the Mephistophelean nature of the compact. The Jesuits in Brazil condemned as the grossest blasphemy any equation between men and animals. Other, equally honourable Fathers of the Church and jurists in the Spanish empire wrote forthrightly to Philip II on the unspeakable, unchristian, evil of enslavement. But other councillors and clerics were prepared to justify enslavement on the pious pretext that it was a way to bring the heathen Africans to the Gospel. And, besides, were they not captives from their own tribal wars? The arguments were transparently defensive and sometimes disingenuous, but imperial Spain (which had incorporated Portugal in 1580) was desperately short of funds, and it was more expedient to listen to the permissive, than the prohibitive, arguments. By 1630 there were probably over 60,000 African slaves working in the sugar estates of Brazil, and the investment was paying off handsomely for all concerned except its traumatized, brutalized victims.

Since the reign of Elizabeth, English interlopers (competing with the Dutch) had been buying slaves on the coast of West Africa and selling them to Hispanic America. But by the middle of the seventeenth century envious glances were being cast in the direction of Brazil (where the Portuguese and Dutch were slugging it out for sovereignty), and where it was obvious immense fortunes were to be made. The Dutch—as any quick visit to an Amsterdam baker or confectioner would have made apparent—had already succeeded in introducing sugar as a staple of daily diet rather than a rare and expensive luxury. And the English were aware that, even if it were highly volatile in the early stages of production, sugar was extremely stable in shipping and warehousing. It was marvellously versatile and market-adaptable, yielding not just two qualities of sugar (refined and cruder 'muscovado') but also molasses, treacle and rum. As a commodity for long-distance trade it was impossible to beat.

But where could the English find a place to grow it, safe from the long arm and the heavy hand of the Spanish? Early attempts were made in Bermuda, but the tiny island off the coast of South Carolina was too dry, too cool and too remote. Barbados, on the other hand, seemed the answer to their prayers. Hanging out in the ocean, on the extreme windward edge of the Antilles, its annual rainfall averaged 60 inches (over 1500 mm) a year—all the moisture the sugar cane could possibly need; and its breezy exposure could be harnessed to turn the sails of windmills to crush the cane. It was as far as it could be from the Spanish centres of power in Cuba and Hispaniola while still being in the Caribbean, and it was the first port of call for ships coming across the Atlantic from either Africa or England. Even its topography seemed perfect, with lowlands sloping down to a

222

coast with some hospitable natural harbours in the south and a wet, upland northern plateau quickly named 'Scotland'.

Perhaps sugar may have been on the mind of the mariner John Powell when he first made landfall on Barbados en route back from the Guianas in 1625. But the colonial product of choice at this time was tobacco, and for a generation or two efforts were made to grow a crop on Barbados. Competing with Virginia and Maryland, however, was hard work. The island was covered with a dense canopy of rainforest—mastic and ironwood, poisonwood, hoe-stick wood and locust—which took twenty years to clear for adequate growing space. Even then, the leaf never managed to achieve the vaunted quality of Virginia tobacco. And there were the same labour troubles that plagued the Chesapeake Bay plantations. The Irish indentured labourers were especially restive under their crippling regime of toil, and the teenage boys who came from England wilted and collapsed in the heat. In 1649—the year of revolution in England—there was a slave plot on Barbados, suppressed with merciless, characteristically Cromwellian brutality. Even before the rebellion some of the first-generation planters such as James Drax, a landowner of Anglo-Dutch background, had been experimenting with slave labour shipped on his own account from Africa. Now the slave–sugar nexus seemed a much better bet than the struggle with tobacco, especially when the Dutch were prepared to advance planters capital for milling equipment and even show them how to use it. The crop took off. As early as 1647 an owner of 50 acres reported that 'provisions for the belly

. . . at present is very scarce [since] men are so intent upon planting sugar that they had rather buy foode at very dear, rather than produce it by labour, soe infinite is the profitt of sugar workes'.

As early as 1655, three years after that first coffee-house opened in London, Barbados was shipping 7787 tons of sugar back to England, and there were already 20,000 slaves on the island against 23,000 whites, well over half of whom were probably indentured servants. When Richard Ligon arrived two years later, the well-founded reputation of Barbados as a gold-mine had already been established. Drax had built himself a Jacobean manor house on the upland plateau and 'as we passed along the shoar', Ligon wrote, 'the Plantations appeared to us one above the other like several stories in stately buildings which afforded us a large proportion of delight'. It was common knowledge that an up-front outlay of £1000 (advanced from the Dutch) invested in 200 acres, a windmill (sometimes, along with the boiling house, shared with a neighbour), a distillery to make rum and a hundred odd slaves would yield, within a very few years, an annual income of £2000. No wonder, as Henry Whistler noted in 1655, 'the gentry here doth live far better than ours do in England'. They were, by far, the richest men in British America.

It was precisely between 1640 and 1660, when the rhetoric of liberty was being most noisily shouted at home, that the slave economy of the British Empire was being created in the Caribbean. (Cromwell's baffled disappointment that God had somehow decided that Hispaniola should not, after all, be British was partly consoled by the capture of Jamaica in 1655.) And this timing was not, alas, a coincidence. For if making an 'empire of liberty' meant keeping it clean of Catholics, no one wanted this more than the hard-nosed, coffer-counting men of the Protectorate (in many cases, of course, identical with the hard-nosed men of the Restoration). The impeccably Puritan Earl of Warwick had, after all, been among the most enthusiastic pioneers of settlement and slaving in the Caribbean two decades earlier. So Barbados filled up with shackled Africans while its white Assembly resounded with the pieties of self-government. The island became a little Commonwealth, but without the gloomy inconvenience of the morals police. Barbados was divided into parishes, each run by a vestry (as is still the case), and its manorial gentry, in their magisterial role, adjudicated the common law much as they did in Berkshire or Cheshire. But they also adjudicated the slave code, which declared the punishment for running away to be mutilation and the penalty for theft of any article worth more than a shilling death. Wilfully killing a negro might incur an inconvenient fine, but it was virtually impossible to prove it. And with Bridgetown and its other harbours made easily defensible, the island was safe from the Catholic scourge. It was a planting full of blessings, an Ulster in the sun.

The restoration of the monarchy only made things better. On vacation from losing battles, Prince Rupert of the Rhine went slaving up the Gambia in West Africa and made a tidy profit on it. Once his cousin Charles II was king he became instrumental in founding the Company of Royal Adventurers into Africa in 1660. Initially chartered

225

with a 1000-year monopoly of trading rights in western Africa, it was re-chartered in 1663 as the Company of Royal Adventurers Trading into Africa, commonly known as the Royal African Company. By the time its ships deposited their first human cargoes at Bridgetown there were already well over 30,000 slaves on Barbados, twice as many blacks as whites on the island. By 1700 the number had risen to around 50,000. (A century later the slave population on Barbados would number some 70,000, with roughly another 400,000 on Jamaica.) Barbados had become the forcing house of high-end, fast-profit, industrially organized slave capitalism. The patchwork landscape of relatively small farms—10 acres or so on average—worked by racially mixed gangs of indentured servants and slaves had gone forever. In its place were 350 large estates of more than 200 acres and scores more of about 100 acres, all of them worked almost exclusively with African slave labour. Quakers like George Fox visited Barbados, preached that 'all blacks, whites and tawnies' were equally God's creatures and asked the planters to use the slaves gently and free them after a period—but stopped short of demanding abolition. The indefatigable old Puritan Richard Baxter, though, was more damning in 1673 when he asked, 'How cursed a crime is it to equal men to beasts. Is this not your practice? Do you not buy them and use them merely as you do horses to labour for your commodity . . . Do you not see how you reproach and condemn yourselves while you vilify them all as savages?' But even when they were occasionally embarrassed into conceding the human cost, the planters (and indeed the merchants at home) shrugged their shoulders and asked what a Negro would do with liberty. The bottom line, always, was money. Daniel Defoe, as usual, was shockingly blunt and absolutely truthful: 'No African Trade, no Negroes; no Negroes, no Sugars . . . no Sugars . . . no Islands, no Islands, no [American] Continent; no Continent, no Trade; that is say farewell to all your American Trade, your West Indian Trade.' The poet William Cowper was later to write a little comic verse on this predicament:

> I own I am shocked at the purchase of slaves
> And fear those who buy them and sell them are knaves
> What I hear of their hardships and tortures and groans
> Is almost enough to draw pity from stones
> I pity them greatly but I must be mum
> For how could we do without sugar and rum?

In the century and a half of the slave trade, from the 1650s to 1807, between three and four million Africans were transported out of their homelands to the New World in British ships. Between nine and twelve million were abducted and sold as chattel property by the traders of all the European nations involved: it was the single largest mass abduction in human history. A million and a half of those died en route during the hellish crossing known as the Middle Passage, the second leg of the Britain–Africa–West Indies–Britain route that gave rise to the term 'triangular trade'. Of course, it was not only white Europeans and Americans who were responsible for this enormity. It had been the Portuguese discovery of a thriving trans-Sahara

227

slave trade, harvested and delivered by African warrior dealers, which had made the traffic possible in the first place. But the demand for slaves trans-shipped to the New World became so voracious in the late seventeenth and eighteenth centuries that it created incentives for the raiders—usually native or Portuguese—to reach far beyond their traditional catchment zones, to make opportunistic descents on stricken and defenceless villages. By the early eighteenth century, raiding parties were moving well north of the Niger and deep into western Sudan. And a region already suffering from repeated plagues of locusts and droughts was now made even more insecure. In some of the worst-hit areas it was not uncommon for desperate villagers to sell their children or even themselves.

There was another sense in which the transatlantic slave trade was qualitatively more inhuman than the norms of slavery prevailing in the Islamic and pagan African worlds. For slaves in these regions, while indisputably unfree, were made into status objects, attached to the households, court and military retinues or seraglios of their owners. They were, in every sense, prized. And this had also been true for slaves in urban Europe: blacks in Dutch or English households were shown off and cosseted as if they were exotic pets. Never before, though, had masses of one particular race—black Africans—been treated as mere units of production in the calculus of profit. By definition, slaves had always been property. But now they were inventory: priced, sold, packaged, freighted, resold, amortized, depreciated, written off and replaced. They were, as Baxter had said,

228

nothing more than beasts of burden. Perhaps the most shaming aspect of that dehumanization was the retrospective adoption of a set of racist commonplaces in the apologetic literature claiming that Africans were animal-like in their incapacity to feel pain or even emotion in the same manner experienced by the white races.

Who knows when the awareness of their bestialization made itself inescapably clear to the terrified Africans themselves? By the time they reached their first selling point—from the holding pens at places like Cape Coast Castle—they had already endured a succession of traumas. Olaudah Equiano, the Ibo who wrote his memoirs in the mid-eighteenth century under his bizarre slave name of Gustavus Vasa, taken from the Swedish kings, had been well aware of the dangers of abduction as a child. When the adults of his village were away at work in the fields he would climb trees to sound the alarm when suspicious persons made an appearance. One day, none the less, he and his sister were taken. It was when they were separated that misery first took hold: 'I was left in a state of distraction not to be described. I cried and grieved continually and for several days did not eat anything but what they forced in my mouth.' Though he was to see his sister again, it was a moment of false hope, for Equiano, like countless others, was deliberately uprooted from any kind of familiarity—country, customs, language, kin. When he was taken on board the slave ship and 'tossed up to see if I was sound', the sense that he had been reduced to a workhorse must have been unmistakable. The master of the *Hannibal*, Thomas Phillips, who wrote an account of a typical

229

voyage of the 1690s, described even more degrading procedures when inspecting the shipment supplied by the African dealers at Ouidah. Searching for signs of the yaws that 'discovers itself by almost the same symptoms . . . as clap does for us . . . our surgeon is forced to examine the privities of both men and women with the nicest scrutiny, which is a great slavery but what can't be omitted'. Once purchased, the slave was branded on the breast or shoulder with the letter of the ship's name, 'the place before being anointed with a little palm oil which caused but little pain, the mark being usually well in four or five days, appearing very plain and white'.

There were other regrettable inconveniences that marred the smoothness of the loading process: negroes who were 'so wilful and loth to leave their own country that they have often leapt out of the canoes, boat and ship into the sea and kept under water till they were drowned, to avoid being taken up and saved by our boats which pursued them, they having a more dreadful apprehension of Barbados than we can have of hell'. Once on board there were still possibilities for suicide, especially since the slavers usually prowled the coast to take on extra cargo: the Africans would jump overboard, shackled or not. 'We have . . . seen divers of them eaten by the sharks,' wrote Phillips, 'of which a prodigious number kept about the ships in this place [Ouidah] and I have been told will follow her to Barbadoes for the dead negroes that are thrown overboard in the passage . . . I am certain in our voyage there we did not want the sight of some every day . . . we had about twelve negroes did wilfully drown themselves and others

230

starvd themselves to death for 'tis their belief that when they die they return home to their own country and friends.'

Other accounts register the inconsiderateness of negroes who went 'raving mad', or mutilated themselves during the passage, or who had the audacity to refuse to eat, thereby jeopardizing the value of the cargo. When the young Equiano declined his gruel of horse beans and vegetables, he was flogged until he changed his mind. But what the slavers and their surgeons described as 'melancholy' was almost certainly the semi-catatonic state characterized by sunken eyes, swollen tongue and extreme torpor that is induced by extreme, potentially fatal, dehydration. The average adult male weighing around 150 pounds needs under normal circumstances about 4 pints (2.3 litres) of fluid a day to recover losses from urine and sweat. The standard ration for slaves on the Middle Passage—a journey lasting anything from thirty to seventy days in anything but 'normal circumstances' —was a pint of water and 2 pints of soup. That ration was seldom if ever given in full, but even if it were the slave would still be in fluid deficit. If, over a long journey, he or she lost just 10 per cent of their body's 80 pints (just under 50 litres) water content, they would certainly die. Between 10 and 20 per cent of slaves on board died this way.

Fluid loss from extreme perspiration was the first cause. When the ships were out in the open ocean, the slaves were taken up on deck twice a day for air, water and soup. If the sea were too rough, however, they would be kept in the stifling heat of the cramped holds, shackled in pairs and given less space (according to the Royal Africa Company

231

specifications) than for a European pauper's coffin. If the ship was still sailing the West African coast (one of the hottest and dampest regions of the world) picking up more cargo, the climate below decks was even more dangerous. Olaudah Equiano recalled:

> The closeness of the place and the heat of the climate, added to the number in the ship, being so crowded that each had scarcely room to turn himself, almost suffocated us. This produced copious perspiration so that the air soon became unfit for respiration from a variety of loathsome smells and brought on a sickness among the slaves, of which many died, thus falling victims to the improvident avarice, as I may call it, of their purchasers. This deplorable situation was again aggravated by the galling [chafing] of the chains, now become insupportable; and the filth of necessary tubs into which the children often fell, and were almost suffocated. The shrieks of the women and the groans of the dying rendered it a scene of horror almost inconceivable.

Equiano is describing a perfect environment for faecal contamination, in which both shigellosis or bacillary dysentery, the 'red flux', and, more ominously, amoebic dysentery, the 'white flux', could rage. Commonly chronicled by surgeons aboard the slavers, both triggered violent spasms of vomiting and diarrhoea, which would induce further fluid loss. No wonder that when he was taken below decks for the first time Equiano 'received such a salutation in my nostrils as I had never experienced in my life'. Amoebic dysentery,

232

which had a longer incubation period, attacked the victim in mid-voyage and was the more serious of the two infections since it lasted for weeks rather than days, with its victims suffering around twenty evacuations a day. Fluid losses would have been massive, triggering rapid sodium depletion and the excretion of potassium. Potassium loss in its turn would affect brain function, leading to the strange twilight dreaminess in which sufferers entered before their cardiac function was finally traumatized. Under the circumstances it is surely amazing that the mortality rate on slave ships was only around 12–15 per cent, though it could be as high as 20 per cent for children, who were naturally more vulnerable to acute dehydration than the adults.

What happened to them next, if they did survive to landfall, may have made the young slaves wish they had perished on board. Naked except for loincloths, they were paraded, poked and inspected all over again like livestock, their jaws clamped open for the inspection of teeth. A few were sold directly to planters. But many more were taken by wholesale merchants who confined them once more in a holding yard or pen. There they had to endure another extraordinary ordeal known to the planters as 'the scramble'. At Bridgetown in Barbados, Equiano described the prospective buyers 'on a signal given, such as the beat of a drum', rushing into the yard like bargain-hunters at a sale, sprinting towards the chained slaves and laying hands on them to secure their purchase. The most desirable job lots were young boys, just like Olaudah, between twelve and fifteen, for as David Stalker, a planter's buyer on the island of Nevis, explained, 'they are fully seasoned by eighteen and is [sic] full as handy as them that is born in the country, but them full grown fellers think it hard work never being brought up to it and take it to heart and dye or are never good for anything'. If they were too 'meagre', though, Equiano wrote, they would be put in scales, weighed and sold at threepence or sixpence the pound like cabbages. Bought again, they were branded again. Some of those branding irons survive in the museum at Bridgetown: made of fine silver, delicately fashioned in the form of a monogram, and indecently untarnished.

Now they truly belonged to King Sugar and toiled to make him rich. He was no sparer of age or sex. At least 80 per cent of the slave population worked, in some form or other, on the plantation for seventy to eighty hours a week. Some 20 per cent of those born there failed to survive beyond their second birthday, but if they did they had four or five years before they joined the 'third' work gang of the child labourers, gleaning, weeding, cutting grass and taking care of domestic animals. The 'second gang' comprised adolescents from twelve to nineteen, already out in the fields as well as tending to the animal population. The work on the second gang—around eleven hours of toil from before dawn to night—was so hard that many of the girls, in particular, died before they could graduate to the even more relentlessly back-breaking routine of the 'great gang' of adults. About 60 per cent of the total slave force in Barbados, Jamaica and Antigua worked in the 'great' or 'first' gang drilling holes for the new canes; cutting and stripping the harvest during the

234

frantic 'crop time' between January and May; bundling and hauling the cumbersome canes at a smart-enough pace not to compromise the sugar quality. Looking on to see that the work was going quickly was the overseer, as often black as white, quick to use the whip should he see any laggards. Assignment in the mill or the boiling house was hardly an improvement. The vertical rollers that crushed the cane were notorious for taking hands with them since the cane had to be fed in manually, and hatchets were kept beside the mill to sever an arm before the entire body was pulled in. Slaves in the boiler houses worked in conditions of intense heat, dirt and exhaustion and were in constant danger of being scalded by the boiling syrup as it was poured from larger to smaller copper vats.

One would suppose that economic rationality might mitigate the severity of labour at least to the point where the planters could get full value from their investment, especially since deaths were never made up by births. Reproduction rates on the plantations were notoriously low—possibly 10–15 per 1000 compared with perhaps 20–30 per 1000 in Britain. But neither the balance of the sexes nor the way women were treated was likely to favour a home-grown slave population. Women were outnumbered by men almost two to one, and those who did become pregnant were not spared from work in the fields until they were virtually on the point of delivery. Those women were no more immune than anyone else from floggings administered by overseers if they lagged in the pace of their work. Poor nutrition, damp and vermin-infested huts, exposure to smallpox and yellow fever as well as diseases brought from Africa like elephantiasis and yaws, further added to the toll of miscarriages and low fertility. But it seems unlikely that the managers of the plantations were unduly troubled about wastage, at least until the third quarter of the eighteenth century when prices rose. For while it took at least £40 to raise a slave child to the point when child and mother could become productive, a new slave could be bought from the traders for between £15 and £30. No wonder, then, that, although 1.5 million slaves were imported into the British Caribbean during the eighteenth century, the population never rose above 800,000.

Violence—threatened or delivered—was what made the system work, and it fell with special savagery on African women. In one year, 1765, the estate manager of the Egypt plantation on Jamaica, Thomas Thistlewood, administered twenty-one floggings to thirteen women, each likely to have been no less than fifty lashes. (Equiano wrote that it was common to make the slaves kneel down after such a flogging and thank their masters for it.) Arguably, adult women endured the hardest lot of any section of the slave population, since so much was demanded of them—cooking, caring for infants, mending and washing clothes in addition to field work. And they also had to endure the habitual sexual aggression of masters and overseers who assumed they could copulate with any woman they chose whenever and wherever the mood took them: in the kitchen, pantry or laundry of the houses, or out in the yards and barns. Female field hands, like the men, worked naked but for a loincloth, and must therefore have been especially vulnerable. The fastidious data collector Thistlewood kept a regular slave mistress, Phibbah,

236

with whom he carefully records having intercourse one hundred times during 1765. But in addition to Phibbah he had twenty-three other slave women on fifty-five separate occasions that year, most often out in the cane fields. Despite the resort to abortion by slave women who, forced to take more than one sexual partner, were terrified of alienating any one of them with a compromisingly coloured birth, 10 per cent of all births were in fact mulatto.

A small minority of the slaves of both sexes did manage to escape the punishing toil of the fields, either as domestic servants in the plantation house or as artisans who had brought with them from Africa specialized skills, which were much needed on the plantation. These coopers, masons, carpenters and blacksmiths, along with carters and wagoners as well as fishermen and even sailors, constituted a special class among the slaves, freer to move around and to buy and sell materials for their work. And there were times, too, when the slaves were not utterly dominated by the tyranny of the cane. The planters knew it was in their interest to give them some respite, and on Barbados there were some sixty free days and holidays a year. 'Free time' on Saturday afternoons and evenings was given over to the release of emotions and energies—often in music and dance, which the planters usually characterized as 'howling'. But in these brief moments of freedom business was at least as important as pleasure, for it offered a little taste of independence.

The Sunday market in towns like English Harbour on Antigua or Bridgetown on Barbados was where the African world remade itself. Beneath shady awnings, women and men sold

237

vegetables or chickens that had been legally brought from villages, articles they had made themselves—baskets, pots, wooden stools, hammocks, ropes and gourd bowls, as well as objects they had managed to pilfer (often through relatives working as domestics) from the plantation house—nails and pieces of copper and lead. The 'hucksters', as the whites called them, sold their commodities sitting on the ground, or, if it were more obviously contraband (sugar, tobacco or rum), walking around the market waiting for selling opportunities. Money might change hands, but there were other objects that could be used as currency in the market: beads, copper wire or even cowrie shells, the exchange medium of West Africa.

The world of the market and the coopers' and carpenters' shops created a class of slaves who were more literate and assertive than the field hands, and whose social horizons were a lot broader than the cane fields. Because they depended on the artisans and carters in particular and got to know them well, some of the planters and their managers naïvely imagined that these more enterprising slaves might act as intermediaries between themselves and the mass of field hands. They were badly mistaken. The records of uncovering and suppressing rebellions almost invariably featured ringleaders from this 'slave elite'. Even though there was little chance of any of these revolts succeeding over the long term, especially in islands like Barbados where a potentially sheltering forest had been almost completely stripped to make way for cane, there was a steady drum-beat of rebellion, some of it, as in Antigua in the 1720s and 1730s and in Jamaica in mid-century, flaring into ferocious violence. 'Tacky's Rebellion' on Jamaica in 1760 took the lives of close to 100 whites and 400 blacks, as well as exiling 600 more, before it was finally put down with a great deal of difficulty.

Resistance to being reduced to a cipher in a manager's account-book (bought, worked, died) could also take forms other than violent insurrection. Among the socially traumatized slave community there were those who took it on themselves to preserve some sense of African tradition and cultural memory in a world that had been stripped of it. Different language groups, regions and tribes had been deliberately mixed to pre-empt any kind of potentially threatening solidarity. But the need for shared life, the need to make the scraps and shards of ancient, half-kept memory, was stronger even than slavery. African culture, though pulverized by terror and hardship, was reduced not to fine dust that could be blown away into the wind but to small, resistant grains that could be replanted, regrown, remade. And those new growths were tended by keepers of ancestral wisdom, keepers of the knowledge of religion, obeah healing and music. Because the tribal and language groups—Akan, Twi, Efik, Ewe—could not just be transposed to St Kitts, Antigua and Barbados, the healers, drummers, singers, weavers and carvers had to create unapologetically new forms from many strands of material, some inherited, others discovered, all shared. But it was, none the less, theirs—hard-earned, not the gift of their masters. In fact, the reluctance of the Caribbean masters in the early years to Christianize the slaves—lest literacy and religion produce a sense of presumptuous brotherhood in Christ, and lest the uses of literacy turn seditious—gave the Africans a generation or two to establish their own kind of syncretic culture, free from interference. When, finally, an effort was made to convert them, the missionary gospel was inevitably grafted on to cultural roots that had already sunk deep into the West Indian soil.

Rites of passage figure heavily in this new–old culture, none more important than funerals. From the beginning of the slave experience, cool observers like Thomas Phillips noticed that the Africans invariably treated death as freedom, and, *in extremis*, even shackled, did their utmost to swim to it (on the journey) or run away to it (on the islands). Was this not the ultimate irony of slave culture—that the masters would do what they could to keep their property alive, and the slaves would pay them back by seeking the liberation of death? To die in the Caribbean was to go home, and, to the bewilderment of clergymen like the Reverend Griffith Hughes, in Jamaica in the 1730s burials were occasions for outbursts of joy as well as solemnity. The bodies were laid out in fresh white cloths and were borne to the grave in a slow procession, the women walking in pairs and dressed in white, the West African colour of mourning; 'both men and women which accompanying the corpse sing and howle in a sorrowful manner', as another observer, John Taylor, noted in Jamaica. Once the body was interred, along with it went provisions: cassava-bread loaves, roasted fowl, rum, tobacco 'with fier to light his pipe withal . . . and this they doe . . . in order to sustain him in his journey beyond those pleasant hills in their own country wither they say he is now going to live at rest'. Once the grave was filled up with dirt, the mood of the moment changed to singing, clapping and dancing, using gourd rattles, drums and baffalo, many of the mourners 'desiring the corpse [by kissing the grave] to acquaint their mother, father, husband and other relations of their present condition and slavery as he passeth through their country towards the pleasant mountains'. It was, in effect, a letter home, and the dead would be their courier.

Also deposited in the graves (and recovered now from excavations in slave cemeteries on Barbados) were ornaments appropriate to a happy and ceremonious homecoming. From humble materials—dog teeth, copper wire and pieces of brass, as well as other objects familiar in African jewellery such as cowrie shells and glass beads—amulets and charms were lovingly fashioned. Slaves, who had been dispossessed of virtually everything, not least their humanity, managed somehow to create works of art and then gave them away to the dead so that they might arrive back home in dignity. It was the ultimate retort to the mindless cliché that they were no better than insentient beasts of burden.

By the middle of the eighteenth century, the mercantile 'empire of liberty' was critically dependent for its fortune on the economic universe made from slavery. The sugar produced by three-quarters of a million slaves in the Caribbean had become the single most valuable import to Great Britain, and it would not be displaced from that rank until the 1820s. Huge fortunes had been made, which translated themselves into grandiose country estates and houses in Britain, or the kind of institutional bequest that, from the money of the Codringtons in Barbados and Antigua, created the great library at All Souls College, Oxford, which bears their name. The profits from sugar may not have been a necessary condition of Britain's industrial revolution (as some historians of slavery have always maintained), since the amounts available for reinvestment probably did not exceed something like 2 per cent of the capital ploughed into purely industrial undertakings. But equally it's indisputable that the sugar–slave economy had spun off enterprises of immense importance to Britain's dizzying growth. The elegance of eighteenth-century Bristol was paid for by the trade; and the port of Liverpool, which in the 1740s had sent three times as many triangular trade ships to Africa and the Caribbean as London, owed its expansion entirely to it. The great banking houses of Barclays and Lloyds were equally the creation of the Atlantic trade, but were afterwards able to provide capital to the manufacturers of England and Scotland. While Indian calicoes had once been among the exports shipped from Britain to Africa in exchange for slaves, the huge demand there for brilliant printed cottons was now supplied almost entirely by more cheaply produced British textiles. And the demand for the ancillary products of the sugar industry—molasses, rum and treacle—worked to tie together not just the West Indies and Britain but the continental American colonies and the Caribbean as well.

In the 1750s the swaggering plutocrats who embodied the West India fortunes—William Beckford and Christopher Codrington (the Governor of the Leeward Islands), the Pinneys and

242

the Lascelles—began to throw their weight around back home at Westminster and in the corporation of the City of London. But although the older grandees of the counties may have looked down their noses at the pushy vulgarity of these nouveaux riches, they could not have denied their critical importance to the fate of the empire of the three oceans.

Yet despite what, to most jealous outsiders, seemed its outrageous share of good fortune, at that time the West India lobby did nothing but grumble about the difficulties it faced in preserving the sugar empire. The price of sugar was going down, it asserted, while the price of slaves was going up. Neither was precisely true. Sugar prices had indeed halved between 1713 and 1733 (the low point), but had recovered again by the end of the 1740s. If it was hard to work up sympathy for their purported plight as they bought yet another country house and raked in over 10 per cent annual profits on their investments, there was one item in their litany of complaints that did touch a raw nerve in Britain: fear of the French. For the British attitude towards the impertinence of French imperial competition managed to be arrogant and paranoid at the same time. For many of the apologists and tub-thumpers of Britannia's dominion of the seas, the mere idea of a French commercial empire was a comical oxymoron, for how could a nation so notoriously constituted from craven slaves of papist absolutism be taken seriously as entrepreneurial colonizers? (Never mind the fact that when Malachy Postlethwayt wanted to find a 'Dictionary of Commerce' to plagiarize for his own English version, *The*

Universal Dictionary of Trade and Commerce (1751), he went to a French original.) Mysteriously, the evidence in the 1730s and 1740s pointed ominously to the rapid creation of a French empire in India and America but, especially in the Caribbean, that was becoming so successful so quickly that it seemed to the alarmists like a dagger pointed at the heart of the British imperial future.

They were right to worry. For although the French were late-comers at the colonial table, at least in the boom sector of the West Indies, they more than compensated by the concentrated energy they brought to profit-making. As the British planters never failed to remind the home government, they had the advantage of being able, through the dynastic alliance of the Bourbon monarchs in France and Spain, to piggy-back their settlements in the Caribbean on older Spanish naval bases and colonies. No *guarda costas* were going to board French slavers or sugar ships to damage the property and persons of their cargo or crew.

By the 1740s, in fact, there were signs that the productivity of the French Caribbean sugar empire was beginning to outstrip that of the British. The French had their own slaver fleets built and fitted out at the dynamically growing port of Nantes at the mouth of the Loire; and they possessed their own locked-up sources of supply on the Gambia and in Senegal, pushing the British traders east into the Bight of Benin. In St Domingue, the western half of Spanish Hispaniola, they had a land area incomparably bigger than any of the British islands, even Jamaica; it was cut with rivers, which made the freight of goods easier and cheaper, and boasted both flat coastal plains and cooler uplands. The French plantations seem from the beginning to have been more productive than the British. At any rate they grew and shipped enough sugar to undercut prices in Europe, virtually taking that market away from Britain. And the French Caribbean was also more diversified, exporting coffee, cotton and indigo back home for profitable re-export.

As if this were not bad enough, there was also evidence that the French were being insolent enough to make inroads into the British colonial system of trade, encouraging British American ships to smuggle their own rum and molasses into British America and undercutting exports from Barbados and the Leeward Islands. So when the makers and keepers of British macro-economic policy looked at a map of the world, they could see only serious trouble coming from France. On the coast of southeast India, it's true, the erstwhile juvenile delinquent and disgruntled clerk turned military adventurer Robert Clive, together with Stringer Lawrence commanding the tiny army of the East India Company, had managed to thwart a French attempt to lock up the Carnatic as their own exclusive commercial satellite state. But the lesson in that vicious little war had been that a commercial edge was not protected by trade alone. The French were prepared, indeed they shrewdly assumed, the need to play politics with Indians (whether they were the Native Americans in North America or the Nawabs in the Carnatic), to offer their 'protection' in return for the ejection of the British. If that cost money and lives, so be it. What, then, were the British to do? Flinch from the

245

challenge on grounds of expense and dangerous entanglements and concede the territory to the ambitious French? Or respond, as the gung-ho commanders of the East India Company had done, in kind, give the enemy a bloody nose and post the Keep Out sign on the Indian Ocean? Needless to say, the government at home, presided over by the judicious Pelhams—Henry in the Commons, the Duke of Newcastle in the Lords—were more mindful of oceans of red ink than of blue-water imperialism. What they wanted was damage limitation. The treaty of Aix-la-Chapelle in 1748, which returned Madras to the British and the fort of Louisbourg, commanding the mouth of the St Lawrence north of Nova Scotia, to the French, seemed like just such a rational accommodation—a sensible division of spheres of influence. But no one who was thinking with any honesty or seriousness about global economic strategy could have been fooled. This was a breathing space, not a peace.

No one recognized with more pessimistic clarity that this was a moment of truth in the history of British power than William Pitt. It's easy enough to suppose that he had been born to imperial vision, being the grandson of Thomas 'Diamond' Pitt, the commercial interloper turned Governor of Madras who had become famous for hawking his 410-carat uncut rock for a mere £20,400, a price he described as 'cheap as neck beef'. (By a sublime irony it wound up at Versailles.) But the Pitts were not, despite the give-'em-hell career of the magpie governor, classic imperialist adventurers. They were, rather, country gentry from Dorset and Hampshire who numbered Elizabethan and

Jacobean exchequer officials in their lineage. And they played politics by the rules. The rotten borough of Old Sarum, once the site of the Norman palace where William the Conqueror had been presented with the Domesday Book, but now just so much rubble in a field, was their very own pocket constituency. And though 'Diamond' Pitt had been a furious Whig, his son Robert, to his blustering father's outrage, turned Tory. Young William, by contrast, became a Whig and was to prove himself in politics by being a noisy nuisance to the Walpole interest.

William Pitt was not made for a quiet life. Even during his political apprenticeship friends and adversaries alike noticed that his moods alternated between elated bursts of hyperactive, hyper-articulate energy and deep troughs of paralysing gloom and despair. Contemporaries put this emotional oscillation down to the early signs of gout. And Pitt was certainly a sufferer from a disease that caused him a lot of joint pain. But the description of his switchback alterations of temper also corresponds very closely to the classic symptoms of manic depression, a behavioural disorder that seems to have afflicted an extraordinary number of those pantheonized as the builders of the British Empire, among them James Wolfe and Richard Wellesley.

Pitt's chosen form of neurotic release was the spoken word, delivered in the 'torrents' that so unnerved those who got in its way. It so happened that Pitt's fame as an orator occurred precisely at a time when an interest in Latin rhetoric, in particular in Longinus' treatise *On the Sublime*, with its self-conscious manipulation of the effects

247

of terror and rapture, was much in vogue. No one was more conscious than Pitt that rhetoric was not just an academic art but a potent weapon too in contemporary politics. 'Arm yourself,' he wrote to his undergraduate nephew, Thomas, 'with all the variety of manner, copiousness and beauty of diction, nobleness and magnificence of ideas of the great Roman consuls; and render the powers of eloquence complete by the irresistible torrent of vehement argumentation, the close and forcible reasoning and the depth and fortitude of mind of the Grecian statesman.' Though no one disputed Pitt's often frightening vehemence, he was at his strongest when dropping into an otherwise orotund turn of phrase a pearl or two of perfectly calculated malice. Carteret, once his ally in the anti-Walpole coalition, was now the Hanoverian troop minister 'who had renounced the British nation and seemed to have drunk of the potion described in poetic fictions which made men forget their country'. Listening to him, the Commons became the Colosseum as much as the Forum, and the benches full of overgrown schoolboys watched gleefully as Pitt, tall and statuesque in posture (despite the gout), pointed his beaky nose at some unfortunate time-server, trapped him in the net of his irony and then jabbed away with Britannia's trident.

Even Seneca took a job, though. Conscious of this reputation for Roman uprightness, but hungry for advancement, in 1746 Pitt did something guaranteed to put him in a league of his own. He accepted a government office from the Pelhams, but refused its most lucrative perks. It was not just any office, but the Paymaster-Generalship of the army, one of the juiciest jobs that could possibly have come his way. Through the Paymaster's office went payments for military contracts. Into the Paymaster's pocket went the odd percentage or two for favouring this or that supplier. So turning his nose up at the customary rewards was a flamboyant way to disarm accusations that the patriot had sold out to the hacks. Drawing on the Bolingbroke playbook, Pitt ostentatiously deposited the Pay Office balance (from which Paymasters had been known to siphon the occasional thousand or two) in the Bank of England and declined the usual commission owed to him on arranging a military subsidy for the duchy of Savoy.

Pitt's cultivated pose as the lonely patriot may actually have been more solitary than he would have ideally liked. If he had been betting that he could forgo the windfalls of office because, with George II in his seventies, the bountiful reign of Frederick and his trusted ministers was about to dawn, Pitt was in for a brutal disappointment. His patrons were vanishing. Cobham died in 1749 and Frederick two years later, while the king, who made no secret of his dislike for Pitt, dismayingly soldiered on. In the end it didn't matter. For Pitt's sense of himself as a man meant to steer the course of British history was not, in fact, a sham. He was not a fake Cicero in a bad perruque but, for better or worse, a genuine visionary. And what he saw in his visions—obsessively—was America. Though his grandfather evidently had seen something irresistible (all those glinting carats) about Asia, and though Pitt himself was close to West Indian sugar plutocrats like Beckford, he was convinced that it was America that would be the proving-ground of the empire of liberty. What happened in

America would demonstrate whether the British Empire were to be not much more than an amusement for the tourists at Stowe or a dominion that would change the world.

Like everyone else who cared about naval power, Pitt subscribed to the conventional wisdom that, unless Britain controlled its home waters, its 'liberties' and security would never be truly assured. But unlike more conservative strategists, he also believed that the battle for commercial supremacy (which in the end would determine whether Catholic absolutism or parliamentary government would dominate the world) had to be taken to the French in America if it were to be decisively won. And like the West-Indian planters and the American colonists, Pitt did not think that time was on Britain's side. St Domingue, Martinique and Guadeloupe had already robbed Britain of its European re-export market, and now the massive fortress on Cape Breton Island at the mouth of the St Lawrence threatened the security of the priceless New England fishing industry. (Salt cod, sent to the West Indies, was about the only protein, other than beans, in the slave diet, and in return New England imported rum and molasses.) Pitt entirely subscribed to the view, coming out of America itself, that the French were engaged in a slow but systematic strangulation of British economic and political power in the New World. Native Americans were being suborned to deny New England trappers their share of the fur trade. Today it was beaver, tomorrow America.

So he was happy when a largely volunteer army under Governor William Shirley of Massachusetts, together with a small naval squadron, actually

250

succeeded in taking the major fort of Louisbourg in 1745—one of the few undisputed successes of 'King George's War'. A year later he supported the Duke of Bedford's memorandum urging a more general attack on Canada, to destroy the French fur trade with the Indians and rob it of mast timber for its navy. But not only was the attack shelved—too fraught with danger, too expensive; in the peace negotiations in 1748 Louisbourg was returned to France.

The problem of French America, as Pitt would come to recognize, was in fact much more serious than the battle over the St Lawrence and the eastern seaboard. It was, in essence, the battle for living space. The man who saw most clearly how high the stakes were was the scientist and practical man of letters Benjamin Franklin. His *Observations Concerning the Increase of Mankind* were written in 1751 (though not published until 1755) and went to the heart of what British America was to be. There were already upwards of 1.2 million people living in its several colonies, and that number, through natural increase, could be expected to double within a generation; so British America had to be expansive or it would atrophy in self-destructive claustrophobia. In other words, Franklin shared with the boosters of empire in Britain a conviction that it was an empire of liberty. But Franklin's American liberty was not just so much Whig hot air; it was material and territorial. He could see with a precision rivalled only by the French philosopher de Montesquieu the relationship between geography, demography and freedom; that in America (unlike crowded England) the availability of land gave material meaning to the ideal of self-sufficiency.

And in his Britophil innocence Franklin, at least the Franklin of 1751, assumed that these sunny horizons would be shared by the guardians of the imperial future at home. When, in a century, the population of America actually surpassed that of the metropolis, a population dispersed over who knew how much of the continental landmass, such a moment, he supposed, could only be an occasion for shared celebration: 'What an accession of power to the British Empire by sea as well as land! What increase of trade and navigation! What numbers of ships and seamen.'

There was, however, something other than British obtuseness and self-interest in the way of realizing Franklin's dream of a westward-ho empire of freedom, and that was French strategy. French settlement in America consisted of three regions: 'New France' (Canada), from the St Lawrence to the Great Lakes; the mid-Mississippi 'Illinois country' (claimed as a result of a French expedition, by Sieur de la Salle, to the Mississippi delta in 1682); and Louisiana at its delta. They were all, of course, separated from each other by vast distances, and it was the determination of the ministers of Louis XV and especially his governors in Quebec to connect them with a chain of roads, navigated rivers, portage trails and forts. Critical to making the first connection between Canada and the Mississippi was the broad stretch of territory between the Alleghenies and Lake Erie known as the 'Ohio Country'. And it was in this densely forested land, crossed by rivers and peopled by Native American tribes, such as the Shawnees, Delawares and Mingos—roughly the region of modern eastern Ohio and western Pennsylvania—

that the fate of America would be decided.

The Virginians—who claimed that the hinterland of America, all the way to the Pacific, including 'the island of California', had been included in their original charter of 1609—had formed the Virginian Ohio Company in 1747, to survey and lay claim to trans-Appalachian lands. And the mid-Atlantic colonies—New York, New Jersey, Pennsylvania, Delaware and Maryland, whose own populations had boomed in the first half of the eighteenth century, were themselves acutely interested in preventing the French and their Native American allies moving south from Canada, robbing them of the fur trade there and pre-empting territory for westward expansion. The word most commonly used of French designs (and there were few more damning in the lexicon of colonial competition) was 'artful': the artful extension of 'lines within our colonies'; the artful seduction of the Native Americans to deny the British their proper share of fish and furs. But behind all that art was brute force, the application of a deadly choke-hold, crushing the life out of British America. The time had come to resist or expire.

In 1744 the Treaty of Lancaster was signed at Newtown in Lancaster County, Pennsylvania, and solemnized by the presentation of belts of wampum (freshwater shells used as currency) between commissioners of the British colonies and the Six Iroquois Nations. The Native Americans were given free passage across the British territories to hunt down their tribal enemies like the Cherokee and in return appeared to cede sovereignty over virtually the entire Ohio Country. Trying to remain

253

neutral in the Anglo–French wars, the Iroquois soon indignantly repudiated any suggestion that they had permanently alienated their rights over this enormous area; but it was enough to send a wave of trappers and mappers into the Ohio Country to stake claims for King George, the Ohio Company and not least themselves. The French responded in the ways they knew best, sending out pre-emptive expeditions to lay down little lead plaques on a 3000-mile arc of territory; and followed that in the summer and autumn of 1752 with an intensive campaign of fort building, done on a Roman scale that cost 400 lives and 400 million livres. The French forts may have been built of logs, but, like Fort Duquesne, named after the strategically minded new governor in Quebec, they were serious structures with walls 10–12 feet thick, the corners shaped in the arrowhead projections stipulated in European military text-books, and capable of garrisoning hundreds of men.

By early 1753 the battle of the hatchets and the surveying rods had become official. Even the Duke of Newcastle had become persuaded that something important was at stake in the backwoods of the colonies. The Scottish merchant turned American surveyor Robert Dinwiddie, who was to become Lieutenant-Governor of Virginia in 1754, dispatched a six-foot-two, twenty-one-year-old major with absolutely no command of French to carry a letter to the commandant of Fort Le Boeuf, demanding that the French cease and desist from garrisoning territories self-evidently belonging to King George.

George Washington may have had no French,

but he understood the compelling interests of the British Empire very well. His half-brother Lawrence, after all, had named their property in Virginia 'Mount Vernon', after the hero of Porto Bello, and he first practised his profession as a land surveyor on behalf of the English aristocrat Lord Fairfax, who was the dominant magnate in the northern neck of Virginia. But his early experience of defending those interests was unhappy. At a Native American village on the fork of the Ohio he met up with a French platoon that invited Washington to sup. 'The Wine, as they dos'd themselves pretty plentifully with it, soon banish'd the restraint which at first appeared in their Conversation . . . They told me it was their absolute Design to take Possession of the Ohio & by G— they would do it, for tho they were sensible that the English could raise two men for their one; yet they knew their Motions were too slow and dilatory to prevent any Undertaking of theirs.' At Fort Le Boeuf, Washington had much the same dusty reply, phrased with exquisite courtesy. The following year, 1754, he prepared and led an expedition. An early success (followed by a scalping and general massacre of French prisoners) turned into a much bigger disaster on 4 July, when Washington's soldiers, trapped inside their 'Fort Necessity', found their muskets unusable in a July rainstorm. Leaving wounded and dead behind, they ignominiously marched out from the fort and limped back to Virginia, leaving the French in jubilant command of the Ohio Country.

For those in America and London who were not prepared to accept the French stranglehold on the western frontier, two options were left. Either a counterattack should be mounted by a force raised from all the colonies, in alliance with Indian warriors in substantial numbers. Or a true army, dominated by British regular troops and commanded by a British general, should do the job for them. Franklin, of course, was in favour of the first, more authentically American way and was one of Pennsylvania's representatives at a pan-American congress at Albany in the Hudson Valley, just a week after Washington's débâcle at Fort Necessity. For the first time a working military and political confederation of the British-American colonies was discussed in some detail. But the fires lit by the Albany meeting were immediately doused by the rejection of its agenda by all the separate colonial assemblies, who were too preoccupied with their own sectional interests. (The New Englanders wanted fishery protection; the New Yorkers wanted everyone else to pay for forts guarding their northern frontier.) But the ideals of a federation remained warm inside Franklin's head and heart. Some time during the latter part of 1754 he wrote to Governor Shirley outlining what he hoped for the future of British America. First, the western frontier had to be uncompromisingly defended against the French. But that defence had to be undertaken in a true spirit of the indivisibility of the empire: American citizen-soldiers and British regular soldiers in concord. And if the British government were truly prescient it would understand that its own best interests would be served not by subjecting America but by co-opting it; that it should make good the understanding that Americans were responsible for their own internal government; and that if money were needed for a common defence it ought to come from the consent of their own institutions. Economically, too, the interests of the mother and the children should be seen not as competitive but as complementary, so that the industries of America ought not to be penalized for narrow interests at home but should be regarded as the strength of the common empire.

Franklin's rational and benevolent vision of the British Empire paid its ideological inventors the compliment of taking their rhetoric about liberty at face value. But he presupposed a breadth of understanding, an appreciation of the strengths of American culture and society that had barely impinged on the conscience of the empire-builders at home. Their policies were designed not to respect distance but to abolish it, not to make room for diversity but to impose 'order' and uniformity. By the 1750s, the politicians at Westminster believed they already had a model of orderly, industrious integration, and it was called Scotland.

So naturally it fell to the Duke of Cumberland, the 'Butcher of Culloden', to nominate the general who would take the Ohio Country campaign to the French and sort out, once and for all, who was sovereign. Edward Braddock was the ideal Cumberland protégé: a thorough-going, unsentimental administrator and a stickler for discipline. To show he meant business Braddock would take with him two regiments, the 41st and the 48th. Even the announcement had the British press relishing the assured victory and sketching an early self-portrait of the character of the British Empire: averse to conquest, slow to provoke, but, when roused, frightening in its might. 'We have

257

now shown the world that the Dominion of the Sea is not an empty boast,' trumpeted *Jackson's Oxford Journal*, 'but such a one as we can and dare assert whenever it becomes absolutely necessary. We never disturb our Neighbour with our Intrigues, we never encroach on their Territories. . . . But when we are threatened, deceived and encroached upon ourselves . . . then . . . it [military action] appears to us as Justice.'

The French, it was confidently felt, must be shaking in their shoes. One British force was to retake Louisbourg, denying reinforcements; a second was to capture the forts at Niagara, travelling up the rivers from the Hudson; while Braddock himself would march on Fort Duquesne, where Washington had come to grief. Once that had been dealt with Braddock would advance north, rolling up resistance, and join the Niagara battalions at the lake: simple, decisive, swift. Washington and Franklin met the general at Frederickstown in Maryland just before the march of his two regiments. Washington went as aide-de-camp on the strength of his knowledge of the country, and Franklin had provided a spectacular token of Pennsylvania's appreciation of British protection by supplying each officer with the equivalent of the imperial pantry: 6 pounds of rice, raisins, chocolate, coffee and sugar; a pound each of green and Bohea black tea; half a pound of pepper; a whole Gloucester cheese; 20 pounds of best butter; two hams; 2 gallons of Jamaica rum and two dozen bottles of Madeira. This was what made it worth being British.

Unfortunately it was also what doomed Braddock to bloody fiasco on 9 July 1755. It was

258

not just the 150 wagons and 500 packhorses bearing all these supplies that slowed him to a plod en route to the Monongahela forks. It was the necessity of cutting a laborious way through deep forest, widening tracks to make a road wide enough and level enough to get his supply train through without getting into potentially dangerous difficulties. His Mingo Native American guides had doubtless alerted Braddock to these obvious logistical realities, but as a Mingo chief, Scarouady, noted, he treated them barely better than 'dogs'. The dogs could bite. The 'contemptible savages' fighting for the French did not form up in the open like sporting Jacobites to take on Braddock's light infantry, but raked them with fire from invisible positions deep inside the forest. Weakened by dysentery and suffering acutely from haemorrhoids, Braddock let his training as an officer and a gentleman take over. As his boxed-in infantry attempted to return fire into the piny nowhere he remained imperturbable in the saddle, riding the line, encouraging the soldiers even as they fell in hundreds: a deliberately perfect target for the inevitable musket ball in the chest. Down went the redcoats like lead soldiers in text-book platoon formation, their fellows taking their place in the firing line, staying put as they dropped. By the time a modicum of self-preservation took over, and men actually began running for their lives, two-thirds of Braddock's force was dead or critically wounded. The French and their Native American allies had lost just twenty-three dead and sixteen wounded. Braddock died on the retreat and was buried along the road his sappers had cut. George Washington, who took the general's blood-soaked cloak back to Mount Vernon, did not in fact conclude that Braddock had been woefully mistaken in his tactics, only that his men had been inadequate to the task.

If one kind of Cumberland war guaranteed defeat, another, just as depressing, guaranteed a kind of 'success'. In Nova Scotia the Governor, Charles Lawrence, was engaged not just in pacification but in something more ominously modern: mass deportation. By the terms of the Treaty of Utrecht in 1713 the French-Catholic Acadians had been allowed to live peacefully in southern Nova Scotia, on the wrong side of the Anglo-French divide, provided they refrained from actively assisting the enemy. But as the Franco-British conflict in America heated up, their refusal to take a formal oath of loyalty to King George made them seem like a permanent fifth column, egging on the Native Americans to attack the outnumbered British. Lawrence was determined to get to them before they got to him, and set in motion the appalling policy known to the Acadians euphemistically as '*le grand dérangement*'. At least 6000 of them who had been living on the shores of the Bay of Fundy were forcibly uprooted from farms, homes and land, and assembled for trans-shipment to Massachusetts, South Carolina and Virginia. The move was so sudden and so brutal that, even as the boats were being prepared to take them away, they could not quite believe they were 'actually to be removed'. On 8 October the first group was loaded. The British officer in charge wrote: 'Began to embarke the Inhabitants who went of very Solentarily and unwillingly, the women in Great Distress Carrying Off their Children in their Arms, Others Carrying their Decrepit Parents in their carts and all their Goods moving in Great Confusion and appeared a scene of Woe and Distress.' Colonists from New York and Massachusetts took their place in northern Maine and Nova Scotia. Half of the passengers on the first ship to the Carolinas died on board in conditions of extreme filth and hardship. Some thousands managed to escape to Canada, only to find the country changing hands with the imminent Seven Years' War. Another group made a great odyssey down Duquesne's strategic trail on the Mississippi all the way to Louisiana where they finally resettled, exchanging a diet of lobster and cod for crayfish and catfish as Acadian culture metamorphosed into Cajun.

The dogs of war had been unloosed (even if the American tails had wagged them). And from the beginning it was thought of as a world war, even by the habitually cost-conscious Duke of Newcastle. The strategy, though, was not in fact any different from the way in which the war of the 1740s had been fought. There would be a heavily subsidized European ally, Prussia, whose armies would pin the French down in Europe and divert both men and resources away from the imperial theatres in India, West Africa, the Caribbean and America. The bulk of the Royal Navy would, as always, be assigned to guard the home waters and raid and blockade French ports from the Mediterranean up the Atlantic coast, stopping reinforcements from reaching Canada. In America itself, 'long-injured, long-neglected, long-forgotten,' as Pitt said (exaggerating as usual), the old Braddock plan of simultaneously attacking Canada, the upper New

261

York lake fort at Ticonderoga and Fort Duquesne in the heart of the Ohio Country was revived. But along with it came many of the old mistakes. Braddock's replacement as coordinator of these campaigns was yet another Cumberland stop-gap, the Ayrshire aristocrat John Campbell, fourth Earl of Loudoun, whose enthusiasm for the military life had led him to plant a wood resembling a regiment of the line and who came with a retinue of seventeen servants, travelling mistress and mistress's maid. If anything, Loudoun's contempt for the colonials and their savage allies was even more patrician than Braddock's. Convinced that the whole bloody shower needed smartening up, he courted the hatred of American officers by insisting on the War Office policy of ranking Americans far below their counterparts in the regular British regiments and alienated the men by demanding that the British whip-happy code of military discipline (500 lashes for insubordination, 1000 for stealing a shirt) be imposed on the colonial troops who had never seen it, much less endured it. Exasperated by contraband trade between the French-Caribbean and British colonies, Loudoun's answer was to shut down trade altogether.

Loudoun's way of running the war represented a clear choice and the Americans knew it. An alternative would have been to co-opt the colonial troops and the Native Americans in a genuinely imperial coalition. This would mean entrusting the colonial assemblies and their governors with the power to raise men and money in the ways they best saw fit, and the ways best suited to part-time bachelor soldiers who would want to feel assured that when the worst was over they could get back to

262

their farms and forges. Raising funds for these troops, as the governors knew, was better done through consent than by imperious demand. But men like Braddock and Loudoun saw the assemblies and even the governors as mere subalterns to be told what was needed and when and where to deliver it. To allow them any sort of latitude in military affairs, they believed, was to indulge their natural tendency to insubordination, to compromise discipline and to court defeat. Loudoun continually expressed his horrified astonishment that the colonials, especially the 'leading people', presumed to venture criticism or even opinion on imperial strategy. And the raw material of American troops he believed to be unfit for serious combat. Only integrating them into regular regiments and teaching them, fiercely if need be, how real soldiers conducted themselves would create a viable army.

Even though Loudoun had much of his way, defeat came all the same. In India the irrepressible and brutally efficient Robert Clive destroyed Siraj-ud-Daulah, the Nawab of Bengal, handing (whether it wanted them or not) the revenues of the richest province in Mughal India to the East India Company so that it could balance its books. But elsewhere the first two years of the war against France were a procession of disasters. In the Mediterranean Admiral Byng lost the island of Minorca, thought strategically vital for controlling the routes east to Italy and the Levant. Amid an ugly eruption of patriotic fury, Byng was sacrificed by court-martial to spare the government the odium. Worse, Admiral Boscawen's fleet failed to blockade the mouth of the St Lawrence effectively, so that reinforcements and supplies managed to get through to the armies of New France at Quebec and Montreal. On the New York lakes, it was the French and not the British who were on the offensive, capturing Fort William Henry in 1757.

It was the end of Newcastle. Pitt, who had raised a hue and cry for massive mobilization, had been brought into the administration, but kept (not least by the king's mistrust) from real power. At the end of 1757, though, with the prospects looking grim, Pitt was finally given his moment, and he leapt at it with the full conviction of someone who never for a second doubted that God had personally appointed him for the job. Among his first priorities was to make it clear that he would fight an American war the American way and to repair some of the damage done by the likes of Braddock and Loudoun. The latter was ignominiously recalled, and Pitt won friends in the American assemblies by committing the British government to reimburse the colonials for any expenses laid out for equipment and pay. Over £1 million would be earmarked for this. Whole-hearted collaboration instantly replaced surly assent: Massachusetts, for instance, voted for the supply of 7000 volunteer troops. Likewise Pitt repealed Loudoun's invidious weighting of ranks between the regulars and the colonials. Then he threw good men and pots of money at the job in hand. Generals—some of them, like James Wolfe and William Howe, in their thirties—were suddenly promoted, leapfrogging over their seniors. Others, like Jeffrey Amherst in command of the frontal attack on Canada, were given unprecedented troop strength: some 14,000 alone for the attack on

Louisbourg. The French in America could probably put together no more than some 16,000 of their own soldiers together with whatever Native Americans they could mobilize, but those would now be counterbalanced by Mohawks and other tribes among the Iroquois nation who, seeing the writing on the wall, had gravitated towards the British. By the end of 1757 there were nearly 50,000 British imperial troops committed to the war in Canada, almost two-thirds of the entire population of New France. Almost £5.5 million was spent on the American sector of the war alone, £1 million for the navy and another £1 million on fulfilling the promise to pay for colonial troops. Pitt had succeeded in persuading the country that this time the war had to be all or nothing.

And it was to be a British, not an English, war. The first Highland regiment in the British army to serve abroad had been raised and deployed in Europe in 1745—the year of the Jacobite rising. But those soldiers were predominantly drawn from loyal clans like the Campbells. By the time that additional regiments were formed for the American campaign their recruiting zone was much broader. There were Munroes from Galloway and Murrays from Inverness. It has been estimated that by the time the American war began one in four officers in the imperial army were Scots. They were to undergo a murderous baptism of fire.

In early July 1758 the portly General Abercromby (known unpromisingly to his own soldiers as 'granny'), in command of the expedition to take Fort Carillon at Ticonderoga, decided, while a mile distant from the battle site, to send his troops on a suicidal frontal assault without first

265

setting his artillery up on a hill where it might at least have given them covering fire. The result was predictable. The Black Watch and the Inniskillings quick-marched to the sound of bagpipes right into the tangle of sharpened tree-stumps set in front of the breastworks and never exited. A terrified officer in a battalion of Massachusetts volunteers, Archelaus Fuller, flat on the ground behind a log while French musket shot whistled past his ears, described 'a sorful s[ight] to behold, the ded men and wounded lay on the ground having som of them Legs, their arms and other [sic] lims broken, others shot threw the body and very mortly wounded; to hear thar cris and se their bodis lay in blod and the earth trembel with the fier of smal arms was a mournfull [h]our ever I saw'. This carnage continued for eight hours. Nearly 2000 dead and grievously wounded lay around the timber palisades. At sunset, not having heard anything from their officers, the survivors who had had the sense to lie motionless between logs tentatively rose from their brushy cover and disappeared into the woods like raccoons on the run.

Ticonderoga was, though, the first and last real catastrophe of Pitt's war. Only glories followed: first, the fall of great Louisbourg to Amherst and his brigadier James Wolfe in a conventional siege that unloaded such devastating ordnance on the town that it capitulated before it melted. Among those who witnessed the triumph was the thirteen-year-old Olaudah Equiano, who some years before had been bought by a sea captain, Michael Henry Pascal, as his page and servant. When Pascal went to serve in the Royal Navy in 1756, Olaudah went with him and found himself aboard the same ship as Wolfe en route to Cape Breton. At the end of the siege he was flooded with a kind of terrible wonder at the strange terrors of war: 'A lieutenant of the *Princess Amelia* [one of the ships] was giving the word of command and while his mouth was open a musket ball went through it and passed out his cheek. I had that day in my hand the scalp of an Indian king, killed in the engagement: the scalp was taken off by a Highlander.' Holding the scalp of an Indian king who had been killed by a Highlander, Equiano was getting an accelerated education in the multi-national empire.

The Native Americans would remain adversaries. But the former physician Brigadier John Forbes, yet another Scot, who had been assigned to the Ohio Country campaign, assembled representatives of the Cherokees and Delawares, as well as other tribes, and brought enough of them over in a treaty agreement to make the capture of Fort Duquesne merely a matter of time. The French removed what they could of its munitions and blew it up. The fort settlement built in its place was called Pittsburgh.

In Europe Frederick the Great was more than holding his own against the French and their allies, which was just as well since £200,000 had been allotted annually for his subsidy! But what was a mere £200,000 when everything suddenly seemed to be going Britain's way? Towards the end of 1758, parliament enacted a military budget for the coming year of £12.5 million—a sum that had never before been conceivable, much less granted. Half-borrowed, half-taxed, it sustained an army of 90,000, a navy of over 70,000, a territorial militia of between 30,000 and 40,000. It bought victory.

Sitting on top of all this bounty, Pitt could play around with the world. A raid on West Africa took French slave stations at Gorée and the Gambia; an expedition to the Caribbean, after some real difficulty, ended up taking Guadeloupe with its 40,000 slaves and 350 plantations. Within a year (to the consternation of British planters in Jamaica and Barbados, who were not at all sure they wanted this particular conquest) Guadeloupe sugar was flooding into the London market. In Bengal, Clive (if not the East India Company) was drowning in 'presents' offered by rival Indian nawabs. And in south India, an opportunistic attempt by the Comte de Lally to re-establish a strong military presence on the Coromandel coast was undermined by the inability of the French marine to break a British blockade.

All this, however, was but a sideshow to the main event, which, for Pitt after 1761, became the definitive conquest of Canada. Once this was accomplished, he believed there would be no stopping the future of British America, and by extension British power, which was to say, as he and the graduates of Stowe understood it, British liberty. The elements seemed to be helping, for Canada had suffered almost famine conditions in 1758, and the winter of 1758–9 was the most brutally cold in memory. With Louisbourg and Cape Breton Island fallen to the British, its plight would be desperate unless it was somehow resupplied. In the early spring of 1759 a few ships did manage to cut a path through the ice at the mouth of the St Lawrence, sneak past the British blockade and land some reinforcements and food

268

at Quebec. This breath of life convinced the Governor, the Marquis de Montcalm, to entrench himself on the easily defensible Heights of Abraham at Quebec along with all the manpower he could muster—perhaps 16,000, including Canadian militia—and defy the British, also suffering from shortage of supplies, to come and get him. An alternative strategy would have been to evacuate the city, disperse troops to several different centres and settle down for a partisan war in a country whose natives and settlers could be relied on to be bitterly hostile to the British. But Montcalm's view carried the day at Versailles.

Amherst's was always the main army. But back in London James Wolfe succeeded in persuading Pitt to let him attempt an assault from the St Lawrence. Giving Wolfe 20,000 troops, Pitt perhaps felt he had nothing to lose. But for Wolfe destiny was calling. Sick with consumption, he was already seeing himself carved in marble on a patriot's tomb. But en route to passion play on the Plains of Abraham he very nearly failed in his plan for immortality. Hungry or not, Montcalm refused to be drawn from his massive defences around Quebec, his own bastions reinforced by the precipitous 200-foot bluffs on one side to the river and an equally sheer rock face on the inland side. Thwarted, Wolfe let his soldiers and Native Americans loose on a campaign of ferocious 'cruelty and devastation' on the surrounding countryside. If this were meant to goad Montcalm into emerging, out of concern or anger, it was an abysmal failure. All the French commander had to do was sit tight through the autumn and wait for the ice to close in on the river, trapping Wolfe or

269

forcing him to retreat.

Something desperate was called for, so desperate that no one, not even Wolfe, seriously imagined it could work: a night-time ascent straight up the cliffs along a ravine trail identified by one Robert Stobo, who had been captured during Washington's failed attack on Fort Necessity and had lived in Quebec under easy half-imprisonment for some years before escaping to the British lines. It was only on the eve of the attack that Wolfe deigned to let his brigadiers, with whom he was barely on speaking terms, know what he had in mind. The idea was to feint downstream east of the city but sail in the opposite direction west, then allow the tide to drift thirty flat-bottom landing boats back down to the landing point. At five in the morning, the first hundreds of men scrambled up the slopes. There was a skirmish at the top, but not the all-out battle Wolfe had been assuming. The French soldier who brought news to the garrison at Quebec was unsure whether the British had stayed or gone back the way they came—the venture seemed so bizarre. Wolfe himself was astonished at getting 4800 troops and two cannon atop the Plains, where he lined them up, a scarlet ribbon extending half a mile across the plateau from one cliff to the other. He was set right between Montcalm and his supply lines and reinforcements, all now west of Wolfe. With food and munitions running out, and absolutely no room to manoeuvre around the rear of the British without dropping off the edge, Montcalm was dumbfounded by what had happened. Listening to the British drums and fifes, he realized he had no choice but to engage in something seldom seen in

America: a formal battle. But if the troops he had sent west could be recalled in time, the advantage would suddenly be reversed. Wolfe's line would be trapped between two French forces with no route for retreat except back over the cliff.

By nine o'clock there was no sign of French troops from the west, and the cannon Wolfe had brought were doing damage to the French line. Highland pipes were skirling in the rain. Montcalm could wait no longer. His own numbers matched Wolfe's, but half of them were Canadian militia. They were supposed to advance in drill-order at a steady pace towards the British, halt at about 150 yards and then fire; but when given the order, the militia ran virtually at will towards the thin lines of immobile British troops, making any kind of coordinated advance, let alone re-forming after the inevitable counter-volley, impossible. Wolfe, whose wrist had been shattered by a musket ball, used his other arm to hold his soldiers back until the French had reached as close as 40 yards. The British couldn't miss. An immense volley of fire, 'like cannon', both sides said, tore huge holes in both the white-coated French regulars and the militia. When the smoke cleared they were in full retreat. Wolfe took shot in his guts and another in his chest, realizing the hero's consummation he had been so determined to achieve. He would get his marble sepulchre in the Abbey. As soon as the news reached England, wrote Horace Walpole, people 'despaired—they triumphed—and they wept—for Wolfe had fallen in the hour of victory! Joy, grief, curiosity and astonishment were painted in every countenance.' His cult was a gift to Pitt, who in the House of Commons delivered an oration that was, in effect, an elegy over the bier of a fallen hero from antiquity. Only—as the Stowe 'patriot boys' always wanted—this was better than Rome.

There were other more prosaic, but more decisive, events to come, none more so than Admiral Hawke's destruction in Quiberon Bay off Brittany of a French Brest fleet still capable of threatening a Britain defended mostly by militiamen. The French held out in Canada much longer than anyone supposed after the battle on the Heights of Abraham. It was only the following year, in the summer of 1760, that, finally robbed of any chance of reinforcement and supply, the French Governor, Vaudreuil, capitulated to Amherst at Montreal. Part of his incentive to do so, rather than fight on, was the fairly generous terms offered by Amherst. The 70,000-odd Canadians were required to remain neutral in any future conflict between Britain and France, but in return were to be allowed free practice of their Roman Catholic religion and even the guaranteed appointment of a diocesan bishop for Quebec. As Vaudreuil must have correctly calculated, French-Canadian culture and identity, if not its political existence, would be preserved for generations to come.

Voltaire may have written Canada off as 'a few acres of snow'. But its conquest utterly transformed the sense of the future for the British Empire. Franklin, for one, who since 1757 had been living in London as the commissioner of the Pennsylvania Assembly, was exhilarated and campaigned furiously against any thought of its return. Taking in the storm of patriotic celebrations, the bonfires and the bell-ringing, the feasts and the renderings of Garrick's 'Hearts of Oak' that erupted throughout the country—especially in Scotland—Franklin was utterly convinced of the momentous righteousness of the war. 'If ever there was a national war,' he wrote, 'this is truly such a one, a war in which the interest of the whole nation is directly and fundamentally concerned.' In the *annus mirabilis* of 1759, when triumph followed triumph, and, as Horace Walpole boasted, 'our bells are worn threadbare with ringing of victories', Franklin travelled to Scotland where he made friends with the learned nobleman and writer on political economy and agriculture Henry Home, Lord Kames. To Kames Franklin must have confided his bursting pride on what had happened and the prospect it opened up of the realization of the indivisible empire of liberty. Had he not signed his petition to parliament 'A Briton'? To Kames, he wrote, 'I have long been of the opinion that the foundations of the future grandeur and stability of the British Empire lie in America; and though, like other foundations, they are low and little seen, they are nevertheless broad and strong enough to support the greatest political structure human wisdom ever yet erected.' Just seventeen years later he would put his signature to the Declaration of Independence. What happened?

Peace, in 1763, brought disenchantment. Olaudah Equiano had spent his adolescence on Royal Navy warships as one of the boys who ran for powder for the guns while colossal ships of the line burst into flames. He had watched boys and men torn apart by cannon-balls or pierced by splintering timbers 'and launched into eternity'. At the siege of Belleisle he saw 'above sixty shells and carcasses in the air at once'. Alternately terrified and elated, baptized a Christian, learning to read and write, acquiring books and a Bible, Olaudah had been led by his master, Pascal, to believe that when it all ended he was going to walk away from the terror and slaughter a free man. Instead he found Pascal first accusing him of attempting to run away and then, over his tears and angry grievance, reselling him to a captain who took him to the West Indies. 'Thus, at the moment I expected my toils to end, was I plunged . . . into a new slavery.' Pascal had robbed him of his books, his personal belongings, his only coat—and his hard-won dignity. In bitter distress—and knowing he was bound for the West Indies—Equiano wrote, 'I reproached my fate and wished I had never been born.'

William Pitt was in less extreme straits, but he too was angry, sick and miserable much of the time. On 25 October 1760, George II, who at the very end of his life had finally come to appreciate, rather than despise, Pitt, had finally died of a heart attack. Only good things were expected from his grandson and successor. He had been tutored by a friend of Pitt's, the Scot Lord Bute, in the precepts of Bolingbroke's *Patriot King*. The influence of his mother, the Dowager Princess Augusta, was equally obvious. Unlike his excessively Hanoverian predecessors, George III proudly and publicly 'gloried in the name of Briton'. His apparent artlessness seemed the very model of a Patriot. Doubtless his bust would shortly join the pantheon at Stowe. But in no time at all, Pitt was disabused of virtually all these assumptions. The friend Bute turned into an unfriendly rival, more sympathetic to those who wanted an exit from a war now thought cripplingly expensive. Pitt's obsessive determination to see the French not merely damaged and humiliated but annihilated as a potential imperial competitor, and his goal of destroying Spanish power in the Caribbean as well, looked increasingly irrational. The young king, it seemed, was listening to his tutor and shared his view of the 'mad' Pitt. Worse, the Stowe family was breaking up. When Pitt was forced out in 1761, the new Viscount Temple and one of his brothers-in-law, James Grenville, went with him, but George Grenville, who had become Bute's and Newcastle's poster boy in the Commons, did not. Pitt treated this as a betrayal, and for the next decade the two would be harsh political enemies. In 1763, when the Peace of Paris was signed, Pitt believed that Bute had sold out the interests of the Empire by returning Martinique, Guadeloupe and St Lucia to France, Havana and Manila to Spain, and by restoring the right of the French to fish the precious cod banks off Newfoundland, safeguarded by their possession of St Pierre and Miquelon in the St Lawrence.

But a glance at the map—and British statesmen did more than glance at it—must have confirmed their doubts about Pitt's sanity. The planters of Jamaica and Barbados were eager to restore, not retain, the sugar islands of Martinique and Guadeloupe before they outsold them in the vital American market as well as in domestic markets; and hanging on to a fishing monopoly was not going to alter the inescapable fact that, for all its recent disasters, France was still—demographically and militarily—the pre-eminent power in Europe. Inflicting a Carthaginian peace would only quicken the desire for revenge. When government ministers considered the immense extent of the newly enlarged Empire, from Bengal to Senegal, from Minorca to Montreal—elation at the fact that Britons, as Horace Walpole exulted, had been able to 'subdue the globe in three campaigns', whereas the Romans had taken three centuries, was necessarily tempered with a deep anxiety about how to pay for its defence. The enormous wartime army of over 90,000 had now been halved, but even at that strength was a crippling financial burden on a Treasury groggy with debt. Peacetime had also brought economic dislocation: there was a banking crash in Amsterdam whose effects rippled through the closely connected London money market, making credit suddenly tight; and the demobilization of vast numbers put pressure on employment at the same time that labour-intensive industries had to be cut back to pre-war levels. Harvests were poor, prices high; the populace in ports and towns more than usually riotous. A new round of excise duties on consumer goods would only make an already dangerous situation worse.

So it was inevitable that George Grenville, who succeeded the deeply unpopular Bute as First Lord of the Treasury in August 1763 (to the express disadvantage of Pitt, who had been approached for a return), should turn his tidy mind to the challenge of having the American empire—which he supposed could best afford it—pay for the costs of its own defence. The logic of it must have seemed incontrovertible. Had not British America benefited immeasurably from the war? Had not money poured into its trade and industries from the mother country during the campaigns? Were not its prospects, with the immense territory of Canada added, bright? But now there had to be some sort of reckoning. First, the basic, self-evidently dependent relationship of the colonies to the home country, in which the former existed to supply Britain with raw materials while consuming its manufactures, needed to be restated and reinforced. Whatever Benjamin Franklin thought, no illusions should be held that Britain would tolerate, much less encourage, the growth of American manufactures that might compete with its own, nor would it look kindly on foreign countries that did so, least of all France and Spain, and their colonies. Secondly, if the costs of defending the American empire were not to become uncontrollable, the region of settlement had to be limited to lands east of the Appalachians; lands further to the west must henceforth be reserved to the Native Americans, without whose goodwill continuing and expensive trouble would be guaranteed. Thirdly, it seemed only equitable that the American colonies, for whose benefit it was constituted, should pay for their own defence through some form of additional revenue.

Just what those revenues should be deeply exercised the fastidious Grenville. On looking through the books of the American customs and excise he was appalled to discover that their operating costs were much heavier than their yield. The conclusion was certainly not to abolish them, but to impose a new substantial duty on the foreign commodity most in demand in America. And that, of course, was French sugar, in particular the Caribbean molasses needed for distilling into the ubiquitous American food staple—rum. (British

Caribbean molasses was inadequate in supply and high in price.) Grenville's proposed duty was sixpence a gallon. When protests—especially loud from the rum-happy New England colonies—were voiced, he cut it in half but backed it up by aggressive, quasi-military customs enforcement. In 1761, at the height of the Seven Years' War, when trading with the enemy was deemed a form of economic sabotage, 'writs of assistance' had been used to search and try smugglers in vice-admiralty courts (since colonial ones seemed reluctant to convict them). Now, to the anger and dismay of the commercial communities in Boston and New York—where smuggling was a way of life—those courts were to be continued in peacetime.

The trouble for Grenville—did he but know it—was that he was making trouble for the best-read smugglers in the world. And what they read was history: English history, the epic history of English liberty, the very same history that Grenville himself had so innocently admired in the park at Stowe. Inside the reading clubs of Boston and Philadelphia, and in the Societies for Encouraging Commerce, the crackdown on contraband, the heavy hand of the customs men and the special jurisdiction of the 'vice-admiralty' courts all triggered instant memories of Star Chamber. To resist them was to summon the noble shade of Hampden to defend the imperishable rights of free-born Britons. 'If our Trade may be taxed, why not our lands?' asked speakers at the Boston Town Meeting in the spring of 1764, scenting the whiff of tyranny. 'Why not the produce of our lands and everything we possess or make use of? This . . . strikes at our British privileges which, as we have never forfeited them, we hold in common with our fellow subjects who are natives of Britain.'

And if the Sugar Act (1764) goaded them to complaint, Grenville's second really bright idea—a stamp tax to be imposed on paper used for all manner of articles from playing cards and newspapers to legal documents, broadsheets and advertisements—was the imperial equivalent of Charles I raising his standard at Nottingham. Grenville congratulated himself on the genius of the stamp tax because, unlike customs duties, it was, he thought, self-administering, free of onerous and abrasive searches. The duty would be paid on pre-stamped paper before it was used for whatever purpose. The bill had its first reading in the Commons (before a half-empty House) in early February 1765, and Grenville announced that it would not come into force until November to give time for representations from the colonies. Since, for all their grumbling, most of the colonies had in the end swallowed the Sugar Act, Grenville was still confident that the Stamp Act (1765) would be accepted as well. He had estimated it might bring in £100,000 in the first year, much more in later years. He certainly could have had no idea that he had just inaugurated the beginning of the end of British America.

But then Grenville, like most of his contemporaries in Britain, even those who imagined themselves well read, broad-minded and well travelled, really knew pitifully little about the reality of the American colonies. Those few Americans (like Franklin) with whom they had occasion to come into contact in London were, by definition, those who had the strongest affinity with

279

Britain. Those with whom they had official business as governors in Boston or Williamsburg usually told them what they wanted to hear: indeed often encouraged them in taking a hard line with the colonists to discourage the signs of insubordination and presumptuous liberty they had noticed during the recent wars. When the politicians in London imagined America they imagined, largely, English men and women obediently transplanted. Sometimes they imagined Scots and Presbyterian Irish—but then those countrymen had served the Empire well in its army. Very seldom did they think of about 80,000 Pennsylvania Germans, 40,000 New York and Hudson Valley Dutch, and many other populations —Quakers, Jews, African slaves—all of whom made America a much more heterogeneous, much less Anglo-pinko place than could be imagined at Westminster.

Nor from the fastness of Westminster could they imagine the electrifying intensity of local politics in towns like Philadelphia and Boston. In Boston, 2500 men out of a total population of some 16,000 were entitled to vote at the Town Meeting, whose sessions at Faneuil Hall were rowdily eloquent. Pitt and his generation liked to imagine themselves so many Ciceros. But Boston really was the size of the optimum face-to-face neo-Athenian democracy imagined by Rousseau in the 1760s; and its orators—James Otis, Sam Adams, Josiah Quincy and John Hancock—believed they were so many Demostheneses. Least of all did it really occur to the likes of Grenville and the Whig politicians that somehow the liberty-canon of British history might actually be turned against them—that they would now be cast as Laud and Judge Jeffreys—and that one day some young Virginian would be trawling through the Declaration of Rights of 1689 for a list of accusations to level at King George III.

And in truth that day was still far off. But the fact that Boston, especially, was a book-crazy, news-hungry, astonishingly literate (70 per cent for men, 45 per cent for women), habitually litigious place, with a strong religious disposition to see the world in terms of the embattled forces of good and evil, doomed the Stamp Act from the beginning. The city prided itself on its civic culture: its grammar schools and colleges, gazettes and libraries. And its educated leaders made conscious efforts to reach a popular audience. John Adams, for instance, wrote his articles on the errors and iniquities of British administration in the *Boston Gazette* under the pseudonym 'Humphrey Ploughjogger.' This was the kind of thing that would have been meat and drink to shopkeepers like Harbottle Dorr who read the *Gazette* avidly, scanned its woodcut illustrations and made copious commentaries about the stories that fed his indignation. With a population of 16,000 it was also a city small enough to place a high value on the transparency of politics. John Adams spoke for many in 1765 when he insisted that 'the people have a right, an indisputable, unalienable right, an indefatigable right to that most dreaded and envied kind of knowledge, I mean of the character and conduct of their rulers.' To such Bostonians, the Stamp Act seemed to announce not just an illegal tax but also a gag on the production and distribution of free political information. Yet for all

281

these glaring sources of grievance, no one, least of all the Lieutenant-Governor and Chief Justice of Massachusetts, Thomas Hutchinson (who always had his doubts about the wisdom of the Stamp Act), had the slightest inkling of what was about to happen.

It is true that he ought to have been worried about being hanged in effigy at the 'Liberty Tree' on 14 August 1765. But Hutchinson was used to symbolic demonstrations of hatred. On the 26th the action became much more physically immediate. A riot of extraordinary savagery tore apart his elegant house in Boston, including its cupola, and threw his manuscript history in the dirt. Had he not fled on the desperate pleading of his daughter, the incensed crowd would probably have torn him apart too. There was a long tradition of rowdy, drunken street fighting in Boston, especially when rival gangs from the North and South End celebrated 'Pope's Day'(5 November) with their annual, violent football match. But on this occasion, and on Pope's Day 1765, crowds of tanners, dockers, seamen and carpenters who lived around the harbour combined forces, and with very specific targets in mind: Hutchinson and the distributor of the stamps, his brother-in-law Andrew Oliver. The mob had evidently been mobilized by men like the twenty-eight-year-old cobbler Ebenezer Mackintosh, but he in turn would have been listening to, if not actually taking instructions from, a secret group called the 'Loyal Nine' who had decided that only physical resistance would stop the introduction of the stamps.

The 'Loyal Nine' were in their turn taking their cue from men who were by no means roughneck

282

mob-raisers, but articulate, resolute politicians who knew exactly what they were doing. In Boston they included the merchant James Otis and the ex-tax collector and brewer-maltster Samuel Adams. Their own instincts for dramatic resistance had been fired by the 'Virginia Resolves' moved by a young orator, Patrick Henry, who had compared the introduction of the stamps to the most iniquitous Roman tyranny; by blessings for their cause awarded from the pulpit by Jonathan Mayhew; and, from far off, by the report of an extraordinary speech given in the House of Commons on the day of the Stamp Act's first reading by Isaac Barré, half of whose face had been blown off on the Heights of Abraham. Fixing his one eye and mutilated cheek on Charles Townshend, who had just asserted the 'undoubted' right of parliament to tax the colonies on the grounds that they had been 'planted', 'nourished' and 'protected' by Britain, Barré opened up with a withering counter-attack, replacing the official version of selfless British paternalism churlishly repudiated with an altogether different history of the relationship between mother country and colonies. He thundered:

Planted by your care! No! Your oppressions planted them in America. They fled from your tyranny to a then uncultivated and inhospitable country . . . they nourished up by your indulgence? They grew by your neglect of them: as soon as you began to care about them that care was exercised in sending persons to rule over them . . . to spy out their liberty . . . They protected by your arms? They have nobly taken

283

up arms in your defence, have exerted a valour amidst their constant and laborious defense of a country whose frontier, while drenched in blood, its interior parts have yielded all its little savings to your emolument.

Stirred by this conviction that the most hallowed principles of *British* liberty were at stake, the Stamp Act protests spread throughout almost all the colonies, forcing the distributors of the stamps to have serious second thoughts about the wisdom of their commission. Grenville had also succeeded in provoking a rare example of inter-colonial cooperation, at the Stamp Act Congress convened in October 1765 in New York to discuss measures to be taken. The delegates shied away from physical resistance but adopted a policy (already mooted in Boston) of boycotting imports of British luxury goods, on which so many incomes in the already disturbed home economy depended. In July Grenville's government fell—although for reasons unconnected with the American crisis. The Rockingham administration, which replaced him, was disposed, but not yet committed, to repeal (which even Thomas Hutchinson in Boston was urging). In the winter of 1765–6 debates of immense significance, attempting to grapple with the relationship between Britain and America, took place in parliament for the first time.

Centre stage were the hostile brothers-in-law Pitt and Grenville, both now out of power. Pitt made what for several years afterwards would be a crucial (though in reality arbitrary) distinction between 'external' taxation—the authority to regulate colonial trade—and 'internal' taxation (like the stamps), which trespassed on the right given to the colonial assemblies to raise taxes only with their consent. Grenville replied that if this distinction were to be taken seriously Britain would, in effect, have conceded a vital element of its sovereignty:

> The government over them being dissolved, a revolution will take place in America . . . Protection and obedience are reciprocal. Great Britain protects America; America is bound to yield obedience. If not tell me when were Americans emancipated? The nation has run itself into immense debt . . . and now they are called upon to contribute a small share toward the public expense . . . they renounce your authority, insult your officers and break out, I might almost say, into open rebellion.

Rising on his gout-crippled legs, Pitt then made the speech of his life:

> The gentleman tells us America is obstinate; America is almost in open rebellion. I rejoice that America has resisted. Three millions of people so dead to all the feelings of liberty, as voluntarily to submit to be slaves, would have been fit instruments to make slaves of the rest. I come not here armed at all points with law cases and acts of parliament with the statute book double down in dog's ears to defend the cause of liberty; if I had . . . I would . . . have shown that even under former arbitrary reigns parliaments were ashamed of taxing a people without their consent. . . . The gentleman asks,

when were the colonies emancipated? But I desire to know when they were made slaves.

Pitt asked that the Stamp Act be 'repealed, absolutely, totally and immediately'. And so it was. When the news was learned in Boston, John Hancock laid out a pipe of his best Madeira on the Common for citizens to help themselves. But the cause of repeal in London was perhaps best helped by a dazzling display of expertly informed advocacy from Benjamin Franklin, called before the bar of the House to answer questions from interested members including Grenville. To Grenville's claim that Britain had reimbursed the colonies already for their own outlay of expenses in the war, Franklin pointed out that in his state, Pennsylvania, alone the £313,000 laid out to equip and pay volunteer troops had been compensated by only £75,000 from the Treasury. To Grey Cooper's question on the 'temper' of America towards Britain before 1763 he replied, 'the Best in the World. They submitted willingly to the government of the Crown, and paid in all their courts, obedience to acts of parliament.'

'And to their temper now?'

'Oh,' replied Franklin, 'very much altered.'

Once they considered parliament the bulwark of their liberties; now, much less. When asked what would be the result if the Act were not repealed, Franklin answered candidly but devastatingly, 'The total loss of the respect and affection the people of America bear to this country and of all the commerce that depends on that respect and affection.'

These predictions gave Franklin no joy. As he

wrote to his good friend, the Scottish luminary Lord Kames, 'I have had so great a part of my life in Britain and formed so many friendships in it that I love it and sincerely wish it prosperity and wish to see that union on which alone I think it can be secured and established.' He added shockingly, 'As to America, the advantages of such a union to her are not so apparent.' For Franklin believed that time was emphatically not on Britain's side. His own vision of the future was uniquely informed by a sense that the destiny of nations was shaped, ultimately, less by inherited customs and traditions than by geography, population and social structure. Only the Scots, like Kames, David Hume, James Ferguson and John Millar, who themselves had thought about such things, de Montesquieu in France and some of his other, advanced friends at the 'Honest Whigs' Club, like Richard Price, could possibly comprehend this essentially sociological way of looking at the rise and fall of nations. The facts of the matter for Franklin were that, sooner or later, the immense expanse of America (whether or not officially bottled up by British regulations), the vitality of its natural population increase and the robustness of its immigration, together with the extraordinary possibilities offered by continental economic expansion, all virtually dictated that it would outstrip its parent country. And he probably subscribed, too, to the principle first articulated at the end of the Commonwealth in James Harrington's *Oceana* that, ultimately, the distribution of property determined the balance of political power. Before long the inventory, as it were, of American assets would of itself demand that the British adjust to reality. Even if, in the full flush of their imperial triumph over the French, the British could scarcely conceive of such an eventuality, it was going to happen. That was a certainty. It was up to the British, who chose for the moment to play the sovereign, whether they wanted this extraordinary American future to unfold as part of a genuine empire of the free, built on mutual respect and consent, or whether their short-term needs would blind them to their long-term interests.

To his regret, Franklin was not able to see William Pitt, increasingly infirm, pessimistic and evil-tempered. But even if that encounter had taken place it is extremely unlikely that he would have been able to persuade that 'friend' of the Americans to his view of the inevitable organic development of his country. For as much as Pitt was adamant in his opposition to the iniquitous stamp tax, he was equally adamant that parliament in principle was indisputably sovereign over the colonies. It was that unwavering assumption that led subsequent British administrations, even when making concessions to American grievances, to make categorical reiterations of that sovereignty. The stamps may have gone, but other commercial duties, the Townshend duties, were introduced in 1767, and the customs administration to enforce them became, especially in ports like Boston, notorious for the shamelessness of its smugglers, increasingly militarized. One of the most shameless of them all, the rich young merchant John Hancock, typically converted self-interest into ideology by calling one of his sloops *Liberty* and flaunting his intention of 'running' Madeira ashore. When a ship-of-the-line, the *Romney*, was summoned from Halifax, Nova Scotia, to assist the

288

customs officers, riots in the docks made it impossible for it to do its assigned work.

It was the glaring fact that Boston and New York were not only uncowed by the threat of force but also rapidly becoming ungovernable that triggered the decision to use regular troops as police. The colonial ports had responded to the Townshend tariff of duties in 1767 by mobilizing a boycott of British imports; shippers and shopkeepers found to have violated it were denounced, intimidated, roughed up and sometimes tarred and feathered. Some 3500 redcoats under the command of General Gage were brought to the rowdiest of all the centres of protest, Boston. In a small, tight-packed city, they could hardly help being extremely visible—that indeed was the idea—and were habitually abused by jeering crowds (especially by young apprentices) as 'lobster sons of bitches'. The fact that the soldiers were allowed to moonlight in jobs like ropemaking, which were usually held by the locals, did not help. By late 1769 brawls were common. And sometimes matters got completely out of control. On 23 February 1770 an eleven-year-old boy, Christopher Seider, joined a noisy protest of schoolboys and apprentices outside the shop of an importer, Theophilus Lilley, where he was shot dead by a customs officer. With feelings whipped up by a powerful woodcut of the shooting published in the *Boston Gazette*, his funeral turned into a mass demonstration, carefully orchestrated for maximum tear-jerking by Sam Adams. As many as 500 boys marched two by two behind the little bier, and behind them came at least 2000 adults.

On 5 March the inevitable disaster happened

when a wigmaker's apprentice ragged a soldier all the way to the Custom House for an allegedly unpaid bill. When a guard struck the pursuing youth, a tocsin normally used as a fire alarm was sounded and mobilized a large and angry crowd. A small and frightened platoon of eight soldiers, sent to restore order, was surrounded by the crowd who pelted them with rock-solid snowballs. Terrified they were about to be manhandled or worse, they panicked and started shooting. Five were killed, including a black, Crispus Attucks, and an Irish leather breeches-maker, Patrick Carr. Several more were badly wounded. Only the appearance of Thomas Hutchinson, promising swift and proper legal action and evacuating the troops to Castle Island in the harbour, avoided much more serious bloodshed. Though it was recognized that the soldiers had acted out of fear rather than malice, and though they were defended by at least one well-known 'patriot', John Adams, their acquittal only contributed to the legend of a deliberate 'massacre' carefully cultivated by the widespread distribution of a print made by the engraver and silversmith Paul Revere, showing a line of British soldiers firing in unison at defenceless civilians. The print was also incorporated into an extraordinary front page of the *Boston Gazette*, its dense columns of print lined in funereal black and including images of five coffins, engraved with skulls in the manner of the tombs in the Granary and Copps Hill burial grounds. Though he knew better, Sam Adams (John's cousin) had no hesitation in publicizing the incident throughout the colonies as evidence of the murderous intent of the British to slaughter civilians who refused to truckle to parliamentary coercion.

Even at this point, however, there was nothing inevitable about the separation of America and Britain. Most Americans, even those deeply affronted by the economic and military policies of governments and parliament, still considered themselves in religion, language and historic culture ineradicably British. If anything, they felt passionately that *they* were the legatees of the 'true' British constitution, which had been abandoned in the mother country or somehow held hostage by a vicious and corrupt oligarchy. Some Americans who visited London and were shocked by the excesses of luxury and depravity they found there (while occasionally enjoying a sample of it) explained the lamentable abandonment of the old traditions of freedom by this sorry descent into voluptuary wickedness. But many still hoped the clock could yet be turned back to the days before 1763, a date that began to assume scriptural significance as the first year of iniquity. The virtuous king, evidently misled by wicked counsel, might yet be rescued from his misapprehensions. A changing of the guard at Westminster actually seemed to bode well. The author of the infamous customs duties, Charles Townshend, died. The non-importation campaign against British goods had begun to subside so gratifyingly that in 1770, when Lord North became First Lord of the Treasury, he could announce, without fear of being accused of surrendering to intimidation, that most of the objectionable duties would be repealed. In 1771 Franklin wrote optimistically to Samuel Cooper that there seemed to be a 'pause in Politics . . . should the [British] Government be so temperate and Just as to place us on the old ground where we stood before the Stamp Act, there is no danger of our rising in our demands'.

There was, however, one commodity on which Lord North, in his wisdom, decided to retain the duty: tea. And the storm that stirred this particular cup would overwhelm British America.

Few could have foreseen the repercussions in May 1773 when the Tea Act was passed through parliament. Looked at from London, it seemed merely a pragmatic expedient designed to get the financially beleaguered East India Company out of its difficulties. The Company had been chartered by Queen Elizabeth in 1600 and had established its first trading post on the west coast of India at Surat eight years later. As usual, the expectation had been that some exotic raw materials might be imported to England (and re-exported to Europe) in exchange for the sophisticated manufactured goods of the home country. But India, and especially its dazzling, printed cotton textiles, turned out to be a lot more sophisticated than anything produced in England. There was nothing that India wanted or needed in exchange for those 'calicoes' other than silver. So bullion poured out of England as the calicoes poured in, especially in the second half of the seventeenth century, generating a costume revolution as the light, brilliantly patterned fabrics gripped first the fashionable and then the middling classes. Only the panic-stricken representations of English linen manufacturers stemmed the flow of the imports. Happily, tea came along as a substitute and by the middle of the eighteenth century accounted for almost 40 per cent of its import business.

But—especially in America—heavily dutied British tea, although an obligatory item in the pantry, was expensive compared to virtually identical leaf smuggled by the Dutch. The non-importation campaign of 1768–9 had only made matters worse. By 1773 there was a tea mountain piled high in the Company warehouses in the City of London around Fenchurch and Leadenhall Streets, 18 million pounds of it. East India Company stock was in free-fall, and, as if this were not bad enough, the Company owed the government a substantial debt for unpaid customs duties, as well as the military protection of its trade. Lord North and the government were darkly considering its future. Then someone—a Scot, Robert Herries—had a bright idea. Why not abolish entirely the customs duties on tea imported into Britain, lowering the price to the point where it could undersell Dutch contraband leaf not only in Britain but even on the European and American markets? The answer was yes, but. Lord North had decided that he would repeal all the Townshend duties *except* for tea, if only to preserve the principle of parliament's right to impose tariffs on the colonies. Now, however, it was thought that the drastically lowered price of tea shipped into America through the East India Company would sweeten the modest payment of threepence a pound to the point where the Americans would hardly notice they were swallowing it.

They noticed. On 7 October 1773, when the first ships loaded with tea chests were already on the high seas, handbills signed 'Hampden' were posted and distributed in New York, warning that, under the diabolical guise of cheap tea, Americans

293

were once again being lured to accept taxation without their own consent. The fact that the duty was to be used to pay for colonial administration and that many of the selected 'consignees'—the American merchants who would receive and sell it—were connected to the likes of the Governor of Boston, Thomas Hutchinson, only heightened the sense of a conspiracy. Two of the consignees were actually Hutchinson's sons, a third was his father-in-law. Hampdens suddenly were reborn everywhere. One of them, the Philadelphian Dr Benjamin Rush, his spirit possessed by the ghost of the foe of ship money, declared that 'the baneful chests contain in them a slow poison . . . something worse than death—the seeds of SLAVERY'. In Charleston, New York and Philadelphia the intended consignees were put under such pressure of intimidation as the instruments of reimposed taxation that nearly all backed off, promising not to accept the cargoes.

In Boston, the destination for four brigs, the sudden crisis was a godsend for Sam Adams, whose efforts to sustain the trade boycott against Britain had been meeting with increasing indifference—until the tea was on its way. At just the right time, private letters exchanged among Hutchinson, the Lieutenant-Governor Andrew Oliver and Thomas Whateley were discovered by Franklin and published. The letters sneered at the patriots, and expressed the hope that parliament and the British government would do its utmost to uphold the principle of their sovereign right to regulate trade and tax the colonies. The apparently devious way in which cheap tea was being used to seduce innocent and virtuous Americans to part with their liberty was evidence of the 'diabolical' nature of the design. On 29 November, the day after the first ship, the *Dartmouth*, carrying 114 chests of Bohea, had tied up at Griffin's Wharf, notices in town called on 'Friends! Brethren! Countrymen! The Hour of Destruction or Manly Opposition to the Machinations of Tyranny stares you in the Face!'

Boston instantly turned into a revolutionary hothouse with bells ringing to summon concerned citizens to public meetings. They came from the city, and they came from neighbouring towns and villages—Cambridge, Woburn, even Hutchinson's village of Milton. Thousands of them poured into Faneuil Hall—so many of them that the meeting had to be reconvened in Old South Meeting House, the fine Congregationalist Church, where light washed over the agitated speakers and their flock from high windows. The 'baneful weed' could not, would not be unloaded; nor would the iniquitous duty be paid. It would be sent back to London in proper disgrace. But, the poor merchants who had shipped it, all unsuspecting, pleaded, British law forbids, on pain of forfeiture, the return of any dutiable cargo once shipped out. To send it back would be to guarantee their ruin. Too bad was the majority opinion. In the meantime, Hutchinson and his family consignees had fled to the safety of Castle William, where they too refused to think about returning the cargo. So it stayed on board ships at the wharves, guarded, in effect, by the patriots while the stand-off continued and two more ships, the *Beaver* and the *Eleanor*, arrived.

By the third week in December a deadline loomed. If duty had not been paid by then, the customs officers would (doubtless with the help of troops) seize the tea as forfeit. Knowing that, faced with financial disaster, the consignees would capitulate, pay and unload, the Boston Committee of Correspondence, the organizing arm of the patriots, summoned further meetings. On the 16th Old Southie was again filled to capacity as orators denounced enslavement by the pot and Josiah Quincy attacked Boston's foes for their 'malice . . . and insatiable revenge'. An envoy, the ship's captain, had been sent to Hutchinson at Milton, demanding one last time that the *Dartmouth* be allowed to sail, if not for England, then at least out to the harbour castle so that it could be said to be on its way. Around quarter to six, with the light almost gone, Hutchinson would not be swayed. Sam Adams got to his feet to say that he could not see what more could be done to save the country. It was not so much an utterance as a signal. An Indian war-whoop sounded in the church gallery; there were more at the door from a crowd of fifty or so, their faces crudely blackened with coal-dust, disguised as fancy-dress braves with blankets substituting for native dress. The 'Mohawks' whom handbills had warned might attack the cargoes of tea if a solution were not found were on the war-path, and it led right to the wharf. Most of them, like the shoemaker Robert Twelves Hewes, were working men who had been drawn into the world of direct political protests over the past four years, and they had been deliberately selected by the patriot leaders for their relative anonymity. But they had also been carefully instructed on what to do. The noise they made was enough to stop one merchant, John Andrews, from enjoying his evening cup of tea. Arriving at the door of the Meeting House he collided with a roaring crowd as it exited into the softly falling Boston rain, heading for the docks and the *Dartmouth* and the *Eleanor*.

By the light of lanterns the 'Mohawks' did their work, smashing their way with hatchets through 342 chests containing 45 tons of tea, value £9000: enough to make, it has been estimated, 24 million cups. Once split wide open to ensure maximum damage, the chests were heaved into the water where much of the loose tea escaped. A vigilant eye was kept on anyone who imagined that, for all their patriotic ardour, they might help themselves to a little by stuffing it down their coats or breeches. There was so much tea that before the job was done it began to back up against the sides of the ships as if the vessels were becalmed in some monstrous tide of Bohea slurry. The next morning, by the light of day, little boats went out into the water to make sure none of the cargo remained undamaged, using paddles to push the wooden chests and free-floating rafts of the stuff down into the muddy water. As they were drifting through the muck John Adams wrote in his diary, 'This is the most magnificent Movement of all . . . there is a dignity, a Majesty, a Sublimity in this last Effort of the Patriots that I greatly admire . . . the Destruction of the Tea is so bold, so daring, so firm, intrepid and inflexible, and it must have so important Consequences and so lasting, that I cannot but consider it as an Epocha [sic] in History.'

He was right. The Boston Tea Party was a classic instance of an issue and event, apparently trivial, even absurd, in itself, becoming floodlit into a great drama of national resistance. This was the way it was described in the instant accounts written in Boston for distribution throughout the colonies and carried there by a network of fast-riding couriers, not least the silversmith Paul Revere. Not everyone was impressed, of course. There were many, even on the patriot side, who were outraged by the wanton destruction of property and believed that those responsible ought to pay compensation. For a while at the end of 1773 and the beginning of 1774 it seemed possible that the action might isolate Boston rather than automatically win it sympathy in the other colonies. That, at any rate, was what Lord North's government was calculating when it decided to punish the city and colony in the most draconian manner possible. The port of Boston was to be closed until compensation was paid for the tea, guaranteeing financial ruin for its mercantile community and real hardship for its citizens. The 1691 charter of the Commonwealth of Massachusetts was to be called in and reissued so that a more orderly government would be established. A Quartering Act authorized the billeting of troops in unoccupied buildings and barns.

It was this act of coercion beyond anything that had happened before, which convinced waverers and sceptics who had doubted Sam Adams' insistence that they were facing not a reasonable and well-intentioned home government but a selfish and brutal tyranny that he was, in fact, right. George Washington, a stickler for the sanctity of property, wrote, 'The cause of Boston, the despotick Measures in respect of it, now is and ever will be the cause of America (not that we approve

298

their conduct in destroying the Tea).' In the weeks and months that followed, as regiments landed and a naval blockade took up position outside the harbour, America was created. Planters as far away as South Carolina sent rice to Boston; farmers in Connecticut, New York and Rhode Island established wagon convoys to get food supplies to the inhabitants, represented as the innocent victims of British retribution. Most seriously, the first inter-colonial Continental Congress since the Stamp Act Congress convened in Philadelphia in September 1774 to consider a coordinated response. By the time the Congress opened in Carpenters' Hall in October, another action of the British government had added to its suspicions and fears. By the terms of the Quebec Act, passed in August, parliament had agreed to preserve the French system of civil law and to allow the 70,000 Francophone Catholics of Canada to practise their faith without penalties, their Church to be supported by tithes. To the overwhelmingly Protestant Americans this heralded trials without juries, the effective end of habeas corpus and a government instituted in America without any kind of elected assembly, only a nominated council. It was 'slavery and wooden shoes' entering by the back door, or more precisely up the St Lawrence and down the Hudson. And it was the most obvious confirmation yet that George III was indeed a Stuart in all but blood. No wonder he displayed so many Van Dycks of Charles I at Windsor Castle.

What the king *ought* to be, wrote Thomas Jefferson in his *Summary View of the Rights of British America*, prepared for the Congress, was 'the chief officer of the people', who presumably

299

could be dismissed and replaced if he failed to honour his contractual obligations to his subjects. But Jefferson was too ill to go to Philadelphia and those radicals who did—some of whom demanded that citizens begin military training—did not dominate the proceedings. Cooler heads argued for a breathing space in which parliament and the king might be petitioned to hear the justified grievances of America. It was, moreover, a long, deep breathing space. Only if redress of those grievances had not been made by 10 September 1775—a year hence—would the Americans begin a general cessation of all trade with Britain from 1 December.

It was a last, priceless opportunity for reconciliation, and it was not taken. Not, however, for want of statesmen on both sides recognizing that such a grace period might never come again. Even Lord North was attempting to hammer out some sort of middle way in which, if the colonies would agree to the sums needed for their own defence, they would be free to raise them in their own fashion and through their own assemblies. But could the British government, North asked an American representative, be assured that the several colonies would agree to their respective apportionments? No such assurance could be given. And, in any event, America had already gone past the point where it could be expected to accept even the *principle* of being taxed by the parliament at Westminster. For the king himself these last-minute efforts to cobble together some sort of agreement were so much sticking plaster over an open wound. Was it not evident, George asserted, that the colonists' pretence of disputing this or that imposition was so much disingenuous tomfoolery; that they had all along conspired to throw off the entire authority of parliament altogether? The only question now, as far as he was concerned, was whether the Americans were to be allowed to remove themselves from the allegiance they owed to their sovereign—king and parliament—without at least a fight.

Opinion inside Britain in the winter of 1774–5 was bitterly and frantically divided, especially in the mercantile cities whose trade faced catastrophe should war break out. Rival groups petitioning for reconciliation or military action contested for the same meeting halls in Manchester and Bristol and for the same signatures of mechanics and shopkeepers. Parliament was dominated by calls to inflict on the wicked and ungrateful children across the Atlantic a hiding they would never forget. On 20 January 1775 William Pitt, now Earl of Chatham, and tormented by sickness, arrived at the House of Lords in the company of his fifteen-year-old son William and Benjamin Franklin—with whom, at last, he had had earnest conversations about what, if anything, could be done to halt the march towards imperial self-destruction. Franklin was turned away from the door on the grounds that he was neither the eldest son nor the brother of a peer. Chatham entered, remarking as loudly as he could, 'This is Dr FRANKLIN whom I would have admitted.' He then put a motion to withdraw General Gage's troops from Boston, in other words to stop a war before it started. Though few of his peers believed it, he promised them it would be unwinnable. What he then went on to say proved just how carefully the old man had listened to

301

Franklin. For the first time he was staring at the vast expanse of America, and he knew he was staring at defeat. 'What, though you march from town to town, and from province to province; though you should be able to enforce a temporary submission . . . how shall you be able to secure the obedience of the country you leave behind you? . . . to grasp the dominion of 1800 miles of continent, populous in numbers, possessing valour, liberty and resistance?'

And where did the peers who denounced the Americans for their temerity imagine their stubborn attachment to representation came from? Had they looked in the mirror lately? Had they read any good books about their own history lately?

> This resistance to your arbitrary system of taxation might have been foreseen . . . it was obvious . . . from the Whiggish spirit flourishing in that country. . . . The spirit which now resists your taxation in America is the same spirit which formerly opposed . . . ship money in England; the same spirit which called all England on its legs and by the Bill of Rights vindicated the English constitution. . . . This glorious spirit animates three millions in America . . . who prefer poverty with liberty to gilded chains and sordid affluence; and who will die in defence of their rights as freemen.
>
> To such united force, what force shall be opposed?—What, my Lords—a few regiments in America, and seventeen or eighteen thousand men at home! The idea is too ridiculous to take up a moment of your Lordships' time. . . . It is

not repealing a piece of parchment that can restore America to our bosom; you must repeal her fears and her resentments and you may then hope for her love and gratitude . . . We shall be forced, ultimately, to retract: let us retract when we can, not when we must. . . . Avoid then this humiliating, disgraceful necessity. . . . Make the first advances to concord, to peace and happiness.

But the first advances were to Concord, Massachusetts, where, so General Gage had heard, the 'rebels'—for so they were already dubbed in the British garrison—had stored arms and ammunition. Throughout the late winter, not only in Massachusetts but in Virginia and Pennsylvania as well, the committees of correspondence had been taking steps to organize the defence of their own communities in citizen militias, hastened by rumours that not only British but foreign mercenary troops too (the armed lackeys of satanic despotism!) were on their way to America. On 18 April 1775 John Hancock and Samuel Adams were in Lexington where a company of 'minutemen'—a militia of farmers who could be instantly summoned in the event of an emergency—had been formed, guarding a cache of munitions. It was already known that Gage intended to march troops west to Lexington to arrest Adams and Hancock and seize the weapons. And the fact that for three days grenadiers and marines had been taken off duty and boats made ready was unlikely to keep the raid a secret. The only unknown was when this descent on the hamlets across the Charles river would take place; hence the famous arrangement by which a signal lantern would be set in the steeple of Old North Church to alert patriots in Charlestown to the departure of the soldiers—two for an approach by water, one by land. Three riders were to be dispatched to warn Hancock and Adams. One was arrested before he could depart; the other two, William Dawes and Paul Revere, got out of Boston, Revere rowing across the Charles beneath the guns of a British warship. Picking up a horse at Charlestown, he took the longer route but arrived first at the Reverend Jonas Clarke's vicarage just by Lexington Green. In the moonlight the green looked then (as it still does) the epitome of an English village, the kind of place that seems to describe the perpetuity of British America and not its imminent death-rattle.

Revere tried to carry his warning to Concord but was arrested by a British patrol before he reached there. But word was out. Hancock and Adams departed swiftly for Woburn and safety, the beginning of what would be a long journey through America, publicizing the events of the morning about to dawn. All around Boston, alarm bells and signal guns were sounding. When the six companies of British troops arrived at Lexington, just before light, they were confronted by about seventy minutemen drawn up on the green. One of the officers shouted, 'Disperse, ye rebels!', and the militia officer, Captain Parker, did apparently order a dismissal. While it was happening, a shot was let off, from which side, no one was sure. But the grenadiers let fly a musket volley. When the smoke cleared, eight men were dead and ten wounded.

At Concord the British cut down a Liberty tree

and then faced a serious firefight, shot at from a hilltop by the Old North Bridge. Their retreat back through Menotomy to Charlestown turned into a nightmare as they were riddled with gunfire by more than a thousand militia often firing from behind walls and the cover of trees. This was not going to be an easy war.

News of the events of 18 and 19 April were carried 'on wings of wind' through the colonies, not least by Hancock and Adams who had been singled out by General Gage as the only rebels to be exempt from a pardon. By the time they reached Manhattan island, the streets were thick with impassioned crowds. In May the second Continental Congress, held in Philadelphia, appointed a Virginian, George Washington, to take command of their army of defence, signalling that Boston's war was now America's. Throughout the summer, the British found themselves effectively besieged by an American army whose size and strength they had never remotely anticipated from rude colonials. In June, Gage sent a formidable army up Breed's Hill to break the American position on Charlestown Heights, and in the process lost 92 officers and nearly 1000 men. They included Major Pitcairn, who had been at Lexington on 19 April and had sent a letter to London that had been shown to the king, who shared the major's opinion that 'once the rebels have felt a smart blow . . . they will submit'. By the time George III read it, Pitcairn was dead. Stunned by the casualties, Gage wrote to Viscount Barrington, Secretary-at-War, that the Americans were 'spirited up by a rage and enthusiasm as great as ever a people were possessed of . . . The loss we have sustained is greater than we can bear.' In response he was heavily reinforced, so that by July there were 13,500 British troops in Boston together with many thousands more loyalist refugees. But even with this enormous force it was not clear how long they could hold the city.

There was a war, but there was not yet anything like agreement among the Americans on its ultimate goal. The second Continental Congress remained divided. Could union with Britain be preserved if its government took America back to the halcyon days before 1763 and agreed to a broad degree of self-government including the right of self-taxation? Or was absolute independence now the only possible option? In early July 1775, Congress produced a declaration of 'the Causes and Necessity of Taking up Arms', which said that: 'We have not raised armies with ambitious designs of separating from Great Britain and establishing independent states. We fight not for glory or conquest. We exhibit to mankind the remarkable spectacle of a people attacked by unprovoked enemies.' Two days later an 'olive branch' petition from Congress, drafted by the Pennsylvanian John Dickinson, was sent to the king through the hands of the grandson of the colony's founder, William Penn. It began with a profuse statement of loyalty:

Attached to your Majesty's person, family and government with all devotion that principle and affection can inspire, connected with Great Britain by the strongest ties that can unite societies . . . we solemnly assure Your Majesty, that we not only most ardently desire the former harmony between her and these

Colonies may be restored, but that a concord may be established between them upon so firm a basis as to perpetuate its blessings, uninterrupted by any future dissensions to succeeding generations in both countries.

It was the last, best chance to save British America, and George III's ministers were having none of it. At such critical moments in the fate of nations and empires the historian wants to reach for some deep, sophisticated structural socio-political explanation. But what turned the corner, what made reunion out of the question, was, all too simply, the king and his government. They let it be known that the king was not interested in any communication from an assembly of rebels. On 23 August the Americans were formally proclaimed to be in a state of 'open and avowed rebellion'. On 26 October they insisted that the revolt was 'manifestly carried on for the purpose of establishing an independent empire'. It was George III and his advisers, then, who spelled it out, who in effect uttered a declaration of independence; and figures like Jefferson who, even as late as November 1775, were professing their deep reluctance to make a complete break, were also calling the king 'the sceptred tyrant' and 'the bitterest enemy we have'. The trouble was, this time no William III was at hand to appear as a constitutional king of America.

For Thomas Paine, whose *Common Sense* appeared in January 1776, no more kings need apply. Delude yourselves no further about the sainted British constitution, he argued. It is a sham and a ruin. Have no more to do with it: ' 'Tis time to part.' But though Paine's tract sold a staggering 150,000 copies, the founding fathers—John Adams and Jefferson in particular—were not so much men of a new democratic age as to be able, yet, to unhitch themselves from the great tradition of expressly *English* Liberty. If they were at war with the British Empire it was because it was the wrong empire: not the empire of liberty at all, but an unrecognizable perversion of the principles on which it had been founded. Even when they did take their pens in hand and finally draft declarations of independence in the late spring and early summer of 1776, after the British had evacuated Boston and the British government still refused to spell out the terms on which peace might be made, the nation builders instinctively reached back, not forward, to their pantheon of heroes. They were the same heroes who had appeared in Lord Cobham's monument at Stowe—Hampden, Milton and William III. In 1774, after hearing the news of Boston's coercion, and thinking about the future constitution of their state, Jefferson and some of his colleagues in the Virginia House of Burgesses trawled through John Rushworth's *Historical Collections* of documents from the epic of parliament's struggle with Charles I. And when he came, finally, to draft the Declaration of Independence, Jefferson's model for the long list of accusations against George III was the Bill of Rights of 1689 written to justify the removal of James II.

No one felt the irony more sharply than Chatham. He had repeatedly attempted to stop the war in its tracks, to no avail. Even in the unlikely circumstances that it would be won, it would, he told the Lords in January 1777, be a pyrrhic victory, for 'we are the aggressors. We have invaded them.' Everything he had made, even the triumph over France, was now unmade, for the old enemy was merely biding its time to profit from the débâcle. After the failure of the Saratoga campaign to isolate New England from the other colonies in October 1777, when North was desperate to resign and even George III was beginning to look for an exit from disaster, Chatham was spoken of, crippled as he was, as the logical man to make a simultaneous peace with an independent America and war with a newly threatening France. On 7 April 1778, in extreme pain, the famous vessel of his voice broken and halting, Chatham spoke in the Lords, still hoping that some sort of connection might be preserved between America and Britain, but ready to face, if necessary, a hostile alliance of France, Spain and America. 'Any state is better than despair . . . if we fall let us fall like men.' What use is valour, said the Duke of Richmond, when we have no navy, no army, no money? Chatham looked as though he would reply. He struggled heavily to his feet, swayed, staggered a little, clutched his hand to his heart and fell into the arms of peers sitting close by, one of them the master of Stowe, Lord Temple. When he died on 11 May the empire of liberty, the right empire, died with him.

*   *   *

On 12 September 1786, Charles, second Earl Cornwallis, stepped from his pinnace on to the Calcutta dockside. As befitted a new Governor-General of Bengal who was also, for the first time in the history of British India, a peer of the realm and Commander-in-Chief, his uniform was dress scarlet. Never mind that it was the same scarlet he had worn five years earlier at Yorktown, Virginia, when his capitulation to Washington and the French General Compte de Rochambeau had sealed the fate of the American war. It was a new day for His Majesty's Empire in Hindustan, and Calcutta was sweatily festive. Though the monsoon season was over, the town had not dried out. The cottony mist clinging to the surface of the Hooghly river was already heavy with sopping moisture and cadet regiments of mosquitoes, primed to puncture the rosy flesh of the sahibs, were hatching from larvae on the brim-full tanks and ponds. The British affected not to notice either the steamy heat or the buzzing pests. Cornwallis, forty-eight years old, rotund and genial in a militarily correct way, was greeted by music, cheering, bands, flags and boats draped with bunting; he cordially pumped handshakes from senior officers, junior officers, Council Members, senior merchants, junior merchants, surgeons and chaplains; and heard whispered welcomes from ladies in broad-brimmed, flower-bedecked hats. After breakfast at Fort William he was reverently greeted, with stooping bows, by the native bankers, banians, kazis, judges and revenue men without whom, he was given to understand, the government would be a nullity. Everyone seemed so very obliging. Could these same persons, British and babu, truly be the ravening 'birds of prey and passage' he had heard Edmund Burke denounce in parliament in December 1783, the vultures whose wings he had come to clip?

If Cornwallis were himself perspiring into his linen that morning in September, it may not have been a mere effect of the climate. He had only agreed to accept the king's commission after twice declining, in 1782 and 1785, and even now he was not without deep misgivings. He knew very well that he had been appointed by the young Mr Pitt and his Foreign Secretary of State, the Marquis of Carmarthen, to redeem in the east what had been lost in the west. Even before the Treaty of Versailles (1783) recognizing the independence of the American states had been signed, the French, whose intervention in the war had made it inevitable, had seized the opportunity to pounce on the wounded lion, returning to India to sponsor the Sultan of Mysore in his war against the British. On Cornwallis' shoulders now fell the responsibility of staving off further imperial collapse. It was a weighty thing.

Not that he felt he had anything with which to reproach himself, except for abandoning his Jemima who had implored him, tears in her eyes, not to go to America in 1778. When he had come back the following year, full of success and honour, she had again begged him not to agree to another command. But his suspicions of the capacity of the British generals in America, by turns reckless and timorous, would not let him decline. When he received news that she was deadly ill he hurried to return. With every dip of the ship into the resisting Atlantic trough, his anxiety and guilt grew more acute. She had asked, ordered in fact, that a thorn bush be grown at her wordless tombstone, and Cornwallis had honoured the mute reproach. He felt its pricks even now.

While Jemima was dying, so was British America. It was a cause of the deepest anguish for Cornwallis, who had been one of the most determined critics of the foolishness of successive governments' policies that had led to the separation. In the House of Lords he had been one of just four peers who had voted against parliament's assertion to tax its American colonies without their consent or representation. Throughout the years of embittered intimidation Cornwallis had shared Chatham's despairing sense of the futility of the government's coercive policy. But once the war had begun and Cornwallis was asked to serve, his disagreement, however severe, immediately took second place to his sense of duty. God knows he had tried to discharge it as well as he could, even while chafing at the irresolution of his seniors—first General Sir William Howe and then General Sir Henry Clinton. He had won the battles they had allowed him to fight—at White Plains and Brandywine— but they had turned a deaf ear to his wish that the northern and southern armies unite and strike, rather than disperse and dig in. At the Delaware, had they done so, they might have finished off Washington before the French had arrived. Once French ships had begun to command the entrance to the Chesapeake and land thousands of troops and supplies, Cornwallis understood that the British faced an entirely new war. Second in command to Clinton, he had vainly attempted to persuade him that only a union of the armies in Virginia—his marching north from the Carolinas and Clinton's south from New York—could strike a decisive blow before it was too late. Clinton had sent but a feeble part of his force under General William Philips, who had died shortly after their arrival, and with this inadequate army had ordered Cornwallis to an ultimately indefensible position at Yorktown. Surrounded, outnumbered, his men already exhausted from their pyrrhic victory at Guildford in March 1781, their supplies cut off by a French fleet sealing the Chesapeake, Cornwallis had held out for three weeks. When the outer redoubts of their fort were stormed, he had made the fateful decision to forgo the pointless sacrifice of his men's lives. Worn out and deeply depressed, his own health collapsed along with the fate of his army. On 19 October 1781, it was General O'Hara who made the formal surrender to Washington and led his troops away, their colours furled, drums beating, fifes playing (as well they might) 'The World Turned Upside Down', while the French lined the road out of Yorktown dressed in insultingly fresh white uniforms and black gaiters, the dandies of victory.

At home hardly anyone seemed to bear him ill will for the disaster, other than Clinton against whose public recriminations Cornwallis was painfully obliged to defend himself. But the king restored him to his office of Constable of the Tower. Barely a year later had come that first request to go to Bengal. Britain was smarting from the humiliation of what had happened in America; indeed, it was still actively embattled against an alliance of the French, Spanish and Dutch. Even from those who had opposed the war, there was no gloating over the outcome. Instead, public opinion had recoiled into a posture of wounded self-justification, professing astonishment that its

313

purposes in America had been so badly misunderstood. It had not been a 'tyranny' that they had been defending, but the most liberal and enlightened constitution in the world: that of parliamentary sovereignty. The European monarchs in Madrid and Versailles who had colluded with rebellion would one day rue their reckless irresponsibility and cynical opportunism.

But although Cornwallis evidently shared the public need to reassert the disinterested nobility of the British Empire, he wondered whether India was truly an auspicious place to plant its flag. Was it, as the vituperative critics of the East India Company's rule claimed, so steeped in venal selfishness, a racket disguised as a business, as to be entirely beyond redemption? Could virtue, he wondered, survive the tropics? What was it the philosophers said about despotism thriving where the orange grew? He was unsure if oranges grew here, but it was obvious that in the Indies, East as well as West, liberty was insecurely planted. Stupendous fortunes had been made, not by making men free but by making them servile; not by probity but by corruption; not by a benign and responsible diffusion of that wealth to the natives but by the most shameless coercion and extortion. After Lord North's government had been sent packing, Charles James Fox had proposed legislation for the East India Company. His East India Bill made provisions for a parliamentary commission. The reforming Act that resulted made a clean separation between commercial and governmental activities. Company administration was now accountable to a Board of Control in London that would include members of the Privy

314

Council and a Secretary of State. The regulatory act was designed to contain and reverse the personal empires of power and fortune that, Edmund Burke (who had largely written it) claimed, had been created under the pretext of securing a fair field for trade. In the parliamentary debates on India on 1 December 1783 Burke had hurled one of his rhetorical thunderbolts against the infamies perpetrated, so he said, by the Company and its servants on the helpless and much abused body of long-suffering Hindustan.

The violence and rapacity of the Company's conduct could never, Burke asserted, be excused or explained by any savagery it claimed was threatening the peaceful prosecution of commerce, for the 'thirty millions' of British India, he said, were not

> an abject and barbarous populace . . . but a people for ages, civilized and cultivated— cultivated by all the arts of polished life while we were yet in the woods. There have been (and still the skeletons remain) princes once of great dignity, authority and opulence. . . . There is to be found an ancient and venerable priesthood, the depository of their laws and learning and history, the guides of the people while living and consolation in death; a nobility of great antiquity and renown, a multitude of cities not exceeded in population and trade by those of the first class in Europe; merchants and bankers, individual houses of whom have once vied in capital with the Bank of England.

What had happened to this magnificent civilization

following the intrusion of the Company? If it had weakened, had the East India Company made it sturdier? If it were beset with strife, had the Company given it peace? If it were impoverished, had the Company brought the blessings of prosperity? Not a bit of it. India had been subjected to the squalid adventurism and wanton cruelty of arrested adolescents, banditti in tricorn hats.

> Our conquest there, after twenty years, is as crude as it was the first day. The natives scarcely know what it is to see the gray head of an Englishman. Young men (boys almost) govern there, without society and without sympathy with the natives. They have no more social habits with the people than if they still resided in England—nor, indeed, any species of intercourse, but that which is necessary to making a sudden fortune, with a view to a remote settlement. Animated with all the avarice of age and all the impetuosity of youth they roll in one after another, wave after wave; and there is nothing before the eyes of the natives but an endless, hopeless prospect of new flights of birds of prey and passage, with appetites continually renewing for a food that is continually wasting. Every rupee of profit made by an Englishman is lost forever to India.

Nor had the English compensated for power with the execution of good works. No bridges, highways or reservoirs had been built, Burke insisted (not altogether accurately): 'Were we to be driven out of India this day, nothing would remain to tell that it

316

had been possessed, during the inglorious period of our dominion, by anything better than the ourang-utang or the tiger.'

And Cornwallis knew, with a sinking feeling, that he was supposed to make this right; that if the British Empire was to rise again, like the sun in the east, it would have to be through the imposition not of force but of justice and virtue. He would have to be the first of the true proconsuls of Bengal, not the convenient instrument of his countrymen's rapacity. He was under no illusions how difficult this would be. Perhaps the task would be impossible. In 1784 he had written:

> The more I turn it in my mind the less inclination I feel to undertake it. To abandon my children and every comfort this side of the grave; to quarrel with the Supreme Government in India, whatever it might be; to find that I have neither power to model the army or correct abuses; and, finally, to run the risk of being beat by some Nabob and being disgraced to all eternity, which from what I have read of these battles appears to be a very probable thing to happen—I cannot see in opposition to this, great renown and brilliant fortune.

In short, Cornwallis did not need another Yorktown, another America.

When William Pitt, the twenty-five-year-old son of Chatham, whom Cornwallis had so much admired, pressed, his resolution had wavered. 'Inclination cries out every moment, "Do not think of it; why should you volunteer plague and misery?" Duty then whispers, "You are not sent here merely

317

to please yourself; the wisdom of Providence had thought fit to put an insuperable bar to any great degree of happiness; . . . Try to be of some use; serve your country and your friends."' In the end, once he had gained the government's agreement to place both civil and military supremacy in his hands (being only too aware that his predecessor, Warren Hastings, had faced personal enmity and political obstruction from the Calcutta Council), Cornwallis had accepted the commission. 'I have been obliged to say yes and exchange a life of ease and content, to encounter all the plagues and miseries of command and public station.' He would do his best to be a good Roman, an Aurelius beneath the banyan.

But when the English had first set their sights on India they had meant to be Carthaginians, not Romans; traders, not conquerors. No doubt the gentlemen relished the grandiose title bestowed on them by Queen Elizabeth's charter of 1600 as 'The Governor and Company of Merchants of London Trading into the East Indies'; but really they were commercial adventurers after a little something on the side to pay for the deer park or the fashionably gilt Thames barge. As a descriptive phrase, the 'East Indies' was deliberately indeterminate, for any fortune hunter with an eye to economic geography would not be looking to the subcontinent at all, but further east, to the Indonesian archipelago whence came the high-priced treasures of pepper, mace, nutmeg and cloves. But between them the Portuguese and the Dutch seemed to have locked up the spice islands. When the English struggled to establish toe-hold trading posts at Bantam in Java and on the South

Moluccan island of Ambon, they had been outgunned by the hostile Dutch fleets. In 1622, they had decided to cut their losses and leave the Moluccas when a punitive Dutch expedition razed the factory and executed the ten English merchants in 1623 to make their point. It was to pre-empt being at the mercy of a Dutch spice monopoly that the English settled for an easier entry via the back door—India itself. There, they believed, they could negotiate with the representatives of the Mughal emperor on equal terms with the Portuguese and the Dutch, rather than deal with local sultans who had pre-emptively committed themselves to enforcing a commercial exclusion zone. From a trading base or 'factory' on the Indian coast the English would be able to import some spices directly, but also acquire silk and cotton textiles, which could be used to barter in Bantam. Surplus textiles could always be exported back to England and re-exported to Europe. It was not exactly the silver mines of Peru, but it was a start: worth, at any rate, the investment of the 200 or so stockholders who came together as the 'General Court' of the East India Company at Leadenhall Street and elected, every year, twenty-four directors to manage their common enterprise.

In 1608 the Company ship *Hector* anchored off the prosperous, busy port of Surat on the Gujarat coast of western India. Despite the truculent opposition of the Portuguese, whose 'factory' had been established not far away at Goa a half century before, the English managed to secure from the Mughal governor the licence they needed to trade in spices and cloth. But the grandiose aim of the Jacobean gentlemen-merchants was some sort of formally negotiated treaty with the Emperor Jahangir himself, and in 1615 Sir Thomas Roe was sent in the capacity of an ambassador bearing letters from James I. The governor of Surat was unimpressed, and it was only a year later that Roe managed to obtain an audience with Jahangir, who was duly bemused both by Roe's refusal to prostrate himself in the accustomed way before the Peacock Throne (instead doffing his hat and bowing from the waist) and by the very idea of a far-off 'king' who would allow himself to be represented by common merchants. On the other hand, the emperor's councillors believed they had nothing to lose from the grant of a *firman* licence, allowing trade under immunity from imperial taxes. There was obviously nothing these *Feringhis* could bring that India might want except large quantities of silver, which the government was happy to have added to its coffers. Besides, cloth exports would provide work for the weavers, bleachers and dyers of the Mughal empire and spread the unquestionable splendours of their arts about the world. Might these new traders be an annoyance? No more, surely, than the buzz of a gnat around the hindquarters of a war elephant.

For two generations dividends were declared in the Company sales rooms at Leadenhall Street. As the seventeenth century wore on, however, they were shrinking, offset by heavy operational costs, not least those of defence against competitors and pirates. But although the outlook for the India trade was uncertain around 1660, its champions, like Josiah Child, who had made a fortune fitting out the fleets of the Commonwealth and Protectorate and who sailed on into the mercantile world of the Restoration, remained optimistic—always provided, he insisted, that the Company understand it would have to act with political and military boldness if its commercial operations were ever to be secure. By the 1680s there seemed to be something substantially worth defending. The Company had settled into a number of Indian commercial centres such as Masulipatnam in the southeast and Hooghly in west Bengal. In those cities it built warehouses and one-storey houses for its 'factors' and 'writers' (clerks), usually near the protecting shadow of the Mughal fort. But in the second half of the seventeenth century there were other sites—Bombay on the west, transferred to English control as part of the Portuguese Catherine of Braganza's dowry as queen of Charles II; Madras on the Coromandel coast; and, from 1690, Calcutta in west Bengal—where the Company custom-built its 'factories' inside a fortified bastion, facing the sea on one side and garrisoned with a handful of Company soldiers, Indian, Portuguese–Eurasian and other Europeans. Either within its walls or protected by them, clusters of one-storey houses were built from the mixture of matted hemp, brick-dust and lime called *pucca*. Facing them was a church in the reassuring English manner, complete with colonnaded porch, steeple and rows of boxed pews made of tropical hardwoods. Behind it lay a churchyard, its graves more populous than the pews. Beyond the walls of this 'White Town' a 'Black Town' of Indian merchants, clerks and money-lenders lived, while a third community of maritime workers—boatmen, stevedores, carters and fishermen—gathered closer to the harbour. Betwixt and between them all were

321

small but extremely important communities of Armenians and Jews who acted as brokers and intermediary agents.

By 1700 the daily round of British life in India was already established: a hard ride before breakfast; morning prayers courtesy of the chaplain; business till the communal dinner (around two or three o'clock), with a tiffin of light curries staving off the pangs between; siesta after dinner; a little more business, then another ride, a fishing or fowling expedition, and cards and a light supper before bed. That was the official version, at any rate. But from less demure accounts, the colonies of bored, badly paid younger sons forced to come to India and brave the terrifying mortality (some 460 deaths in one hot season in Calcutta in a British population of 1200) behaved much as one would expect: gambling heavily; sinking vats of arrack while they did so; fighting and duelling among themselves; and either keeping Indian or Eurasian mistresses or visiting the Black Town brothels between doses of mercury to cure the maladies they acquired from over-indulgence there. Ostensibly in charge of all this was a president—not in any sense a true governor, but the senior merchant (in settlements where promotion came strictly by seniority), attempting to do the bidding of his masters in London while necessarily winking an eye at the extensive private business carried on by its servants in India to compensate for their niggardly salaries. At least the presidents knew how to put on a good show, never leaving the fort without an escort of armed Indian soldiers, two Union flags and the blare of 'country musick', loud enough, one commentator said, to make the natives believe we had gone mad.

It was not all bugles and bombast at Madras or Calcutta, however. For the prospects of British business in India had been transformed by the calico revolution in Europe. During the last third of the seventeenth century, virtually all social classes other than the rural poor discovered lightweight Indian fabrics—brilliantly dyed and figured silks for the well-to-do, and cottons, printed, painted or plain, for everyone. Calicoes and the more expensive silk-cotton mix chintzes changed lives. For the first time, materials other than heavy woollens and linens were available at prices to suit almost every income level. Calicoes, whether in bold prints or sheer gauzy muslins, were strong yet soft and, most important of all, were washable. No part of the male or female, adult or child's body, including the most private, was untouched by them. 'Few think themselves wel-dresst,' wrote one observer, 'till they are made up in calicoes, both men and women, in calico shirts, neckcloths, cuffs, aprons, nightroyls, gowns, petticoats, hoops, sleeves and india-stockings.' In London, as hundreds of thousands of pieces were sold every year, dividends at last became serious, and Company stock soared. Predictably, success bred resentment. Silk weavers at home angrily petitioned the government, and 'calico-chasers' mobbed wagons full of the textiles. The government responded by banning imports other than goods for re-export and plain fabric, which could be patterned up at home. But despite the ban, unofficial calico trading went on, and there was certainly enough demand in continental Europe for the rosier forecasts of business to seem realistic.

The only problem was India. An onward and upward commercial trajectory—the realization of the blue-water empire of trade, unencumbered by costs of territorial conquest or government—presupposed the stable and hospitable business environment provided by the omniscient dominion of the Mughal empire. Although the emissaries of the Stuart monarchs and the first generations of merchants who came to the Mughal court resented the lordly superiority of their emperors and privately still believed their empire to be a peculiar mixture of barbarism and voluptuous decay, they needed its authority to hold the ring against their European competitors and maintain their protection against extortionate local potentates. But in the historical mind-set of men like Sir Josiah Child, putting the Company's trust, not to mention its inventory, into the safe-keeping of a permanent, stable Mughal government was a dangerous delusion. Either empires were on their way up (British) or they were on their way down (Mughal). The rebellion of the Hindu Maratha cavalry war-lords in central and western Bengal, led by their charismatic prince Shivaji, had persuaded Child that the decline of the Mughals was indeed going to be swift and irreversible. Their passing would leave great holes in the structure of their empire to be occupied by some potential adversary, either native or European, to British interests. Child's conclusion was for the Company to act before it was acted on, and believing the Mughals to be seriously weakened in the west he launched a disastrous military action in the 1680s. It succeeded only in ruining their establishment in Surat, provoking the blockade and virtual abandonment of Bombay and a grovelling submission to the Emperor Aurangzeb.

Child's understanding of the changes taking place in India was grotesquely misinformed, save the one truism that there was indeed change. The Mughal empire was far from being on its last legs. Nor was the only alternative to its government some sort of howling barbarian anarchy: Huns in turbans about to plunge India into its Dark Ages. Ruled by the descendants of Tamerlane and Ginghiz Khan, it had evolved from a Turkic horseback warrior state into one of the great sedentary Muslim civilizations. At its height, under the Emperor Akbar I in the second half of the sixteenth century, it governed virtually all of north and central India through a unified system of law based on the Islamic Shari'a and on a centralized, Persian-language administration. Great palaces were built, none more extraordinary than Fatehpur Sikhri; and the Arabic and Persian court culture produced a great flowering of poetry and painting. But although the authority of the Mughals owed a great deal to the fearsomeness of their cavalry and artillery, to the lustre of their court and the energy and probity of their administration, they were governing an immense territory, major parts of which were not Muslim but Hindu. Their success at containing disaffection, then, rested on a careful balance between central authority—not least that of the omnipotent aura of the emperor himself, said to be infused directly with the light of God— and the co-opting of regional princes and peoples.

The key to that collaboration was the land tax, equal to as much as a third of the livelihood of

India's many million farmers and peasants. In return for his obedience and military cooperation, the emperor would assign to a subordinate governor, or nawab, the land revenue of a particular province. After delivering to the imperial treasury the empire's portion (in silver, naturally), and after paying the costs of assessment and collection, the nawab would be free to enjoy what was left. Similarly the nawabs—of Bengal or Awadh, for example—contracted in advance with hereditary collectors, the *zemindars*, for the amounts due from their respective territories. They too made money from the difference between the sum due on their contract and what they could actually extract from the cultivators. In similar fashion, the empire actively encouraged the development of sophisticated and specialized commercial centres around its dominions, so that Bengal indigo or Gujarati cottons often travelled along the great trunk roads to far-distant urban markets.

For a century this seemed a magically self-sustaining system. But after the death of the combative Aurangzeb a decided shift occurred in the delicate equilibrium between central and local power. The drift towards greater regional autonomy was accelerated by the empire's evident inability to defend itself against the onslaught of brutal horseback invasions from both the Afghans and the charismatic Persian despot Nadir Shah, who in 1739 sacked Delhi in a storm of elaborately horrific cruelty: Nadir Shah watched enthroned before the city gates as throats were slit and bodies mutilated. Within central and western India itself the imperial armies were unable to prevent the

Marathas from consolidating their power. And the various tribal raids on India were worse for being hit-and-run expeditions, their perpetrators uninterested (unlike the original Mughals) in settling amid the conquered and establishing something more than a cycle of extortion.

In the circumstances, it was inevitable that the Muslim officials and administrators to whom the empire had entrusted the government of whole regions should look out increasingly for themselves and their immediate subjects. Driven by both necessity and ambition, the nawabs of Bengal and Awadh, formidable men like Alivardi Khan and Shuja-ud-Daulah with their own provincial courts at Murshidabad and Faizabad, which disposed of revenue, law enforcement and soldiers, inevitably became more self-sufficient. Though they still thought of themselves as loyal to the emperor, they made their own offices hereditary and appointed their own men to their governments, irrespective of Delhi's wishes. Instead of responding to orders from the imperial treasury as to how much of the land revenue they were to keep and how much to pass on, they themselves increasingly decided on the shares.

As the struts and armature of the empire began to shake loose, it was these local potentates who became the focus of European attention in bids to outmanoeuvre or exclude their competition. In Bengal the late-comer but energetic French Compagnie des Indes had established a trading settlement at Chandernagor, and its ambitious governor, Joseph, Marquis de Dupleix, courted the nawab in Murshidabad to get an edge on his British rivals in Calcutta. Naval vessels from both

327

countries—summoned, it was said defensively—began to manoeuvre for position and, once the War of the Austrian Succession (in which, in the line-up of European alliances, Britain and France were on opposing sides) began in earnest, to exchange fire. In 1746, in return for the capture of French ships, the French under Bertrand-Francis La Bourdonnais, operating out of their factory at Pondicherry, captured Madras, the jewel of the Company's possessions, and held it for two years. At the Treaty of Aix-la-Chapelle it was returned to the East India Company amid scenes of jubilation at Fort St George. But the initial skirmishing had escalated the struggle. For no one had taken Josiah Child's instruction that the achievement of profit was conditional on the exercise of power more seriously than Dupleix.

When Dupleix made his first intervention in the internal politics of southern India, he was in fact merely applying the kind of conventions used by the French with the native tribes of North America to sustain and reinforce their position. But in India they looked much more ominous. When the most powerful figure in the region, the Nizam of Hyderabad, died, a contest was triggered for control of the Carnatic. Dupleix backed Chanda Sahib, a veteran administrator, and was prepared to support him with regular French troops and Indian levies. Should he prevail, the British could look forward to the end of Madras and their calico fortunes. In competition they gave their support to Muhammad Ali Walahjah, the son of a mercenary soldier. Even more fateful for the future, Dupleix planned to finance his campaign with the proceeds from local land taxes. He insisted to his understandably anxious directors in Paris that the purpose of all this was ultimately commercial: that the creation of a fiscal–military power in south India was the last thing he intended. It would work out otherwise, though—and not for the French, but for their enemies.

The odds on the British prevailing in this struggle must have been steep. For a start, the credentials of their candidate to govern a predominantly Hindu, southern territory were not strong. Muhammad Ali was, as his name suggests, a Muslim, and his family came from northern India. But, famously, there appeared in Madras in the 1740s someone who, even as he built a personal empire that, by comparison, made Dupleix's strategy look timid, likewise protested that he was just the loyal servant of the East India Company. Robert Clive had never really been meant for trade. In Market Drayton in Shropshire he had been so ungovernable a child that his beleaguered parents, over-burdened with a swarm of offspring, had sent him away to relatives in Manchester. He liked it, but it didn't like him. Back in Market Drayton the adolescent Clive pelted passers-by from the church steeple and ran a minor extortion racket against local shopkeepers, who were obliged to fork over to Clive's gang in order to protect their stores from pillage and destruction. He was, obviously, good material for Company service in India and ended up, nineteen years old, in Diamond Pitt's Madras on the lowest rung of the hierarchy: the writer. For some years Robert Clive clerked away, bunking down in the sweaty collegiality of the bachelor boys, hating every minute ('I have not enjoyed one happy day since I left my native country'), pining for Manchester and relieving the tedium with the standard distractions of arrack, cockfights, fistfights, gambling and (unless he was an unlikely exception) sex. The opium habit that, in all likelihood, ended up contributing to his death thirty years on, almost certainly began then and there. In the broiling heat his manic swings between elation and depression (virtually a job qualification for British empire-building) became wilder. Twice he tried to end it all with a pistol pressed to his temples. Twice—the story goes—the gun jammed.

In the war with the French, in which they and the British respectively acted, ostensibly, for Chanda Sahib and Muhammad Ali Walahjah, Clive's gangsterish intelligence and brutality found the perfect career opportunity. Careless of life, beginning with his own, he took chances that no one a little saner would ever have contemplated, gambling that if they came off he would be a god to his soldiers. When the French besieged the bastion of Trichinopoly rock, instead of marching directly on it Clive ordered a counter-march of his tiny troop of Indian and European soldiers to invest the fortress of Arcot and then dared the French to come and get it. They rose to the bait, drawing troops away from Trichinopoly and spending two months failing to take Arcot while Clive defended the stronghold to the last sepoy! It was not necessarily the turning point of the war, but it was a spectacularly tough feat of endurance, and it made him, at twenty-five, a Company hero. It also had the desired effect of allowing a British force to relieve the siege of Trichinopoly, capture Chanda

Sahib and have him beheaded in the shadow of the rock. Dupleix's credibility in France collapsed; the British installed Muhammad Ali Walahjah as the nawab of the Carnatic and were guaranteed the domination of southeast India.

But what for? For the dividend, of course; for the Company; what else? Clive and his fellow-soldiers always insisted that the force they were applying was just enough to pre-empt the Company from being locked out of whole commercial territories by the French. Even by the operational standards of the twentieth, never mind the eighteenth, century, a carefully measured degree of intervention could be justified as sound business practice in a part of the world where free trade and perfect competition were fantasies, and where abstaining from intervention was to cede the field to one's adversary. And there were, always, interested Indians—rival potentates, bankers and brokers, disaffected generals and revenue lords—ready to encourage the British, piggy-backing the redcoats to fortune and power. The danger, of course, for both the Company in London and the Indian opportunists, was that, once mobilized, military action and political involvement would come to be the master, not the servant, of business opportunity and would end up generating unanticipated problems that in turn would call for further and deeper military engagements until the point when a quick killing would no longer mean a trade opportunity. This is exactly what happened in Bengal, and what happened in Bengal landed Britain the wrong empire.

No one saw it coming, not even Robert Clive, back in England after the victory in the Carnatic, relishing his fame and fortune as the hard man of the East India Company, his pockets jingling with spare silver. Neither he, nor the court of directors, were under any illusion that the French would be content to cut their losses in the south of India without trying to compensate in the potentially much richer trading zone of the northeast. Their own factory at Chandernagor had the makings of a Gallic Calcutta, and their growing fleets could compete for control of the Bay of Bengal, sail by sail, with those of the East India Company. But the kind of spiralling competition that had caused so much damage in the south seemed to be contained by the much tougher and apparently more stable regime of Alivardi Khan, the nawab of Bengal. Taking advantage of the impotence of the Mughal court at Delhi to defend the empire, the nawab governed effectively from Murshidabad, 300 miles (400 km) up the Ganges from Calcutta, as a mini-Mughal, carving out a virtually autonomous kingdom that included not just Bengal itself, but also Orissa to the south and Bihar to the west. It was, in its own right, a huge, economically dynamic territory, and it was getting bigger by the year as estuary lands were reclaimed and put under rice, indigo or sugar. The European trading communities, which included the Dutch at Chinsura, were confined within their 'factories' and given limited licences to trade up-country (which meant, in effect, buying printed cottons and silks and handing over silver), and the idea that there might be some sort of break-out into an aggressive, free-wheeling armed state within a state seemed, even in the mid-1750s, inconceivable and, for everyone concerned, undesirable.

But the status quo was actually much shakier than would have been apparent to any visitor to Alivardi Khan's elegant court. He too was over-extended and had difficulty in preventing the Marathas from invading western Bihar and western Bengal. To generate the funds needed to shore up his army meant either becoming further indebted to bankers like the house of Jagat Seth, or putting heavy pressure on the *zemindars* with the predictable result of making enemies. The new defensiveness applied to the Europeans, too. With another round of Anglo-French hostilities coming, the two companies were determined to deprive each other of another Bengali speciality that had become strategic treasure: saltpetre. As they were manoeuvring for position in 1756, Alivardi Khan died and was succeeded by his twenty-year-old grandson, Siraj-ud-Daulah.

'Sir Roger Dowler' (as schoolboys of my generation still knew him) was the first official villain of imperialist history, the sadistic fiend who immured innocent Britons within the living tomb of the Black Hole of Calcutta. Pictures of the monster gloating over his victims, which illustrated Victorian and even twentieth-century 'empire stories', featured stereotypes of the oriental despot: curled mustachios as black as his heart. 'Early debauchery had unnerved his body and mind,' wrote Macaulay (which certainly could not be said of his own childhood) '. . . it had early been his amusement to torture beasts and birds and when he grew up he enjoyed with still keener relish the misery of his fellow creatures.' But Siraj-ud-Daulah was, of course, just your standard eighteenth-century Indian princely post-adolescent: impulsive, spoiled rotten, ill-informed and politically out of his depth. Given what had happened in the Carnatic, it was not, in fact, unreasonable for him to try to ensure that the ostensibly commercial companies stayed just that, by demanding that the European trading posts dismantle their fortifications at Chinsura, Chandernagor and Calcutta. The Dutch and the French obliged. The British did not, perhaps because Calcutta was now much more than a service extension of the trade depot. In the sixty years since Job Charnock had planted himself beneath his banyan tree by the Hooghly, in what was acknowledged then and ever since to be the unhealthiest climate in all India, it had grown into a sizeable city, in its own right with a population of at least 100,000. It was no longer just a strung-together agglomeration of weaving and fishing villages along the Hooghly but a tight little economic powerhouse.

Rightly or wrongly, the British felt that Calcutta was their creation and that it lived or died with the capacity to buy, up-country, the products that the Company needed to ship home (which its servants liked to trade, not always legally, to line their own pockets). The mere existence of the crudely built Fort William was the bargaining chip they needed to press claims for the protection and expansion of that trade, and they were not about to hand it over on a platter to the young nawab. The defiance was poorly timed since the ditch being dug to complete its defences had not been finished before Siraj-ud-Daulah marched on the city to enforce his will. He took it without much trouble, the president and most of the councilmen and inhabitants (about 450 of them) managing to flee before its capture. One of those who did not was Zephaniah Holwell, who along with a group of civilian and military prisoners was imprisoned on 20 June 1756 in a cell about 18 by 14 feet (6 by 3 metres), used for offenders in the Fort and long known by the British as 'the Black Hole'. It was Holwell's graphic account, *A Genuine Narrative of the Deplorable Deaths of the English Gentlemen and Others who were Suffocated in the Black Hole*, written on the journey home a year later that gave Britain its first imperial atrocity melodrama, perfectly tuned to the contemporary taste for the macabre and the sentimental, and complete with sons expiring as they held the hands of their fathers. Holwell claimed that 146 had been incarcerated and 43 survived. The best-researched modern evidence now suggests that he doubled the number of both prisoners and survivors. But this is still by any standards a grim reckoning, and the revisionist argument that some of the bodies were already dead, casualties of the fighting, does not make it any prettier. Some of Holwell's account must have been true: the stifling heat; and unhinged victims, their clothes torn off to give them a fraction more room, dying and making air available for others. But—as any survivors from among the Jacobites imprisoned in Carlisle Castle in 1746 would have confirmed—this kind of treatment was, unhappily, nothing unusual for the eighteenth century.

It was not, in any case, outraged humanity so much as strategic necessity that brought retribution down on the head of Siraj-ud-Daulah. Clive had been recalled to Madras to try to extend Company influence to another state, Hyderabad, but was now diverted north to Bengal in a combined operation with the ships of Charles Watson. Calcutta was taken from the sea in January 1757, and the nawab forced to reinstate all the Company's privileges and fortifications. At which point the gambit, which had been used successfully in the Carnatic, was reapplied in Bengal. A senior general in Siraj's army, Mir Jafar, angry at being passed over and alienated by the petulant antics of the nawab, let it be known that he would not be excessively grief-stricken were Clive to bring him down. The money-men, Jagat Seth above all, without whose resources any nawab was a broken reed, simultaneously gravitated to the power they instinctively thought to be a better long-term bet. At Plassey on 23 June 1757 Clive's force of 2000 red-coated native sepoys and 1000 Europeans appeared to be massively outnumbered by an opposing army of 50,000, complete with elephant cavalry. But the disparity was a mirage, for only perhaps 10,000 of the nawab's troops were actually prepared to fight. Once it was obvious that Mir Jafar and his commanders would stand aloof from the combat, the entire army, critically dependent on command, collapsed. Siraj-ud-Daulah was swiftly murdered, and Mir Jafar was made nawab in his place.

There was, of course, a reckoning to be made for services rendered, and when Clive presented his bill (probably in advance of the battle) it was not for the faint of heart or shallow of pocket. The general was to be 'reimbursed' for his pains to the tune of a cool £234,000, a sum that instantly made the hooligan from Market Drayton one of the richest men in Britain, as well as 'Baron Clive of Plassey'. In addition he was assigned a revenue territory that would yield him an annual income of nearly £30,000. The fact that, of the £80 million purported to be in Siraj-ud-Daulah's treasury, no one could find more than £1.5 million had no effect at all on the scale of the confiscations.

Beyond the opportunism of personal plunder lay a much deeper question and one that the British Empire would face time and time again in its march across the globe. Was its military power to be used to strengthen or to weaken the native government they claimed to be 'assisting'? Which *truly* served the interests of a trading empire, the empire of liberty—a strong Indian regime or a weak one? The view in Leadenhall Street habitually voiced by the directors and their fiscally conservative chairmen like Laurence Sulivan was invariably one of damage limitation: stabilizing the situation to the point where Indian institutions could be depended on to provide the stability and peace needed for commerce to flourish. The immunity of Calcutta from Indian authority that was demanded after Plassey seemed to fit this bill. But, 15,000 miles and six months' sailing-time away, few of the Company men in India itself gave much time or credence to the practicality of self-containment. And some thought it the counsel of the weak. In a telling piece of advice, Clive told the directors in 1758 that 'such an opportunity can never again be expected for the *aggrandisement* of the Company'.

Specifically, did the Company want a pliable nawab (as in south India), or did it want to all intents and purposes to *be* the nawab? The Company men could tell themselves that, by stripping Murshidabad of an army and making it pay for British troops instead, they were only

337

reacting defensively to the experience of 1756–7. But even the most ill-informed of them knew that the legitimacy of the nawab's government depended critically on shows of force—not just armoured elephants in battle array but also guards and police who could descend on a district or *zemindars* to pry loose the silver for the government treasury. Without that force, Indian administration was a hollow shell. Dictating to Mir Jafar that henceforth the Company would collect land revenue directly from the large district known as the 24 Parganas, and that *banians* (middlemen) trading under the Company flag should be allowed up-country to do business without the inconvenience of paying taxes—and doing all this on the grounds that the instability of the regime required this prudent measure of security—was, of course, to make a self-fulfilling prophecy. Predicting the collapse of viable Indian administration, the British did everything to ensure it happened. When, inevitably, Mir Jafar failed to meet his financial obligations and in desperation searched around for alternative allies, even the Marathas, he was replaced by his son-in-law Mir Qasim in 1760. When he in his turn presumed to lay down the law to British private traders, he was likewise disposed of and his aged father-in-law bounced back to Murshidabad.

Summoning or seeing off nawabs, manipulating the polity of Bengal until it frayed and tore and fell apart altogether may have suited the short-term interests of the British. Clive and his associates may even have imagined it gave the Company greater freedom of action. But in fact it locked Britain into a cycle of intervention, war and yet more intervention which it had expressly rejected, a syndrome that transformed an empire of business into an empire of military coercion. There was a particular kind of Indian soil on which soldiers did their very best to avoid pitching tents that was known to them as 'cotton ground'. For if it should rain at night while they were sleeping, what had in dry weather seemed to be a solid surface subsided first into dirty froth and then into a cavernous liquid sinkhole, swallowing tents, occupants and possessions. Though they imagined that what they were doing was 'laying the foundations' of something—and though their exploits have been treated by imperial historians as just that—Clive and his fellow-conquistadors in India were in fact setting those foundations on cotton ground. While they were airily hiring and firing nawabs, a much more decisive drama was unfolding to the northeast. On 14 January 1761, 60 miles (96 km) northwest of Delhi near the small town of Panipat, an immense battle took place between rival claimants to the legacy of the crumbling Mughal empire. On one side was the most formidable army the Brahmin Marathas had yet managed to assemble from their confederation of cavalry dynasts. On the other was an Afghan army under the command of Ahmed Shah Durrani. Like the Persian despot Nadir Shah in 1739, Ahmed Shah had invaded India essentially for the time-honoured purpose of ransacking the cities of the north. But he too had been drawn into a politically mobilized Muslim alliance—with the nawab of Awadh—to stop the Hindu Marathas from taking control of north and central India. The Muslims won the day as the Maratha horsemen were mown down by Afghan guns. But once victory was achieved the Afghans withdrew northwest along their looting route, ensuring that the result of Panipat was to open a great vacuum of power in the Mughal heartland that none of its potential successors—Bengal, Awadh or, further south, Hyderabad—was strong enough to fill.

Of course if the East India Company's plan all along had been to move right into that space, then the decade after Panipat was too good to be true. By the time Company armies had defeated Nawab Mir Qasim and the nawab of Awadh at Baksar on the Awadh–Bihar border in 1764, it seemed to have become an unstoppable machine. By paying Indian soldiers higher wages than they were accustomed to receiving from the nawabs, and by paying them regularly, the Company was able to take on sepoys from the traditional pools of military recruitment in the villages around Banaras and southern Awadh, whose men now wore the red coats. After the nawab of Awadh's defeat, his own treasury was required to pay for those troops who obliged him with their 'protection'. It was the Market Drayton racket gone subcontinental. In Bengal, the army was able to be equipped with muskets, artillery, bullock trains and cavalry horses because from 1765 it became the direct recipient of the bonanza that was the land revenue. In an improvised ceremony at Allahabad that year, for which Clive provided a 'throne' in the form of one of his chairs set on top of his dining table, the Mughal Emperor Shah Alam had formally invested the Company with the power of the *Diwani*: the authority to collect taxes in his name. Though the nawab in Murshidabad still ostensibly retained powers of

340

police and justice, the Company was now in effect the governing power, inserted into the moribund body of the Mughal empire from which it proceeded to gnaw its way out, parasitically and insatiably.

The paradox was that Clive had been sent back to India in 1764 by the Company not to expand its power and territories but as the agent of retrenchment. And to those in London who were painfully exercised by the costs—both financial and political—of William Pitt's empire, the experience in India was every bit as sobering as that in America. If you were the unfortunate person responsible for balancing the books in London, acquiring an empire could be every bit as disastrous as losing one. Needless to say, this is not how it seemed to the men on the spot, their brows garlanded with victory, their exploits celebrated in songs and paintings exhibited in Vauxhall Gardens, their coffers swollen to bursting with extorted Indian silver. With Clive himself setting the pace they began to spend freely in Britain itself, buying country houses and sometimes, as at Sezincote in Gloucestershire, hiring architects to give them the air of an Indian palace. They began to throw their weight about in London and their money at parliamentary seats. As the 'nabobs', they displaced the West Indian planters as the most envied and detested plutocrats of the age.

Acutely aware of the debate about the costs of empire in America, in the two years that Clive remained in India he continued to rationalize this metamorphosis from business to self-perpetuating military state as a golden fiscal opportunity. 'Bengal is in itself an inexhaustible fund of riches,'

341

he wrote to the Directors, 'and you may depend on being supplied with money and provisions in abundance.' Specifically, the difference between what the Bengal land revenues would reliably yield, and what it cost to administer and police them, would be, he cheerfully predicted, pure profit, perhaps £1 million a year. And that profit would, in turn, provide all the capital needed to invest in the Company's cargoes, destined to be auctioned off at its London sales rooms. If you believed this then you believed in dreams come true, specifically the dream of equalizing the terms of trade rather than endlessly pouring silver down the great Indian drain. The self-sustaining neatness of the plan must have seemed even more irresistible when compared to the fiscal nightmare in America, where British troops and armed customs men had to wrest taxes from an infuriated population who accused the home government of instituting tyranny. In India, the Company reasoned, no one expected anything *but* tyranny, and under the auspices of the Union Jack they were likely to get less of it than under the nawabs. Better yet, they would do all the collecting themselves as they had since the beginning of the Mughal empire. What could go wrong? The peasants would go on complaining. That's what peasants did. But they would cough up. The *zemindars* would hand over cash in advance to the Company and turn their men on any recalcitrant villages as they always had. Nothing was going to change except the ultimate ownership of the teak chests into which all this Bengal bounty would be spilled.

But everything did change. Seen from their palanquins borne along the trunk roads by a tottering quartet of bearers, or from the plush of their river barges, the countryside may have looked impervious to trauma, soaking up fiscal punishment along with the monsoon rains and still able to feed itself. But what would happen if the monsoons failed to deliver? This is exactly what happened in 1769 and 1770 when northeast India was plunged into desperate famine. Between a quarter and a third of the population of Bengal and Bihar died in those two years. Travellers remembered seeing saucer-eyed living ghosts, unfleshed ribcages sitting waiting to expire, massed flocks of kites descending on the carcasses— nothing quite fit for recording in Company school paintings. The famine was not the fault of the British regime. But the havoc and misery it had unleashed in Bengal during the 1760s had not helped the countryside to survive the blow.

It had been picked clean by the fortune-seekers, both native and British. In the face of the threats posed by the Marathas and the French, the pressure for land revenue had been fiercer than ever. The government in Calcutta had leaned on the *zemindars*, who had leaned on the villages. The proportion of their produce taken rose; their ability to save for the following year's seed dwindled. If they lost a cow to the collector, or because there was no straw to harvest, they lost milk, draft labour and dung bricks for fuel. Freed from all oversight, merchants with their own armed entourage flying the Company flag would invade the villages looking for cloth but imposing prices on the weavers and dyers—another species of legalized extortion. Burke's scalding polemic against 'the just and punctual hand that in India has torn the cloth from

343

the loom, or wrested the scanty portion of rice and salt from the peasant, or wrung from him the very opium in which he forgot his oppression and his oppressor' was, to be sure, hyperbole. But it was not altogether misplaced. A much less partisan commentator who knew whereof he spoke, Richard Becher, confessed that 'the fact is undoubted . . . that since the accession to the dewanee, the condition of the people of this country has been worse than it was before'.

What Robert Clive had done in 1765 was to set a will o' the wisp scampering through Anglo-Indian history, the vain pursuit of which would decide the fate of its empire. For although at the very end of his career he insisted that the British should not recklessly extend their governmental supervision deep into the Mughal empire, he had held out the promise that grasping the nettle of Indian finances would sting only for a moment. Thereafter it was the answer to the Company's prayers—not just the harbinger, but the condition, of commercial profitability. By 1800 this principle had hardened into an unchallengeable truism, notwithstanding the fact that the Company's finances were turning an ever deeper shade of red and that it was the reverse of every principle that had been laid down by the founders of the empire of liberty and commerce. It was also, of course, the opposite of the precepts being codified in Scotland by the economist Adam Smith, that the less a government imposed itself the more easily the Invisible Hand could do its work (although Smith himself would make an express exception for military contingencies and for the 'special' circumstances of India). In a crude sense, of course, Clive was right, since no one coming from Devon or Dumfries who managed to survive their stay in Calcutta or Madras was likely to get poorer by the experience. Even as he pretended to have the interests of both colonizers and natives at heart, Clive himself stood out as the most outrageous profiteer of all. Reproved for his conduct in parliament, he typically brazened it out with a famous defence. After Plassey, 'a great prince was dependent on my pleasure, an opulent city lay at my mercy; its richest bankers bid against each other for my smiles; I walked through vaults which were thrown open to me alone, piled on either hand with gold and jewels! Mr Chairman, at this moment I stand astonished at my own moderation.' Moderation, though, was not a word anyone else used of the Baron. In 1774, immoderately sunk in opium, Clive's life ended in an overdose.

Paradoxically, Clive's personal notoriety spared the logic of his interventionist imperialism from the scepticism it deserved. For if, somehow, with the best will in the world, British government in Bengal had failed to bring about general peace and prosperity, it could only be because wicked men, selfish men, perhaps led astray by greedy, opportunist natives, had abused their trust in order to line their pockets. The proper correction was not to examine the assumptions behind the proposition, but merely to find the right men and the right measures. The rest of British history in India was a search to do just that.

If the Company was looking for someone who represented the polar opposite of Robert Clive's brutal flamboyance, they could not have done any better than Warren Hastings. The son of an improvident clergyman who ended up in Barbados, he was from the beginning a solemn outsider. The clever but impoverished Westminster schoolboy, painfully shy, carried with him a tight-wound sense of dignified superiority that provoked, often on first encounter, either admiration or hatred. A writer with the Company at seventeen, Hastings worked his way through the ranks, spending some time at Murshidabad. It was there, necessarily dealing with the nawab's administrators, judges and money-men, that Hastings realized, to a degree still unusual in the Company, that its fortunes would depend on plunging, not just into the politics of late Mughal India, but into its culture too. After learning Persian, Arabic, Hindustani and Bengali he became familiar with both the Hindu and Muslim codes of law and with the great works of their sacred and mythic literature. Whatever his other failings, it could not be said that Warren Hastings suffered from any of the cultural arrogance that became the hallmark of later generations of Britons in India.

For all the dourness of his demeanour and his bewildering habit of watering his wine (to Calcutta society yet another irritating sign of his moral loftiness), Warren Hastings was a man who fell in love easily and hopelessly. After his first wife died he fell for the blonde wife of a German artist calling himself 'Baron' Imhoff, and when the Baron returned to Europe Marian stayed behind and became the second Mrs Hastings in 1777. It was a love-match that endured as long as they did. But in a much more fatal way Hastings fell for India: its gorgeous clamour; the battered beauty of its shrines and temples; its heady, aromatic disorder. He wanted desperately to be a Mughal, or at the very least a nawab. He wanted to make the Company Indian. The East India Regulation Act (1773) steered through parliament by Lord North on the eve of the American Revolution seemed to give him the authority of his heart's desire, since it promoted him from governor of Bengal to the first holder of the new office of 'Governor-General', with seniority (much to their intense chagrin) over his fellow governors in Madras and Bombay. But what the Act gave it also took away. For the Governor-General was to rule in tandem with a council composed of four men appointed by the Crown and Company, his own vote counting no more in decisions than theirs.

This, on the face of it, contradictory decision, both to concentrate and to disperse the governing power, was in fact in keeping with shifting definitions (much tested by America) of the theory of constitutional checks and balances. To have even a faint chance of practical success presupposed an essential community of interests between the Governor-General and the council, with differences arising only on details. But from the very first day of their encounter relations between Hastings and the councillors thrust on him, three of whom had not the slightest working knowledge of India prior to arriving, were an unmitigated disaster. By giving them four salvoes short of a twenty-one-gun salute on their arrival in Calcutta, Hastings had given immediate offence to the likes of the spluttering Lieutenant–General John Clavering. In fact, their grasp of the meaning of protocol correctly divined that the mild humiliation was entirely intentional, for while Hastings, justifying his action to the directors at

347

home, laughed it all off as absurdly 'frivolous', he made sure to say that he could not have done anything else without compromising the 'dignity' of his office.

In the tight little world of white Calcutta, such snubs and slights were the equivalent of undeclared war. (What a loss to English literature that Jane Austen never walked Tank Square or sat observantly beneath a banyan on Garden Reach!) And if the councillors took a dislike to Hastings personally, they were—with the exception of the amiably profligate Richard Barwell—no more enamoured of his policies. When he purged the revenue administration they believed he had done it to put in his own creatures in the place of those dismissed. When he launched a war against the Afghan Rohilla tribes on behalf of the Nawab of Awadh, they assumed he was doing it as a mercenary to take a cut of the proceeds. Company business became hostage to the playing out of personal vendettas, none more ferociously pursued than that between Hastings and another councillor, Philip Francis. When a Bengali–Hindu revenue administrator named Nandakumar testified (almost certainly falsely) in public that the Governor-General had taken bribes (although he might have taken unauthorized allowances), Hastings retaliated inciting a prosecution against Nandakumar for embezzling the estate of a deceased debtor. Nandakumar was arrested, indicted for forgery, tried by the new British Supreme Court in Calcutta and, after a mockery of an eight-day trial, sentenced to be hanged, on the authority of a British statute passed in the reign of George II that had little meaning in Hindu law or custom.

The travesty of justice was atypical of Hastings' governance, which was criticized for paying too much, not too little, attention to indigenous law and institutions. Part of the distaste felt by his enemies for Hastings was precisely that, in his eagerness to go native, he had forgotten himself, the Company and the commission he was supposed to discharge, which was to bring British government and justice to the Indians and not the other way about. It would be a sentimental exaggeration to say that the generals and the judges and the Francises barged in on an Anglo-Indian world that was genuinely pluralist. Like its sister cities Madras and Bombay, Calcutta was obviously and aggressively segregated between White and Black Towns. In so far as Indians filled the houses on Garden Reach and Chowringhee, they did so as servants: palanquin bearers, gardeners, cooks, watchmen, runners, sweepers, gatekeepers. But from the paintings of Tilly Kettle and Johann Zoffany (who came to India to repair his career after offending the royal family) it's apparent that for a brief ten or twenty years the boundaries between races and cultures were looser and more elastic, even mutually sympathetic, than at any time before or since. Sex is no sure guide to multicultural tolerance, but with European women still relatively scarce, and very prone to tropical infections, especially during pregnancy and childbirth, it was not uncommon for Company men to take long-term Indian mistresses or even in rare cases (like the Hyderabad resident James Achilles Kirkpatrick, who conducted a politically dangerous love affair with a young woman from the local

349

Muslim aristocracy) to marry them. The lawyer William Hickey, who left a chatty diary of Calcutta in the 1780s and 1790s, wrote tenderly of his long-term lover Jemdani, for whom he bought a country house on the Hooghly where the two of them entertained their mutual friends. She was, he wrote, 'respected and admired by all my friends, by her extraordinary sprightliness and good humour . . . unlike the women in general in Asia she never secluded herself from the sight of strangers, on the contrary she delighted in joining my male parties, cordially joining in the mirth which prevailed'. What happened to the children of these unions suggests both the possibilities and the limits of relationships across the racial border, for, while the offspring were usually looked after very well and educated, whether that education took place in India or England depended very much on the darkness or fairness of their skin.

Though none of the Company men posed for their portraits along with their Asian mistresses, they did choose to have themselves depicted together with the *banians*, who managed private trade for them (circumventing official restrictions) and were a crucial source of both commercial and political intelligence. Many of them, like the *banian* shown with the trader John Mowbray, came from the culturally sophisticated gentry class of the *bhadralog* in Bengal, the dynasties that produced the Tagores. In Britain there was a presumption that new money was philistine, but the commercial shrewdness of these men kept company with a devotion to poetry and to mythological and sacred texts. It was natural, then, for Warren Hastings to believe that effective Company government required more than information about the cultivation of indigo. It also needed a working familiarity with Indian languages, both classical and vernacular, with religion, law, history and politics. So, from the mid-1770s to his foundation of the Asiatic Society in Bengal in 1784, Warren Hastings became the first great patron of Indian scholarship for Europeans. A group of protégés, many of them very young, were commissioned to produce the works that he hoped would be the foundation of educated and disinterested government. Nathaniel Brassey Halhed's 'Gentoo Code', a digest of Sanskrit law-books, appeared in 1776. Some eleven years later, the first English–Hindustani dictionary, *A Dictionary, English and Hindoostannee,* was published in two parts from 1787 to 1790 by the Scottish physician John Gilchrist who had gone from Bombay to Faizabad, grown a long beard like a *sannyasi* (religious mendicant) and 'assumed for a time the dress of the natives'. Gilchrist spent years listening intently to his language teachers or *munshis*, working out the phonetics of the language, and went on to become the first Professor of Hindustani at the College of Fort William, founded by Governor-General Wellesley in 1800.

None of this is to say that Hastings or his oriental scholars—Halhed, Gilchrist, Colebrooke and Wilkins—seriously believed Indian languages, law and literature to be the 'equal' of the accumulated wisdoms of Europe. Part of their determination to educate their countrymen in Indian culture was to liberate them from excessive dependence on native informants who could use their monopoly of knowledge for untrustworthy

351

ends. Ideally, Hastings would have liked European judges qualified to preside over, or at least perfectly able to understand the proceedings of, Hindu and Muslim courts, which under the regime of the 1770s were still the principal recourse of judgement for the vast majority of Indians. But neither is this to say that his 'orientalism' was simply another tool of domination. Hastings and his colleagues took their power as given. What they wanted to do was to exercise it with some sympathy for the place of their government. Was it, for example, the act of a crudely manipulative 'orientalist' to sponsor the first English translation of the *Bhagavadgita*, to make sure its translator got Company leave in Banaras to study Sanskrit and then to provide a preface? In a letter to the chairman of the court of directors, proudly introducing the work, Hastings made it clear that the value of such a translation was not just that it was 'useful' for 'social communication with people over whom we exercise a dominion founded on the right of conquest'. It was also, he wrote in a telling phrase,

> the gain of humanity . . . it attracts and conciliates distant affections; it lessens the weight of the chain by which the natives are held in subjection and it imprints on the hearts of our own countrymen the sense and obligation of benevolence. Even in England this effect of it is greatly wanting. It is not very long since the inhabitants of India were considered by many as creatures, scarcely elevated above the degree of savage life; nor I fear is that prejudice wholly eradicated, though surely

352

abated. Every instance which brings their real character home to observation will impress us with a more generous sense of feeling for their natural rights and teach us to estimate them by the measure of our own. But such instances can only be obtained by their writings and these will survive when the British dominion in India shall have long ceased to exist, and when the sources which it once yielded of wealth and power are lost to remembrance.

Whether the recipient at Leadenhall Street, Nathaniel Smith, got the message, humane and optimistic as it was, is open to doubt. A few months later Hastings was in England—not as he expected, honoured, but violently and publicly vilified as a ruthless and corrupt martinet. If one were to believe the parliamentary indictment drawn up in the spring of 1786 by Francis' friend and ally Edmund Burke, so far from conducting his administration wisely and benevolently Hastings had acted with 'gross injustice, cruelty and treachery against the faith of nations' (the Afghan Rohillas, whom Burke fantasized as noble horsemen caught in the trap of Hastings' personal aggrandizement); had turned Awadh 'which was once a garden [into] an uninhabited desert'; and had indulged 'a wanton, and unjust and pernicious exercise of his powers and the great situation of trust which he occupied in India in overturning the ancient establishments of the country'. In Burke's fulmination, the wise owl had been turned into the vulture.

Though no one, least of all Burke, had the clarity or honesty to see what in fact was obvious, and though the purported charges were all about the Rohillas and Awadh, Warren Hastings was subconsciously being impeached for losing America. Who else was there, after all, to be used as scapegoat? Not King George, who somehow escaped from the ruin of his Atlantic empire with his popularity untarnished; not Cornwallis, who was on his way to succeed Hastings in Calcutta. Putting Hastings in the dock for all kinds of infamies purportedly inflicted on the Indians enabled Britain to exorcise its uneasy conscience about what it had *actually* done in America. What was said about Hastings would have been more accurately said about Gage's and Hutchinson's and Cornwallis' own ferociously terrorizing Lieutenant-Colonel in the Carolinas, Banastre Tarleton. Hastings was even reproached for having nearly lost British India, when in fact he had saved it. In 1780 he had been facing the triple threat of the Marathas; the aggressive Muslim Sultan of Mysore, Haidar Ali, who would come very close to taking Madras; and the French. At precisely the moment when the British Empire was going down to defeat in the west, it had been the urgency and intelligence of Hastings' strategy, buying off the Marathas from any temptation of an alliance with Mysore and then pouring troops into south India, that had prevented an 'American' disaster from occurring in the east. But since, in the stinging aftermath of Saratoga and Yorktown, it was impossible to criticize those actually responsible for the débâcle, the need to create a home-grown oriental despot—bungling and corrupt—became irresistible. This was the straw man whom Burke indicted as 'a Pacha with three tails'. 'Do you want a criminal, my lords?' he thundered at the impeachment.

> When was there ever so much iniquity ever laid to the charge of any one? . . . I impeach him in the name of all the Commons of Great Britain whose national character he has dishonoured. I impeach him in the name of the people of India whose laws, rights, and liberties he has destroyed, whose country he has laid waste and desolate . . . I impeach him in the name of human nature itself which he has cruelly outraged, injured, and oppressed, in both sexes, in every age, rank, situation and condition of life.

Anything else? No wonder poor Hastings was confused by his predicament. The man who had surrendered at Yorktown was on his way to the Governor's House at Calcutta while he himself was in the dock, pilloried as some sort of Ginghiz Khan in knee breeches, fighting for his reputation and his life. At least, unlike the situation with so many scapegoats before, there was no summary rush to judgement. When the ugly mood of post-American chauvinist breast-beating had passed and Britain was once more in a real shooting war with the French, Hastings, having served his turn as whipping boy for wounded national self-esteem, was duly acquitted. But it took ten years of his life, and he never really recovered from the shock and shame. For his part, the plumply well-meaning Cornwallis did what he was supposed to do in India, which was to fly the flag of the chastened but resurgent British Empire as breezily as he could.

The myth of his predecessor's infamy was, in fact, necessary to Cornwallis' pose, provided for him by Burke and by Pitt's Secretary of State, Henry Dundas, as the sweeper of the Augean stables. He would be the man come to bring True Britishness to India; to hear its groans; to repair the damage done by the occido-oriental despot Hastings. Away, then, with the parasites infesting the revenue department (and away they went). Also, no more of this nonsense about the government going native. Cornwallis' own view of the Indians' capacity for government was famously expressed by his statement that 'every native of India I verily believe is corrupt'. What the country needed was a good stiff dose of reform: not an orientalized Briton but a Britannicized oriental; not an English nawab but a sensible JP in the Governor's house. And to keep his officials out of the way of temptation, they had to be decently paid and their sphere of action uncontaminated by low matters of trade. Henceforth those who did business and those who governed would be utterly different personnel. From the increasing indifference, even stigma, attached to Company business came a new sense of altered mission for British India. Whatever might be taken from India in the way of commerce would be repaid a thousandfold with something incomparably more precious than silver coin—the blessings of British institutions, the accumulated wisdom of its justice and the sound benevolence of its society. So when Cornwallis looked at the heart of the matter—the land revenues of Bengal—and saw (as there undoubtedly were) criminal abuses and a dismal panorama of dispossessions and famines, he concluded that what he had to do first was to forget all about pandering to native traditions. A new beginning had to be made, one based on sound first principles.

Those principles were those of the solid English landowner, which, beneath the epaulettes and the frogging, Charles Cornwallis undoubtedly was. To own land, he supposed, was not just proprietorship; it was trust. The progress that could be seen inscribed in every Norfolk village, in every rippling acre of wheat, was owed to the mutually beneficent relationship between the wise, ingenious gentleman–farmer (beginning with Farmer George) and the thrifty, enterprising tenant farmer. (Never mind, of course, that this happy tableau owed just as much to the brutal dispossessions of eighteenth-century enclosures.) In this smiling, rustic Britannia, the parties to this self-sustaining economic miracle could be assured of reaping the harvest of their efforts through knowledge of the fixity of both their tenure and their taxes. All that was needed to make rural India fortunate was for Cornwallis to provide the necessary measure of stability. Stability, it need hardly be said, was a product of settled social hierarchy. 'A regular graduation of ranks', wrote Cornwallis, 'is nowhere more necessary than in this country for promoting order in civil society.' It also went without saying that this solid social order would have to be anchored by the Bengali equivalent of the English gentry, who could be depended on to meet their obligations to the government without unduly burdening their tenants. The Governor-General imagined he found them in the *zemindars*. Historically, under the Mughals, the *zemindars* had been able to inherit and pass on their land allotments within their families. But this didn't mean they were true and outright owners of those lands, as in Britain. They had been assigned the income from them (after the emperor had had his due) as tax officials of the empire, not as aristocrats. But for Cornwallis, all these ambiguities were swept aside by his thirst for cleansing simplicity and his indomitably sunny view of the moral invigoration of ownership. So the *zemindars* were turned into the absolute proprietors of their estates, conditional only on them paying to the government the allotted sum on the appointed day. The assurance of passing on estates to the next generation in England was, after all, the incentive to improve them. Once these 'landlords' had some sense of the ceiling of their tax obligations, they could set about becoming model country gentlemen, collecting only so much from their 'tenants' (who were, in fact, innocent cultivators, some of whom had owned their own strips and fields) who would be left with a surplus to reinvest in next year's seed and stock. As the 'tenants' became more productive they could produce for the booming cash markets of the towns and an export market hungry for cotton, indigo, sugar and opium. All this would happen, moreover, beneath the mantle of peace and justice provided by an honest and impartial government. Courts based on English law as well as Indian courts would now hear grievances, and government-appointed district officials would protect the natives from extortion and see that the monies collected went where they were supposed to.

As everyone sheltered by this miraculously self-fertilizing system grew more prosperous, equally miraculous cultural changes would begin to take place. Simple peasants would become customers for British-manufactured goods and the new Bengali gentry would begin to assemble libraries, opening their eyes to the indisputable wisdoms of the European (which is to say British) enlightenment. The scales would fall from their eyes. They would abandon their disgusting idols and their devotion to gods with elephant heads, even perhaps receive the light of the Gospel. *Real* civilization was just around the corner. Cornwallis was sure of it.

That, at any rate, was the theory. If it worked in Scotland—and a disproportionate number of the young administrators and surveyors who were left to work out the practical details were, in fact, Scots—why should it not work in Bengal, Bihar and Orissa? But Cornwallis' system presupposed peace and stability. And instead of the promised peace there were almost continuous wars—with Mysore, with the Marathas and then with the French. Pressed hard for funds, many of the traditional *zemindars* themselves went into debt to meet their contracts with the government. Their armed men were sent to the villages to extract the last rupee. And when loans and extortion still failed to deliver what they needed to make good on their contract with Calcutta, they were dispossessed and sold up. The indebted country gentry of England had sympathetic bankers willing to perpetuate their credit, but there was no such facility in India. Not infrequently the *zemindars'* creditors simply moved into their debtors' properties, taking over their contract. So precisely the class whom the bluff Cornwallis most mistrusted—the Calcutta money-men, like the Tagores—were the main beneficiaries of his system, becoming wealthy estate owners at exactly this time. Under their impatient stewardship the capitalization of the countryside accelerated as land, some of it reclaimed from the flood delta of the Ganges, was put under cash crops like opium, silk and cotton that could make money, pots of it, very fast.

In August 1789, when he had introduced his 'Permanent Settlement' of the land revenue, Cornwallis had promised the directors of the East India Company that his plan was 'well calculated to secure and even increase your revenues'. But if the Company and the government had hoped that the profits of the new regime would translate into balanced books, those hopes were buried under the dust-storms of war. Both the directors of the Company and Pitt's government had regarded Hastings' military adventurism as not only immoral but also ruinously expensive, so Cornwallis' brief was to hold the line. But India would not let him. Hastings' prudent decision to make territorial concessions to the Marathas as the price of keeping them out of the arms of Haidar Ali had proved no more than a breathing-space. For in the twenty years after he had seized power from a Hindu dynasty the Sultan of Mysore had built the most powerful south Indian state since the demise of the empire of the Vijayanagars in the seventeenth century. Roads and bridges had been built, and the rural and market economy flourished. And though he remained a Muslim prince, Haidar Ali made sure to patronize Hindu temples and shrines. Even Cornwallis thought it a realm of gardens.

Until, that is, he went to war to uproot it. In

1782 Haidar Ali died and was succeeded by his charismatic son Tipu Sultan. During and after the wars that ended in the annihilation of his state Tipu was demonized by the British as another Siraj-ud-Daulah, an unhinged, bloodthirsty despot, and was habitually referred to as 'the usurper' who had supplanted the 'ancient Hindu constitution'— as if the British themselves were credible judges of legitimacy. But the pattern of rationalizing conquests in terms of saving the Indians from themselves was now well established both in India and especially at home. And what could be even worse than a fanatical Indo-Muslim warlord? A fanatical Indo-Muslim warlord who thinks he's a French republican! There's no doubt that Tipu welcomed overtures from the French, who clung to strategically significant Indian Ocean naval bases on Mauritius and Réunion, and that he was happy to use them to train some of his native and Arab-African troops in more aggressively European warfare. Since the American war it seemed to be a French, not British, empire that was in the ascendant, so why would he not at least flirt with the temptation? What was there about British policy that would lead him to believe that they, not he, were the aggressors?

So in May 1791, for the first time since Yorktown, Cornwallis went to war. In front of Tipu's great palace-citadel at Seringapatam his old nightmares caught up with him. His army floundered helplessly in the monsoon mud. Over-extended, lines of communication broke down. But somehow the army did manage to stay together, and in the cool weather of the following year it launched a new and ultimately successful offensive against the island fortress of Kavery. Tipu's defeat was serious enough to force him to surrender half his territories and his two sons as hostages for his good conduct. The avuncular Charles Cornwallis, taking the hands of the little chaps in turbans, became a standard feature of the iconography of imperial self-congratulation. This was an empire that would be firm but magnanimous.

The good Uncle Charlie Cornwallis left India in 1793. The home verdict was that he had done well by India and well by the Empire. At least he hadn't lost it. But it was a mark of the sea-change in the presumptions about what that empire was supposed to be that, instead of dismay about a cost-efficient trading concern turning into an open-ended territorial government, there was a sense of the historical rightness, the inevitability, of that outcome. The greasy-fingered writer of Clive's day, sweating it out in some inky hole in Madras between bouts of arrack-drenched stupor in the Black Town brothels, had turned into the lordly collector sahib doing the tour of the district in his palanquin, scrutinizing the welfare of the cultivators, consulting the collective wisdom of Edinburgh to see how that lot might be improved. Not so long before, freedom of movement and fairness of treatment for up-country traders meant knowing whom to bribe and whom to beat up. Now there were white men in wigs who would adjudicate such matters from a bench in Calcutta or Bombay. And where once fighting for the Company had rated a poor second to parading in arms on the battlefields of Germany, now it was the field for heroes, the theatre of celebrity.

So, at any rate, the three Wellesley brothers

(born Wesley) from County Meath—Richard, the oldest and the political supremo; Henry, the man of business; and Arthur, the battlefield boy wonder—imagined when they arrived in India at the end of 1797. By the time they left, eight years later, India had made them and they, for better or worse, had made (in all but formal title) the Raj. Robert Clive had never commanded an army of more than 5000 men. By 1804 Governor-General Richard Wellesley, first Marquess Wellesley, was commander of an army of some 192,000, as large as that of many of the most powerful states of Europe. The Company—which was to say now, in all but name, the British government—was unchallenged in the subcontinent as the paramount power. Mysore was gone. The Mughal empire was a pathetic joke, its present head, Shah Alam, a blind and helpless dependant of his British keepers. Delhi had surrendered to Calcutta as the arbiter not just of power but of authority too. Awadh—the mid-Ganges state studded with great cities like Lucknow and Faizabad—was a dependency. The Marathas had been divided and all but their last formidable fighting chief, Holkar, neutralized. A regional ruler who had kept his nose clean and made sure to jump on the rolling juggernaut of British military power, like the Nizam of Hyderabad, was preserved, but with a British Resident *in situ* to babysit his politics and a cantonment of redcoats (paid for by his own treasury) to make sure he wasn't naughty. And the debts of the East India Company had trebled, to the point at which they no longer bore any resemblance to commercial book-keeping and had become an institutionally funded obligation. From his palatial new Government House in Calcutta, a near copy of Robert Adam's neo-classical Kedleston in Derbyshire, Wellesley could deliver imperial utterances as if he were indeed the new Augustus: 'the foundation of our empire in Asia is now laid in the tranquillity of surrounding nations and in the happiness and welfare of the people of India.'

And this is always what Richard Wellesley of Castle Dangan, Eton, Oxford and a nice pocket borough thought he was *supposed* to do. At Eton, Caesar, Livy and Tacitus had been drummed into him. But walking around Rome on the inevitable Grand Tour, Wellesley kept company with the ghosts of Trajan and Hadrian. At Posilippo he made the pilgrimage to Virgil's tomb, the imminence of his own epic romantically flickering inside him. When he met the nawab of Arcot in May 1798—a mere satrap of the Company, after all—Wellesley's head was turned by the sight of the escort of fifteen elephants, 'decorated with superb hammered cloth, embroidered in gold, silver and jewels and with golden turrets on their backs'. Established in Calcutta, the long-faced, charismatic Irishman moaned in letters to his voluptuous French wife Hyacinthe about how sexually aroused he became in the tropical heat. But he exercised his virility in other ways, demanding and acquiring the kind of political and military authority that neither Warren Hastings nor Cornwallis could have dreamed of. The pretext—or, as he would have insisted, the occasion—was the global war with the French that had the home government frantically on the defensive. Bonaparte, whose run of military victories in Italy had astonished and terrified the

Coalition powers, had now sent an immense expedition to Egypt, which, if successful, could directly threaten the lines of communication and trade with India from the Red Sea. No one, least of all Wellesley, was underestimating the continuing French capacity to project their power all the way to Calcutta and to inflict serious damage through their proxies.

The most dangerous, or the most foolhardy, was Tipu Sultan, who, even as he pretended to abide by the terms of his treaty with the British, was plotting with the French to escape its stranglehold on his territories and power. As usual, Wellesley took the betrayal personally and represented Tipu's desperate attempt to cut loose from the shackles of British domination as the action of an unhinged aggressor bent on annihilating the Company: 'Professing the most amicable disposition . . . he has manifested a design to effect our total destruction . . . he has prepared the means and instruments for a war of extermination.' A huge army, with Arthur Wellesley one of the commanders, smashed its way into Seringapatam, where Tipu's body was found buried beneath a mound of the dead at the Water Gate. Among the cartloads of plunder taken by the British was the octagonal throne of the *padshah*— the Muslim emperor that Tipu had declared himself to be—with its canopy surmounted by a golden *homa* bird, the beak glittering with inlaid stones, the eyes and tail studded with pearls. The *homa* was said by some to resemble an eagle, by others a vulture. The same could be said of Wellesley's war machine.

Everything that could be removed from Tipu's

palace—his sword, his battle helmet, the mechanical tiger that when wound up would devour a British soldier and produce satisfyingly plaintive cries—made its way back, first to Calcutta and then to England (where it all ended up at Windsor or at the Victoria and Albert Museum in London), but the real prize was a quarter of a million head of white bullocks and milch cattle. With this huge logistical asset, Arthur Wellesley could deploy a completely supplied mobile army wherever he needed, and, together with Lieutenant -General Gerard Lake, he took the war to the Marathas and the threat of war to Awadh.

Though many of the battles were still intensely fought, Richard Wellesley had brought a new generation of cavalry horses, mostly bred from Arab stock, to India and that, together with an edge in field artillery and supply wagons, told. In September 1800 the generalissimo wrote exultantly to his brother, 'We always kill the chief general and we always have the luck to be able to identify the body . . . truly my star is in the ascendant in India. I ought to leave the country before my luck changes.' To Hyacinthe, whom he suspected of casual infidelity (the suspicion was mutual), Wellesley bragged like an adolescent, as if India had been mastered specifically to impress his wife and keep her out of anyone else's bed: 'Behold me covered with glory . . . I have done in two months [at Mysore] what took three years in Cornwallis's time. Farewell dear soul, now all is quiet I am about to arrange the affairs of a conquered country.' He would disclaim most honours except the Garter, but if the king insisted—well, he might allow himself to be known as 'Viscount Wellesley of Mysore'.

This was a bit premature. Wellesley knew that, when the bills came in, the men whom he called 'the cheesemongers of Leadenhall Street' would have a fit. But the six months it took for news from India to arrive gave him all the time he needed to present the directors and the government with *faits accomplis*. He would make the rhetorical challenge over and over again: who knew better the true state of peril confronting British power in India—the men who were there, or the men poring over maps in an office in Westminster? And once the deeds had been done and the body of yet another Maratha general slung on a cart, what was he supposed to do? Give back the territories? Restore the vanquished to their powers? Lay up trouble for the future? India, he said, did not set much store by magnanimity. India responded to unapologetic supremacy.

For all his instinctive Bonapartism Richard Wellesley was not, in fact, a pure military adventurer, still less someone tempted by visions of personal dictatorship—though some who watched the lantern-jawed magnifico process through Calcutta, led by an escort of sixteen horsemen, wondered (especially in contrast to bluff old Cornwallis, who preferred to drive his own little trap like a country squire off to the whipping fair). However misguided, Wellesley was quite sincere when he claimed that the full-tilt drive to paramountcy could be justified by the long-term economic blessings that would make, as he had predicted in one of his rare speeches in parliament, 'London, the throne of commerce of the world'. The short-term fiscal pain had to be absorbed in order to lay down what we would call the infrastructure necessary for a mutually benevolent economic relationship between Britain and India. If his predecessors thought this could be done by defensive half-measures, they had been deluding themselves. As long as there had been competitive Indian powers capable of causing trouble, neither peace nor profit could ever be expected. It never occurred to Wellesley that an India shared among smaller, internally coherent regional states— Bengal, Awadh, Mysore, Hyderabad—might be at least as viable as his paramount Raj, any more than it would have occurred to the boy from County Meath that a federal Britain of four nations made any sense. He was not interested in an empire run by accountants. Fatehpur Sikhri and the Taj Mahal told him that India had last been happy when ruled by one great authority, and he would see to it that the new Raj would be the proper heir of Akbar and Jahangir.

In 1800, Wellesley set the capstone on the arch of his triumphalism by opening the new College of Fort William. It was, he often boasted, the achievement he was proudest of: the nursery of a new generation of proconsuls educated in the laws, languages and religion of the races and nations to whose government they were now irreversibly committed. Along with *munshis* (teacher-secretaries), many of the young men initially patronized by Warren Hastings now took up posts at the college. After Wellesley had gone the college would be sacrificed to the needs of fiscal retrenchment and replaced by Haileybury College in England, but not before it had inculcated its official version of how what had begun as a commercial company, trading from modest posts on the sufferance of the Mughals, had ended up holding sway over a subcontinent. The chaotic and stumbling route to dominion, strewn with acts of self-deception and self-enrichment, was remade as a broad historical highway at the end of which was Wellesley's classical house of government. Instead of being part of India's problems (perhaps the main problem), Britain was the solution. It was meant to be. 'The position in which we are now placed', Wellesley declared in 1804, 'is suited to the character of the British nation, to the principles of our laws, to the spirit of our constitution, to the liberal and comprehensive policy which becomes the dignity of a great and powerful empire.' Britain would be the new Rome in a subcontinent that the Romans had never reached.

Was it really only seventy years since the inspirational inscription had been set in Stowe's Temple of Gothic Liberty, thanking the gods for not making the free British Romans? Was it only three generations since the founders of a maritime empire had insisted that theirs would be a dominion uniquely blessed by liberty, unencumbered by the pompous trappings of conquest? It was supposed to have been a minimalist empire: no big, expensive standing armies; no regiments of tax collectors; an enterprise built on mutual interest, not on military coercion. Hampden and Milton would bless it for minding its own business.

It had not worked out that way. There was business all right, along with the edicts and the elephants, but it was not exactly what the founders had had in mind when they had imagined a flow of raw materials coming into the metropolis and a

369

flow of manufactures going out to the empire. India had never wanted what Britain produced, and it still didn't. Raw cotton was now being shipped from Bombay to England, but in the volumes and at the prices dictated by the likes of Henry Wellesley. Yet those who turned it into manufactured cloths in the spinning and weaving sheds of the industrial north needed something from Asia to reconcile them to their grinding labour and inadequate wages, and that something was hot and sweet: sugared tea. So East India Company ships sailed back from Canton loaded with black Bohea, and its profits would go some way to paying for 150,000 sepoys (for the fabled bounty from Indian land revenues seemed more than ever a mirage). But the profitability of the business depended on the Chinese being induced to take something other than silver in exchange.

And that something was Indian; that something was a narcotic. Despite a draconian ban on opium, the Ch'ing empire was incapable of preventing smuggling, and the number of chests of Bengal opium that found their way to China rose from hundreds to many thousands a year. The first famous victim of the opium habit had been Robert Clive. It had eaten into him so badly that it had overpowered even his other mainline addiction— for the rushing high of imperial supremacy. Most of those who came later to British India would resist the first craving. But as for the opiate of global mastery, nineteenth- and even twentieth-century Britain would remain helplessly hooked.